# CHILDREN'S
# LITERATURE

# Children's Literature

## CRITICISM AND THE FICTIONAL CHILD

KARÍN LESNIK-OBERSTEIN

CLARENDON PRESS · OXFORD
1994

Oxford University Press, Walton Street, Oxford OX2 6DP
Oxford New York Toronto
Delhi Bombay Calcutta Madras Karachi
Kuala Lumpur Singapore Hong Kong Tokyo
Nairobi Dar es Salaam Cape Town
Melbourne Auckland Madrid
and associated companies in
Berlin Ibadan

Oxford is a trade mark of Oxford University Press

Published in the United States
by Oxford University Press Inc., New York

British Library Cataloguing in Publication Data
Data available

Library of Congress Cataloging in Publication Data
Lesnik-Oberstein, Karín.
Children's literature: criticism and the fictional child/Karín
Lesnik-Oberstein.
Includes bibliographical references and index.
1. Children's literature—History and Criticism.   2. Criticism.
3. Children in literature.   4. Childhood in literature.
5. Children's literature—Psychological aspects.   I. Title.
PN1009.A1L475   1994
809'.93352054—dc20         93-35484
ISBN 0-19-811998-4

Typeset by Cotswold Typesetting Ltd., Gloucester

Printed in Great Britain
on acid-free paper by
Biddles Ltd.
Guildford and Kings Lynn

*This book is dedicated with love to my parents,*
*Max and Margriet Lesnik-Oberstein.*
*Chapter Six is also dedicated to Patrick Casement.*

'If mankind had been able to learn from a direct observation of children, these three essays could have remained unwritten.'

(Sigmund Freud, 'Preface to the Fourth Edition' of *Three Essays on the Theory of Sexuality*)

# Acknowledgements

I FEEL extremely grateful, and very lucky, to have received sustained support from many sources during the research and writing which have resulted in this book. My studies in English Literature have been fostered from the start by Dr Richard Todd and the late Professor Fry, both of the Free University of Amsterdam. From the world of children's literature criticism, Professor Fred Inglis (my former Ph.D. supervisor), Dr Peter Hunt, and Mrs Julia Briggs have generously encouraged me and inspired and challenged my thinking. Mrs Julia Briggs and Professor Terry Eagleton have shown me great kindness in Oxford in reassuring me during moments of insecurity and doubt. It was also Professor Eagleton's suggestion that I should have this book published. I am very grateful indeed to the British Council for a two-year British Council Fellowship (1987–9), and to the University of Bristol for a Full Graduate Scholarship (1989–90). Both institutions gave me much moral as well as financial support. I am also very grateful to Worcester College, Oxford, for electing me to a Junior Research Fellowship (1990–2) and, later, to the Junior Deanship, and to University College, Oxford, for electing me to a Salvesen Junior Research Fellowship (1992–4). The staff and students at both Worcester and University colleges have been generous in sharing their learning and friendship with me during my time in Oxford. I have learnt more than I can say from my own tutorial students through their enthusiastic and committed discussions with me. My friends everywhere have been exemplary: they have not only given me love, but also patiently discussed my work with me over the years, and contributed many ideas. My love and gratitude go to my Bobe and the memory of Zeide: they have always supported me in my life and work in the best way they know how. The love and wisdom of my sisters Sarit, Saskia, and Maaike enriches my life immeasurably. Finally, my thinking has been shaped and influenced fundamentally by the three persons who have taught me most in their profound respect for, and compassion with, the individual: Patrick Casement, who makes it possible for me to learn what it is all about for me; my father, a true scholar and a great (child) psychotherapist; and my mother, who introduced me to children's books and to narratives of life, and knows much more about them than I ever will.

# Contents

# Issues in Children's Literature Criticism

Children's literature and children's literature criticism attract people who often have a strong interest in children's books based on a conviction of personal knowledge and experience of children, childhood, or reading. Even as children's literature and criticism gain increasing academic acceptance as areas of study, they remain a field of study which many students approach with more confidence of their acquaintance with the material itself and the matrix of theoretical discussion than with their courses on, let us say, Shakespeare or literary theory. Nor does this attitude come only from students. Where theoretical physicists may often meet polite silence, or questioning, after revealing their chosen area of work, children's literature draws an opposite response: memories of favourite childhood reading are enthusiastically contributed to the discussion, or experiences with the reading of the speakers' own children or children they are acquainted with. Sometimes there follows an often shy or defiant admission of their continuing reading of children's books. If the speakers have a professional interest in reading or childhood, then this usually forms the basis for their remarks. Librarians, psychologists, teachers, and 'adult' literary critics draw on their area of expertise and on their observations made during practical applications of their skills when commenting on children's literature. As Peter Hunt puts it: 'unlike any other form of the arts, children's literature is *available* to criticism, as well as to amateur writers; people are not afraid to comment, to censor, and to be involved.'[1]

These comments are usually pertinent to the discussions in

[1] Peter Hunt, *Criticism, Theory, and Children's Literature* (Basil Blackwell, Oxford, 1991), 7–8.

children's literature criticism, and often reveal personal emotional experiences and attachments. It is this aspect of children's literature studies which makes the field fascinating for me. Where one might assume complex motivations or sources of interest for most areas of study, children's literature studies reveal these motivations in particularly clear and powerful ways. For all their carefully acquired new academic credibility, they have not yet always settled into an academic discourse characterized by what could be loosely described as liberal disinterestedness.

Children's literature might seem, in a modern multi-media world, to be a marginal, if not positively élitist, field. And yet it is placed, and places itself, at the heart of discussions of vitally sensitive issues: on some levels it claims pertinence to emotional life and experience, control of vision, consciousness, ethics, and morality. Children's literature criticism is about saying: 'I know what children like to read/are able to read/should read, *because I know what children are like.*' Kornei Chukovsky, the Russian writer on and of children's stories tells how he once received a letter from a parent, complaining about his writings of nonsense verse. The letter writer asked of him:

Why do you distort realistic facts? Children need socially useful information and not fantastic stories about white bears who cry cock-a-doodle-doo. This is not what we expect from our children's authors. We want them to clarify for the child the world that surrounds him, instead of confusing his brain with all kinds of nonsense.[2]

Chukovsky's reaction to this view was to 'feel not only depressed but also stifled'.[3] He replies to the accusations in the letter that, on the contrary,

the nonsense that seemed to him [the letter writer] so harmful not only does not interfere with the child's orientation to the world that surrounds him, but . . . strengthens in his mind a sense of the real; and that it is precisely in order to further the education of children in reality that such nonsense verse should be offered to them.[4]

[2] Kornei Chukovsky, *From Two to Five*, trans. and ed. Miriam Morton (University of California Press, Berkeley, 1963), 90.
[3] Ibid.
[4] Ibid.

This exchange hints at the major issues drawn into children's literature criticism. Despite the obvious differences of opinion between Chukovsky and the letter writer, the underlying assumptions they share are much more important: they both ascribe powerful educational and developmental functions to a child's reading, no less than a 'clarification of the world that surrounds him', a 'strengthening in his mind [of] the real'. The exchange further involves ideas about the role of fantasy, realism, education, and society. Both Chukovsky and the letter writer wish to argue for their grip on the child's orientation to the world/word that surrounds him.

The premises on which this correspondence is based still form the core of children's literature criticism, and therefore are at the core of the controversies within and around this field: children's literature is—as has been pointed out exhaustively—written by adults for children. Adults usually also publish, edit, review, criticize, select, and buy children's books on behalf of children. In this position of responsibility and authority adults concerned, in whatever way, with children and reading have been anxious to explain the nature and function of children's reading, as we can see in the exchange between Chukovsky and the letter writer. There exists a large community of people who have an interest in considering children's reading: (children's) authors, publishers, critics, reviewers, booksellers, general readers, and sometimes, in some capacities, teachers and librarians, psychologists and parents, politicians and philosophers. Their interests range from trying to estimate the marketable value of a book, to trying to assess a text's literary qualities, or evaluating the use of a text for a school curriculum.

Children's literature criticism may often be consumed at first hand by adults, but its intended main and final beneficiaries are child readers. How to find the *good* book for the child is children's literature criticism's purpose, whichever way it is dressed up. Some critics are open about their aim: Michele Landsberg, in her popular book *Reading for the Love of It*, declares that 'adult responsibility . . . is not to deny, but to add, enrich, stimulate, amplify. To turn away with an indifferent shrug from helping children to choose books is not good enough. If anything goes, nothing matters. And children's literature does matter . . . intensely.'[5] With this view in mind Landsberg sets out to show in her book 'step by step, how any adult can become a skilled and confident chooser of the best books for the particular child'.[6] There are also critics who are less sure of the certainty with which this skill of choosing books can be acquired, or who have elaborated these doubts into theoretical debates. Jacqueline Rose, in her seminal polemical book *The Case of Peter Pan or: The Impossibility of Children's Fiction*, attacks much children's fiction criticism for its assumption of a 'knowable', unified child reading audience. Rose argues that 'the idea that "children's literature's" main quality is that it speaks to children— all children—ignores the socio-economic, political and cultural divisions in which all of society, including children and language, are caught.'[7] J. R. R. Tolkien in this respect expressed a similar view to that of Rose: 'Children as a class—except in a common lack of experience they are not [a class].'[8]

And yet these critics too are somehow seeking ultimately to benefit children, even if it is only to protect them from being told what is supposedly right or good for them. All of children's literature criticism is in this sense an expression of intention with regard to children: it is saying, in so many different ways, 'this is what we want children to read or not to read so that we end up with the following results . . .'. This intention is even more the case in criticism than in children's fiction itself. After all, the genesis of children's books remains problematical. We cannot actually say clearly what makes a book a children's book or not, or why children like it or not, or even *if* children like a book or not. The definition of a 'children's book' is still variously based on publishers' and editors'

[5] Michele Landsberg, *Reading for the Love of It: Best Books for Young Readers* (Prentice Hall Press, New York, 1987), 6.

[6] Ibid. 4.

[7] Jacqueline Rose, *The Case of Peter Pan or: The Impossibility of Children's Fiction* (series: Language, Discourse, Society, ed. Stephen Heath and Colin MacCabe) (Macmillan, London, 1984), 10.

[8] J. R. R. Tolkien, 'Children and Fairy Stories', in Sheila Egoff, G. T. Stubbs, and L. F. Ashley (eds.), *Only Connect: Readings on Children's Literature* (Oxford University Press, Toronto, 1969), 111–21, 112.

decisions, general trends of style and illustration, supposed or claimed readership, and theories of the creative processes which produce a book. Nicholas Tucker points out that 'although most people would agree that there are obvious differences between adult and children's literature, when pressed they may find it quite difficult to establish what exactly such differences really amount to'.[9] Natalie Babbitt, herself a children's author, attempted to test several suggested criteria and concludes that most of them prove inconclusive. Babbitt argues that children's books are not necessarily concerned with 'simpler' or 'different' emotions: 'there is, in point of fact, no such thing as an exclusively adult emotion, and children's literature deals with them all'.[10] Babbitt also observes that 'war, disability, poverty, cruelty, all the harshest aspects of life are present in children's literature'.[11] The only exception Babbitt mentions is 'graphic sex', although this subject, too, justifiably or not, appears in books intended for ever younger children. Whether a book started as an 'adult' book and ends up as a 'children's' book, or vice versa, or straddles both types (traditional examples of these shifting books range from Swift's *Gulliver's Travels* and Carroll's 'Alices' to Richard Adams's *Watership Down*) we have little ground to be sure why children's books are produced, created, or recreated.

If we think about it, it becomes easier to understand the problems that arise here when we compare the situation with adult readers: we do not actually find it that easy to predict which adults will like which books, or to explain why we like certain books, or respond to them, or what a 'good book' or 'literature' is, and why. These topics are the concern of 'adult' literary criticism, literary theory, psychology, philosophy, and reviewing. It is only the inclusion of the idea of the 'child' as reader that shifts these problems in many critics' minds. Because it is assumed that children can be understood, or known, the problems that adult literary criticism engages with seem simplified. To put it crudely,

[9] Nicholas Tucker, *The Child and the Book: A Psychological and Literary Exploration* (Cambridge University Press, Cambridge, 1990), 8.

[10] Natalie Babbitt, 'Happy Endings? Of Course, and Also Joy', in Virginia Haviland (ed.), *Children and Literature: Views and Reviews* (The Bodley Head, London, 1973), 155–9, 157.

[11] Ibid.

children's literature criticism uses the idea that adults know how children think and feel to 'solve' the problems that adult literary criticism struggles with precisely because it is not sure it is easy for people to know or understand how another person thinks or feels. And that is what reading is about, both with adults and children: thinking and feeling—cognition and emotion.

Now of course many children's literature critics have disagreed with one another about children's thinking and emotions, and some critics, like Jacqueline Rose, have substantially diverged from the view that we (can) know much about children at all. We will be looking later at the grounds for these varying views, but meanwhile we can note that crucial disagreements and doubts persist, and almost the only statement that can be made, as Peter Hunt has observed, is that '"children's books" is a very curious classification, a chaotic collection of texts that have in common nothing other than some undefined relationship to children'.[12]

But children's literature criticism is at least more narrowly occupied with some type of definition, analysis, and judgement of books it takes to be children's books. As such, as I have said, it reveals its intentions and purposes quite openly. Indeed, most works on children's literature begin with an explanation of the writer's aim or interest with respect to the field. We have already noted Michele Landsberg's statements concerning the importance of children's books for children. She explains how she personally experienced books during her childhood:

Books were far more than an amusement in my childhood; they were my other lives, and this visible existence I now lead in the workaday world was touched and transformed by them forever. The spell was never broken . . . [I] confirmed my belief that a child's life without books read for pleasure is a child's life deprived.[13]

There are many more examples: Masha Rudman writes that 'books are important influences on their readers' minds. They can either

[12] Peter Hunt, *Criticism and Children's Literature: Theory and Practice* (Dept. Of English, University of Wales Institute of Science and Technology, Cardiff, 1985), 48.
[13] Landsberg, *Reading for the Love of It*, 4.

help or hinder us when we attempt to construct suitable bases for attitudes and behaviours'[14] and, therefore, these books need to 'be analyzed for their effectiveness as well as for their intent'.[15] Lillian Smith declares her intention of 'consider[ing] children's books as literature, and discover[ing] some of the standards by which they can be so judged . . . They are a portion of universal literature and must be subjected to the same standards of criticism.'[16]

Children's literature criticism has had to come out of a corner fighting: Landsberg and Rudman assert the importance of books for children; Smith asserts the possibility of the serious qualitative assessment of children's books. The defensive tone rings throughout children's literature criticism. Each author claims anew the value of children's literature, and the value of the study of these books. Perhaps the most fascinating and problematic aspect of these authors' statements is that they are based not on *knowledge*, but on *belief*. If children's fiction criticism is relatively clear about its aim to find the good book for the child, then it is not clear about the extent to which this aim is based on beliefs and wishes, not facts. Perhaps it would be fairer to say that many critics appear not to be aware how much criticism is based on assumptions and beliefs, rather than on facts or substantiated knowledge.

I have already noted that critics disagree amongst themselves with respect to their views on childhood, on writing, and on reading, and this already warns us that they are not basing themselves on a common field of knowledge. But, again, it is still a conviction of knowledge which brings many people to children's literature criticism: conviction that they know what children like to read, according to their age and gender; conviction about their own memories of their emotional attachment to books in childhood or adulthood, or indeed of their childhood hatred of books and reading. Now why are there these expressions of knowledge when there is so much disagreement among critics, as we will see?

[14] Masha Kabakow Rudman, *Children's Literature: An Issues Approach* (D. C. Heath, Lexington, Mass., 1976), 3.
[15] Ibid. 4.
[16] Lillian Smith, *The Unreluctant Years: A Critical Approach to Children's Literature* (American Library Association, Chicago, 1953), 7.

Certainly most critics who have any awareness of the disparity of
opinions will try to justify their own opinion, and, of course, try to
show why it is more correct than other views. We might therefore
want to reformulate the 'conviction of knowledge' as *need*. That is,
critics of children's literature (as with many other people involved
somehow with children) usually display an urgency of belief,
asserted as knowledge, which is intricately involved with the need
within Western society to capture, define, control, and release and
protect the 'child', as Jacqueline Rose also argues in *The Case of
Peter Pan*.

It is this need which I would principally like to explore further in
this book. Why is the 'child' so important to children's literature
critics, and to all other people involved in defining what this 'child'
is, thinks, feels? There will be many impulsive 'of course' answers
to this type of question: 'of course people find children important—
they love them, they are responsible for them, children are the
future, they are part of one's life.' And, again 'of course', these are
good reasons for wanting to take the best care of children, and in
order to take the best care of children it would seem desirable to
understand them. But there are two problems (at least!) here: the
first is that we have hardly defined 'love', nor is love inevitable or
self-explanatory. People love children, as adults do each other, in
many different ways and to many differing degrees. An 'of course'
answer obscures this complexity. Secondly, these replies do not
address the remaining difficulty of critics' drawing images of
children and childhood which differ substantially and yet are all
claimed to be 'true' or 'real'. In this respect the 'of course' reasoning
so often applied to childhood and children reflects Clifford Geertz's
analysis of 'common sense':

There are a number of reasons why treating common sense as a relatively
organized body of considered thought, rather than just what anyone
clothed and in his right mind knows, should lead on to some useful
conclusions; but perhaps the most important is that it is an inherent
characteristic of common sense thought precisely to deny this and to
affirm that its tenets are immediate deliverances of experience, not
deliberated reflections upon it. . . . Religion rests its case on revelation,
science on method, ideology on moral passion; but common sense rests its

on the assertion that it is not a case at all, just life in a nutshell. The world is its authority.[17]

We constantly encounter the emphatic claim that children 'exist', that they are 'real', and that at least some people 'know' what children are: Sarah Trimmer, for instance, writes: 'little children, whose minds are susceptible of every impression, . . . from the liveliness of their imaginations are apt to convert into realities whatever forcibly strikes their fancy';[18] Elizabeth Rigby, on the other hand, claims that 'a child's head is a measure, holding only a given quantity at a time, and if overfilled, liable not to be carried steadily';[19] Alice Jordan feels that 'simplicity and sincerity are important factors',[20] while a *Times Literary Supplement* critic argues that 'Miss [Charlotte] Yonge knew very well that children can appreciate what they cannot understand. . . . children themselves prefer unsuitable books. They like to read about grown-ups rather than about their own contemporaries . . .'[21]

In the same way that all children's literature criticism is grounded in this belief—that children exist and can be known—so Western society has an ever-growing, complex, and ambivalent attachment to the concept of the child. It is the central argument of this book that that child does not exist. For the purposes of children's literature criticism, so closely involved with children's supposed emotions and states of mind, I am arguing that the 'child' is a *construction*, constructed and described in different, often clashing, terms.[22] Furthermore, these constructions are the

[17] Clifford Geertz, *Local Knowledge: Further Essays in Interpretive Anthropology* (Basic Books, New York, 1983), 75.
[18] Sarah Trimmer, 'On the Care Which is Requisite in the Choice of Books for Children', in Haviland, *Children and Literature: Views and Reviews*, 4–7, 7.
[19] Elizabeth Rigby, ibid. 8–18, 9.
[20] Alice M. Jordan, 'Children's Classics', ibid. 38–43, 39.
[21] Anonymous critic from the *Times Literary Supplement*, 'Ancient and Modern', ibid. 44–9, 48.
[22] While this book was in press, Rex and Wendy Stainton Rogers's book *Stories of Childhood: Shifting Agendas of Child Concern* (Harvester Wheatsheaf, London, 1992) was published. This book argues that childhood is a construction along similar lines to my own argument here, but with specific reference to the policies and practices of child concern. I regret not having been able to include a discussion of their argument in this book.

production of systems of purpose, which are fuelled by need. Besides arguing and illustrating this point, I will consider the consequences of this view—what do we do with the 'constructed child'? I will return to this later.

As I have indicated, children's literature criticism offers an ideal opportunity to study the operations of the systems of purpose (I hesitate to call them an 'ideology' as I believe that with respect to the child the purposes are too varied and mutually contradictory, and operate on too many different levels, to constitute some sort of coherent ideology): it states its aims and intentions clearly, and places itself at the heart of crucial issues. Children's literature bases its validity, its very existence, on a relationship between the author, or the book, and the child—a relationship which postulates, in many forms, the emotions, consciousness, and morality of the child.

Let me be clear: I am in no sense disputing the visible presence of new-born or young human beings. Rather, I am arguing that these creatures have ascribed to them—become 'carriers' for—a load of emotional and moral meanings. In this I am following what I take to be Philippe Ariès's point of view in his classic *Centuries of Childhood*[23] that through history children and the family have carried different emotional and moral values within society. Ariès argues that, although 'men and women will always go on guiding the first steps of those children',[24] these processes do not take place constantly in the same ways. He points out that 'the great demographic revolution in the West, from the eighteenth to the twentieth century, has revealed to us considerable possibilities of change in structures hitherto believed to be invariable because they were biological'.[25] The use of contraception, Ariès argues, is one of the crucial factors that have allowed people to influence, quantitatively and qualitatively, the nature of family life. The choices which the possibility of contraception and, for instance, improving medical care and hygiene have introduced lead him to further reflection on the structures and functions of the family:

[23] Philippe Ariès, *Centuries of Childhood* (Penguin, Harmondsworth, 1973).
[24] Ibid. 7–8.
[25] Ibid. 7.

For a long time it was believed that the family constituted the ancient basis of our society, and that, starting in the eighteenth century, the progress of liberal individualism has shaken and weakened it . . . the study of modern demographic phenomena led me to a completely contrary conclusion. It seemed to me . . . that on the contrary the family occupied a tremendous place in our industrial societies, and that it had perhaps never before exercised so much influence over the human condition . . . The idea of the family appeared to be one of the great forces of our time.[26]

Ariès argues that the modern idea of the family acquires its force from having become 'a value, a theme of expression, an occasion of emotion'.[27] And he adds, 'our experience of the modern demographic revolution has revealed to us the importance of the child's role in this silent history. We know that there is a connection between the idea of childhood and the idea of the family . . . that is why we are going to study them together.'[28] I have quoted Ariès's classic position relatively extensively because the attitude Ariès takes is fundamental to my own discussion, although the detail of his historical argument is not. Furthermore, some of the criticism which has been levelled at Ariès reveals misunderstandings I wish to avoid from the outset. To restate what I said above: neither Ariès nor I am arguing that there were times or places where there were no children. The point is the shift in, or development of, complex webs of meaning attached to the *idea* of childhood. It is only a realization of the complexity of this meaning-construction which allows for a close examination of shifts in the body of these meanings, or for an exploration of the motivations underlying the meaning-constructions. In other words we are not talking about the 'reality' of the two-month-old baby crying the night through: its parents know it is real—but what they will be much less sure about is why the baby cries the night through. They will devise hypotheses and act upon them: feed or change the baby, turn on its music-box, cuddle it, give it more or fewer blankets. Sometimes they will be successful, sometimes not. Some parents will respond to children differently from others, and some responses will seem to change the status quo more than others. Alongside the 'reality' of the crying baby we build up a complex story about why it cries,

---

[26] Ibid. 8.     [27] Ibid.     [28] Ibid.

what to do about it, and the feelings that accompany this story: anger, tiredness, anxiety, affection, pride, or bits of all or any of these, as well as many other feelings.

It is not only the extreme non-verbality of a two-month-old baby which prompts the complex 'story-telling': the same explanatory activity can take place between two more or less equally verbal adults. The attempt to understand that which is furthest from oneself—most *other*—is difficult. If two adults, however well known to each other or closely related, respond differently to what appears to be the same stimulus, let us say a book or film, then one enters the territory of identity, constructed through personal history. We can see the difficulties attendant upon understanding perhaps most clearly in situations with people who are receiving some form of help for their emotional problems: psychotherapy confronts head-on the complexity of identity, behaviour, emotional life, and response.

The complex controversies which attend the practice of social work and therapy (and much of what I am suggesting here also, I believe, applies to aspects of teaching) reflect in acute form the problems which children's literature criticism involves itself with. If I may just touch on some ideas I will discuss in greater depth later: psychotherapy is usually criticized through its theories; but if its theories are approved of, then it is concluded that the discipline must be effective. A much more accurate description of the complexity of psychotherapy is that it presents itself as based on scientific theory, but often admits that its practice depends to a large extent on art. That is to say: we develop structural concepts of understanding, but the practice of understanding depends a great deal on the skill and artistry of the therapist. There are therapists who know their theory backwards and forwards, yet they may be no more than adequate, if not straightforwardly bad, therapists. Whether it is argued that it is a failing of the theories, or of the teaching of the theories, or of the application of the teaching that causes this fundamental problem, the issue remains. A level of understanding is necessary to living an autonomous life in this world, but some people possess a gift for understanding themselves and/or other people. It is crucial, then, that the suppression of the difficulties inherent in self–other interactions is revealed in children's literature criticism by the realization that the most neglected area of discussion is the issue of how adults should set about learning about children from children. Having proved the great difficulty of eliciting useful responses from children about their reading, the subject is generally dismissed. As Nicholas Tucker tells us:

Trying to discover some of the nature and effects of the interaction between children and their favourite books is by no means easy, though. One simple-minded approach to the problem has always been to ask children themselves through various questionnaires and surveys, what exactly their books mean to them. Turning a powerful searchlight of this sort onto complex, sometimes diffuse patterns of reaction is a clumsy way of going about things, however, and children can be particularly elusive when interrogated like this, with laconic comments like 'Not bad' or 'The story's good' adding little to any researcher's understanding.[29]

I am not asserting that more study of this sort would solve the problems of children's literature criticism; I am merely noting this gap, and the implications of the absence of consideration of this subject. As children's literature criticism largely ignores the construction of the child, so it ignores reading as meaning-construction and interpretation, and so it also ignores the overall construction of understanding. Children's literature criticism abounds in statements about the 'child'. It provides us with various sources—scientific, religious, moral, mystical, commonsensical—backing up these statements. It tells us also to study the child, but it does not tell us how. A 'real child' vanquishes the necessity for self-reflection on the part of the children's literature critic concerning the construction of meaning and interpretative readings of texts and the world. The additional fact that almost no writing on children's literature criticism even notes this gap adds to its interest. Charlotte Huck, in *Children's Literature in the Elementary School*, argues that

The teacher or librarian may be very familiar with the general characteristics and interest patterns of children at various age levels and understand the basic principles of learning. Such knowledge is of value

---

[29] Tucker, *The Child and the Book*, 2.

only if it is applied to guiding each child as a unique individual. . . .
Understanding of the child and the accumulated effect of past experiences
is gained through observing him in many situations. . . . The teacher seeks
to understand the child's perception of himself, for this self-concept
influences his behaviour and his choices as well as his achievement. . . . It
is a poor teacher who has to be told what the children's interests are. It
does take skill and knowledge, however, to link children's interests to the
books they will enjoy.[30]

I am going to disagree radically with Huck and suggest that it is a
great deal more problematic, and takes a great deal more skill and
knowledge, to know what a child's interests are than to link a book
to a child. The problem here is that of the entire field of reading and
children and adults and the world: how we understand. That is:
how we understand each other and the world around us; *how we
make meaning*. For most children's literature critics, we do not make
meaning: we are given meaning by the 'real child'.

Therefore ideas about the dynamics of self–other interaction link
children's literature criticism with such disciplines as adult literary
criticism, philosophy, psychology, and psychotherapy. A denial of
the urgency, importance, and intricacy of meaning-construction—
that is, of the very constructed nature of childhood and the child—
can only revert to claims for the 'self-evident nature' of childhood,
for 'common sense', or for the comprehensiveness of information
supplied by science. While science certainly has an important role
to play *within* discourses of truth, reality, and continuity, 'self-
evidence' and 'common sense' cannot have a place in a study of the
history and dynamics of ideas and meaning (unless they are under
study themselves as cultural concepts—see the quote from Clifford
Geertz above).

I may be labouring this issue, but the 'construction'- versus
'reality'-of-meaning debate persists in creating substantial, mis-
placed conflict. Nicholas Tucker, for instance, criticizes Ariès by
arguing that

history tends to be male oriented . . . and then it . . . usually . . . [describes]
a remarkable child or . . . a particular piece of educational propaganda. It

---

[30] Charlotte S. Huck, *Children's Literature in the Elementary School* (Holt,
Rinehart and Winston, 3rd edn., New York, 1976), 30, 37.

is not altogether surprising that Ariès has sometimes been criticized for constructing his theory too much around a tiny, unrepresentative section of French society . . . What is not always clear in his argument . . . is whether children were once seen as mini-adults by everyone (even their mothers) or simply by the male adults mostly responsible for the surviving historical evidence . . . mothers would certainly know that young children were markedly dissimilar from adults in many ways.[31]

Lloyd de Mause similarly claims that Ariès 'ignores voluminous evidence that medieval artists could, indeed, paint realistic children',[32] and that 'his etymological argument for a separate concept of childhood being unknown is also untenable'.[33] Another historian of childhood, Shulamith Shahar,[34] bases her whole study of childhood in the Middle Ages on the attempt to prove that children did 'exist', and were 'seen', in order to refute what she takes to be Ariès's argument that childhood did not 'exist' because high infant mortality precluded emotional attachment to children.

But Tucker's, de Mause's, and Shahar's types of criticism are unfounded: Ariès makes it quite clear that, contrary to Tucker's and Shahar's assertions, he is not writing about 'realities' (whatever they may be seen to be) of states of childhood-dependency or lack of life-experience, but that he is interested in the development of cultural and social ideas of 'family' and 'childhood' as carriers of social, moral, emotional, and ethical values and motivations. As Ariès states at the beginning of *Centuries of Childhood*: 'it is not so much the family as a reality that is our subject here as the family as an idea.'[35] We can see this approach reflected, for instance, in Ariès's remark that 'in the moralists and pedagogues of the seventeenth century we can see that fondness for childhood and its special nature no longer found expression in amusement and "coddling", but in psychological interest and moral solicitude'.[36] All the personal expressions of affection that Shahar collects do not

---

[31] Tucker, *The Child and the Book*, 16, 19, 20.
[32] Lloyd de Mause, *The History of Childhood* (Psychohistory Press, New York, 1974), 5.
[33] Ibid.
[34] Shulamith Shahar, *Childhood in the Middle Ages* (Routledge, London, 1991).
[35] Ariès, *Centuries of Childhood*, 7.
[36] Ibid. 128.

refute the basic shift of attitude that Ariès is attempting to chart. It might also be noted that the evidence on which Shahar bases her claims, mainly male-produced saints' 'Lives', letters, and writings on child-raising, clashes with Tucker's critique of Ariès on its own level and on its own terms: Tucker dismisses Ariès by claiming that male evidence (such as Ariès uses) pertains usually to 'a remarkable child' or to 'educational propaganda', but Shahar takes precisely the male expressions of affection and interest in children as reflecting a generally present social and emotional status of childhood.

However, even if historians such as de Mause and Shahar are correct in their more detailed criticisms of Ariès's use of pictorial, etymological, and written evidence, Ariès's point still stands solidly: throughout history, and across cultures, ideas pertaining to morality, ethics, and emotions have shifted, and attitudes toward persons at the beginning of the life-cycle have been subject to similar changes. Indeed it is these very shifts and differences which constitute 'history' and 'culture'. Tucker, Shahar, and de Mause can only defy historical and cultural changes with respect to children by assuming they can know the 'true' or 'real' child, a 'real' child which has been eternally present. Ariès is nowhere claiming that young humans were not seen to exist in one capacity or another: as he says, 'men and women . . . will always go on guiding the first steps of those children'.[37] What he *is* trying to do is chart some of the changes in ideas of how and why those 'steps' should be guided and the context in which these changes have taken place:

The point is that ideas entertained about these [family] relations may be dissimilar at moments separated by lengthy periods of time. It is the history of the idea of the family which concerns us here, not the description of manners or the nature of law . . . *The idea of childhood is not to be confused with affection for children*: it corresponds to an awareness of the particular nature of childhood, that particular nature which distinguishes the child from the adult, even the young adult. In medieval society, this awareness was lacking.[38]

It is on Ariès's level of discussion (the history of ideas), then, that I

[37] Ibid. 7–8.      [38] Ibid. 8, 125; my emphasis.

wish to operate for the purposes of examining children's literature criticism further.

Before the examination of the premisses of Ariès's methodology I suggested that children's literature criticism is based not on 'substantiated knowledge', but on beliefs and need. I may now be in a position to emphasize that I did not mean to suggest by this formulation that it would be desirable to replace the beliefs and the need by substantiated knowledge. I did not mean to imply that my project is to correct incorrect knowledge of the child used by children's literature critics, and neither do I intend to supply some hitherto obscured or unrevealed facts. Most critics set out to do this, as I have pointed out, with varying results. For the purposes of discussing children's literature criticism I am questioning whether the pursuit of 'knowledge', or determining the thoughts and feelings of childhood, is at all the aim we should be striving toward. Of course, again, I mean this specifically with reference to children's literature criticism, although we will see that ideas about the application, or acquisition, of this type of 'knowledge' also occur in other fields, such as (child) psychotherapy.

A brief example extrapolated from that discipline, which we will be considering in Chapter 6 in relation to the issues of children's literature criticism, may illustrate what I am arguing with reference to this 'knowledge': we do have information and theories about the origins and dynamics of child abuse, albeit still incomplete and sometimes hypothetical. Nevertheless, despite the knowledge available many workers involved in this field function in a problematic way when it comes to the actual diagnosis and treatment of abuse. Further knowledge of the scientific or theoretical kind will not necessarily illuminate their predicament. It may be more important for them to come to terms with their own feelings about working in a field which is such a clear and acute example of many of the problems that the discourse of childhood generates in society. Social workers, therapists, police officers, and lawyers working in child abuse and neglect have their own 'systems of purpose', benign and malignant (of course I am including unconscious motives), with regard to working in this field. One could say they need to acquire a different type of 'knowledge', that is, a better knowledge of themselves and their 'systems of purpose' with regard to child abuse and neglect (in this context, we might call this counter-transference, but more on this in Chapter 6). In other words, the problematic acceptance of 'knowledge', in this context, shares many attributes with the problematic acceptance of 'understanding' I outlined above. I think the emblem of the situation with regard to child abuse and neglect, and that of the knowledgeable but bad therapist described earlier, may be kept in mind during my discussion of children's literature criticism, until I discuss them in their own right later. I would like to stick to the terminology I have suggested, however, for our purposes, and avoid the use of the word 'knowledge' with respect to that knowledge of one's own purposes and motives: I think this confuses the discussion. Also, I do not want to suggest at this point what the precise relationship is that I want to formulate between children's literature criticism and (child) psychotherapy before discussing it at greater length.

Instead, I would like to examine how discussions about the child are filled with what I am calling 'beliefs *expressed as knowledge*'. Why is the child so often portrayed as 'discovered', rather than 'invented' or 'constructed'? I do not think that considering the child as 'invented' constitutes, as we will see some children's literature critics imply, or argue openly, a disregard for the needs and suffering of feeling beings. My example concerning the necessity of thoroughly understanding one's own feelings, conscious and unconscious, when working in child abuse and neglect, also argues this point. It seems to me that exploring purposes and their expression in discourse—in essential invented narratives— can constitute an intense attempt to *listen*: whether it is a listening to stories (again, crucial and essential 'stories', not fictional stories) of selves or to stories others tell of other selves is a matter of belief or conviction at that given moment. In other words, can literary criticism, a system of 'telling' and of asserting views, be examined, or listened to, to learn why it tells the stories it does? This is what I intend to do.

The 'knowledge' problem is not only thrown into relief by the clear intentions of children's literature criticism, but also by its being rooted within discussions on *reading*. Though the mechanics of the reading process have been explored to an extent, as well as the learning of reading, neither is fully explained. We see this partly reflected in current British debates on the preferred teaching-methods for reading: 'whole word' methods versus phonic methods, for instance, or the debates surrounding 'real book' reading. The psychological and sociological aspects of reading, especially the reading of fiction, remain subject to even more differing views and attitudes. What is it that we do when we read? Why does a reader enjoy a book or find it meaningful? Do readers' interpretations of the meanings of a book vary, and how, and why? What is a good book? What is literature? The complex interactions between an individual reader and a text, and their relation to surrounding social, historical, and cultural circumstances, remain open to many interpretations and explanations: the psychologist Jerome Bruner argues that

we may . . . wish to discover how and in what ways a text affects the reader and, indeed, what produces such effects on the reader as do occur . . . Can a 'psychology' of literature describe systematically what happens when a reader enters the Dublin of Stephen Daedelus [*sic*] through the text of 'Portrait'? The usual way of approaching such issues is to invoke psychological processes or mechanisms that operate in 'real life'. But such proposals explain so much that they explain very little. They fail to tell why some stories succeed and some fail to engage the reader . . . And above all, they fail to provide an account of the processes of reading and of entering a story.[39]

Children-as-readers have been allocated particular relationships to these issues by children's literature critics, in the same way that the broader field of adult literary criticism has developed theories about reading to support practical criticism.

As Bruner points out, ideas about reading are crucially connected to ideas about how we know the world in its broadest sense: textual understanding, interpretation, and response are taken to reflect, literally or metaphorically (depending on your theoretical basis), the processes of understanding, interpretation, and response in, and

[39] Jerome Bruner, *Actual Minds, Possible Worlds* (Harvard University Press, Cambridge, Mass., 1986), 4.

to, the 'real world'. Thus we find theoretical approaches comparing reading to conversing with another person, to the process of therapy, to making love, to collaboration or resistance. What *is* it that we do when we read? Literary criticism and literary theory have made many suggestions. What is it that controls the meaning of a text, when not all readers interpret it in the same way, but when there may be limits to how it can be interpreted? The author, the text, and the reader have been allocated the control of meaning at different times. Originally, the author functioned as God in determining the meaning of the Bible: the text meant what the author wanted it to mean. The language of the text effected a response, as T. S. Eliot, for instance, suggested with the idea of the 'objective correlative': the juxtaposition of words in poetry corresponded to the evocation of emotion and imagery. But the problems of determining the intention of an author, and the proliferation of seemingly valid interpretations patently beyond the author's possible intentions, led to rejections of the author as the locus of stability of textual meaning. Some theorists, such as E. D. Hirsch Jr., have defended the idea of the intentions of the author as limiting interpretation, but New Critics such as René Wellek introduced the notions of the 'intentionalist' and 'affective' fallacies, and saw the text as a self-contained, autonomous system of meaning. The linguistic relations between words, sentences, or couplets determined genre and meaning: the text controlled its own meanings.

Diversity of interpretation still nags at literary theory, however. Much practical criticism still makes use of primarily the language of New Criticism and its approaches, especially 'close reading', I would argue, even when the critic does not consider himself to be a New Critic. But theoretically the reader has increasingly been allocated the responsibility for meaning in reading. Both the author and the text seem unable to restrict meanings, or even to create them. The reader most clearly activates the text and interprets it, and therefore criticism has sought to explore the readers' reading as the responsible agent of meaning-construction and reception. The 'aesthetics of reception' of a Constanz-school critic like Hans-Robert Jauss places the reader within 'horizons of reception' where historical context plays a leading role in controlling the fund of meanings a reader can resort to in reading. Wolfgang Iser is an example of a critic who argued that the text contains 'gaps' which a reader has to 'fill in ' to fulfil the meaning of the text. The amount of gaps, and the variable fillings-in of these gaps, lead to multiplicity of interpretation. The sections between the gaps in the text in turn structure and restrict interpretation to an extent.

Critics known as (Derridean) deconstructionists are interested in multiplicity of meaning as the reflection of the unstable, dynamic attributes of all meaning—textual and extra-textual (strictly speaking there is no 'extra-textual' to deconstruction). Deconstruction, incidentally, has had a varied press within the various academic disciplines, but whatever importance we accord it, it has frequently been misrepresented. Deconstruction does not, by my reading, strive toward the nihilism of 'everything means everything, therefore nothing means anything', as is so often claimed (hence the frequent equation of deconstruction with 'destruction'). This view of deconstruction, I think, comes forth out of some critics' inability to take seriously, whether they ultimately agree with it or not, deconstruction's rejection of a 'real' world outside constructed meaning. I take deconstruction to work with the notion of a type of three-dimensional, ever-moving ball of electrical sparks of meaning: meaning is not located 'in' the poles between which the sparks jump—indeed to deconstruction these poles do not 'exist'— it is the streaks of light left behind by the sparks, the 'traces', which represent meaning.

The paths the sparks seem to draw create relationships of 'différance' which are what meaning *is*. Hence each meaning (for instance, 'male', 'logic', 'nature') is determined by what it is and is not ('female', 'object', 'absence', 'madness', 'chaos', 'irrationality', 'civilization', 'freedom', 'presence'). If the electrical activity of the network ceases, or exhausts itself, 'aporeia' is achieved—the draining-away of meaning. But this is a final stage, and since deconstruction presents itself as non-teleological, I do not think we have to worry as much about 'aporeia' as some critics have. It is a necessary concept theoretically to this philosophy, but is impossible to achieve in practice. Neither is deconstruction an obfuscated form of liberal humanist 'close reading' as some critics have claimed. Deconstruction does not accept that stability of meaning is maintained by any form of non-textual 'real world'. I am putting in my tuppence worth on this subject because ideas from, and about, deconstruction (or actually from Freud and Nietzsche, who have both been an influence on deconstruction in particular respects) impinge on my approach to 'childhood' and 'adulthood' in this book. With reference to my rough sketch of some ideas from literary theory, however, it should be mentioned that deconstruction has since been developed in other directions, and other approaches, such as Wayne Booth's attempts to re-establish a basis for morality in literary interpretation, are countering the previous influence of deconstruction.

The main point of this brief overview is to illustrate how reading has been made to play various roles in theories of interpretative activity: children's literature criticism derives its overall authority in making claims about children's understanding and emotional life from the use of unquestioned assumptions about similarities and differences between the interpretative strategies claimed to be used in reading and those which are claimed to be used in 'reality'. In other words, children's literature criticism has made an uncritical and often confused use of ideas about relationships between narrative and 'reality'. In both adult and children's literature, reading has been discussed using terms such as identification, empathy, learning, constructing, conscious and unconscious response, imagination, reflecting the frequent mixture of terms which actually derive from differing theories about the ways reading can or cannot function as an analogue of systems of interpretation which are claimed to be employed with extra-textual 'realities'.

One way in which the difficulty of mixing references to interpretative strategies supposedly used in reading and those used in 'reality' is addressed is by arguing (as we saw in my thumb-nail sketch of deconstruction) that reading is what we do to the world-as-text, or life-as-narrative: that there is no polarized separation or difference between a narrative and a 'reality' with respect to interpretation. Roland Barthes has suggested, for instance, that 'I am the story which happens to me'.[40] But, as we saw in the overview of literary critical approaches, there are various ways, and several levels, of relating narrative to meaning: differing approaches preserve different relationships to ideas of extra-narrative 'realities'. Many theorists who otherwise do preserve a level of extra-textual 'reality' still also include a large role for narrative in their theories of meaning. They tend to argue that in so far as humans lead a life beyond pure practical survival, but deal with emotions, some kind of self-consciousness, and interrelationships on that basis, narrative is a means of discussing both experiences of reality and symbolic life: values, morals, ideals. Ernst Cassirer, for instance, describes such a view of language and story-telling when he writes that

the functional circle of man is not only quantitatively enlarged; it has undergone a qualitative change. Man has, as it were, discovered a new method of adapting himself to his environment. Between the receptor system and the effector system, which are to be found in all animal species, we find in man a third link which we may describe as a 'symbolic system' . . . a new dimension of reality . . . No longer in a merely physical universe, man lives in a symbolic universe. Language, myth, art, and religion are part of this universe.[41]

But within this system too Cassirer warns that, as I am arguing with respect to children's literature criticism, the attempts to 'connect the fact of symbolism with other well-known and more elementary facts . . . has become the bone of contention between the different metaphysical systems: between idealism and materialism, spiritualism and naturalism'.[42]

Cassirer's point on the uses of language explains much of the relevance argued by critics for the use of story-telling and reading in childhood as well as in adulthood. Wilhelm Dilthey, by whom Cassirer was strongly influenced, formulated the idea as follows:

the immense significance of literature for our understanding of spiritual

[40] Roland Barthes, *Roland Barthes by Roland Barthes*, trans. Richard Howard (Macmillan, London, 1977), 56.

[41] Ernst Cassirer, *An Essay on Man: An Introduction to a Philosophy of Human Culture* (Yale University Press, New Haven, Conn., 1944), 24–5.

[42] Ibid. 27.

life and history lies in the fact that the inner life of man finds its complete, exhaustive, and objectively comprehensible expression only in language. Hence the art of *Verstehen* centers on the exegesis or interpretation of human existence contained in writing.[43]

In these ideas reading is intimately involved with *identity* and *consciousness*, and these concepts are in turn central to the construction of such concepts as 'childhood' and 'adulthood'. Because of the way reading is seen to be involved with learning, understanding, and response, the nature of the influence and effects of reading are the central concern in most children's book studies. The desire to foster humanitarian or liberal attitudes and feelings in people, or the capacities for, for instance, love, compassion, tolerance, and truthfulness (as we will often see reflected in discussions about children and their reading), are crucial to the importance attached to ideas about books for children, which are attributed with containing emotional values and evoking emotional reactions to an almost unique extent.

Clearly present in this context is the idealism concerning the enlightening and ennobling functions of art and literature, which encompasses the complexity of values and ideals anyone engaged in educating and raising children attempts to transfer and preserve. This liberal humanist faith in the ennobling function of literature is obviously expressed by literary critics such as I. A. Richards, F. R. Leavis, and the earlier Wayne Booth. It comes as no surprise that these critics were also powerfully interested in education as such. In other words, the value that children's books are attributed with having for children is a particularly concentrated form of the values attached to child-raising in general. Children's literature criticism uses the arena of the interaction between the child and the book to make claims and express ideas about who children are, how they grow, and how, what, and why they learn.

Because children's literature criticism is therefore constantly articulating ideas about reading and readers simultaneously, critical attention has recently realized that the visible nature of the process

---

[43] Wilhelm Dilthey, *Introduction to the Human Sciences*, trans. and intro. essay by Ramon J. Betanzos (Wayne State University Press, Detroit, 1988), 28.

in this field can contribute to thinking in literary criticism and literary theory in general. As Julia Briggs puts it: 'the study and interpretation of fiction for children pose, in an acute form, the fundamental questions raised by all fiction: who writes, for whom and why?'[44] Peter Hunt quotes Aidan Chambers's view that 'I have often wondered why literary theorists haven't yet realized that the best demonstration of all they say when they talk about phenomenology or structuralism or deconstruction or any other critical approach can be most clearly and easily demonstrated in children's literature.'[45] In so far as all reading relates to cognition and emotions, to identity and consciousness, children's literature critics, who have been so involved with these aspects of reading above all, may have contributions to make to thinking about 'adult' reading.

Children's literature and its criticism are inextricably and reciprocally connected with 'adult' literature and criticism anyway. Chris Jenks points out, in examining the sociology of childhood, that 'the difference between the [child and the adult] indicates the identity of each; the child cannot be imagined except in relation to a conception of the adult, but interestingly it becomes impossible to produce a well defined sense of the adult without first positing the child.'[46] Jenks gives some examples of the changing relationships between the 'adult' and the 'child', arguing that society continues to theorize about

whether to regard children as pure, bestial, innocent, corrupt or even as we view our adult selves; whether they think and reason as we do, are immersed in a receding tide of inadequacy or are possessors of a clarity of vision which we have through experience lost . . .; whether they are constrained and we have achieved freedom, or we have assumed constraint and they are truly free.[47]

By defining and discussing the nature of children adults are

[44] Julia Briggs, 'Awkward Questions', *Times Literary Supplement* (1–7 April, 1988), 372.

[45] Hunt, *Criticism, Theory, and Children's Literature*, 5.

[46] Chris Jenks (ed.), *The Sociology of Childhood: Essential Readings* (Batsford Academic and Educational Ltd., London, 1982), 10.

[47] Ibid. 9–10.

expressing, formulating, and projecting ideals and ideas about themselves and the not-themselves.

Children, in culture and history, have no such voice. In this and other respects, this engagement of the dominant concept of adulthood with that of childhood has strong parallels with Michel Foucault's interpretation of the role of insanity within society. In *Madness and Civilization* he writes that 'what is originative is the caesura that establishes the distance between reason and non-reason; reason's subjugation of non-reason, wresting from it its truth as madness, crime, or disease, derives explicitly from this point.'[48] 'Childhood' does not perhaps carry quite such a heavy load of negative meaning as madness or insanity (though madness, too, has at times been held to be a privileged state of contact with the divine, or with unbearable knowledge or ecstasy), but it, too, functions as an exponent of the 'non-adult' and 'non-reason'. Childhood can speak only through the memories, observations, or selections and interpretations of adults, just as 'the man of madness communicates with society . . . by the intermediary of an equally abstract reason which is order, physical and moral constraint, the anonymous pressure of the group, the requirements of conformity'.[49]

Children's books operate in this realm of interpretative tension: in being assigned to children, these books are held to be one of the central repositories of what, at different times, in different places, are considered to be thoughts and emotions *either present in, or lacking from*, childhood. Children's books change as the interaction with historical and socio-cultural needs and ideas relating to childhood change, or different books move into or out of the category of 'children's books'. The shifts remain dependent on authors' and critics' notions of what they are and are not: in so far as aspects of both of these sides are reflected in views of 'childhood' they are expressions of a wish to use children's books either as a means of educating the 'non-adult' to conform to the 'adult' (as Jacqueline Rose, for instance, argues), or as a means of articulating

[48] Michel Foucault, *Madness and Civilization: A History of Insanity in the Age of Reason*, trans. Richard Howard (Tavistock Publications, London, 1967), xii.
[49] Ibid.

what is considered, hoped, or feared to be the 'non-adult' still in the adult (or both): in other words, as a means of maintaining a pathway of contact and communication between the adult and the child without, and/or between the adult and the child within. Jacques Derrida writes:

man *calls himself* man only by drawing limits excluding his other from the play of supplementarity; the purity of nature, of animality, primitivism, childhood, madness, divinity. The approach to these limits is at once feared as a threat of death and desired as access to a life without différance. The history of man *calling himself* man is the articulation of all these limits among themselves. All concepts determining a non-supplementarity (nature, animality, primitivism, childhood, madness, divinity, etc.) have evidently no truth-value . . . They have meaning only within a closure of the game.[50]

The concepts of 'adult' and 'child' interact in an immensely complicated process of adult self-definition. The dominant role of the adult in this relationship is maintained and repeated throughout culture and society. In the Western industrialized nations, at least, ideological, political, and moral issues assert themselves with concentrated vigour with regard to children. This near total dominance of the adult world over children, established at its most fundamental level by chronology, creates an uneasy field of tensions relating to control, self-control, and the pressures, joys, and uncertainties of power. It is a complex hierarchy: in so far as any society and culture are dynamic systems when a child enters them, an inevitable interaction is established and maintained, as between any novice and some form of establishment. Rousseau, for instance, comments on this power structure repeatedly in *Émile*. Regarded as one of the central figures in developing modern attitudes towards children, he writes that 'there is no subjection so complete as that which preserves the forms of freedom; it is thus that the will itself is taken captive.'[51]

Whereas we have already observed that 'knowledge' of children

[50] Jacques Derrida, *Of Grammatology*, trans. Gayatri Chakravorty Spivak (Johns Hopkins University Press, Baltimore, 1976), 244–5.

[51] Jean-Jacques Rousseau, *Émile*, trans. Barbara Foxley (Everyman's Library, no. 518, J. M. Dent and Sons, London, 1911, repr. 1950), 84.

is expressed through the sciences, social sciences, and children's literature criticism, the regulating forces exercised by adults over children are most obviously visible throughout our society in the shape of the laws concerning the child's place in the family: adoption and custody; fostering; laws pertaining to ownership and transfer of property; laws concerning child abuse and neglect; and rules organizing the child's place in public life (legislation on child education and child labour). The story adults tell about a childhood which is largely mute itself determines its function and meaning within society. Yet, crucially, as members of a substratum of the structures of Western industrialized society, the adults within the child–adult hierarchy do not have the option of withdrawing from their positions of power and responsibility with respect to children: their absence would, in that case, only constitute another form of use of power (as we saw Rousseau noting, even the freedom we give children is a product of an exercise of power). We must somehow, instead, further examine the adult–child hierarchy and, in constantly acknowledging the responsibility of power, determine what we want to do with it. Although the hierarchy of domination of adults over children has its very dark sides, such as child abuse and neglect, child exploitation and misuse, and indoctrination, this structure also, I would argue, provides the only means of protection and nurturing necessary within a version of society (*whether or not* it would be necessary to 'children' in some form of Utopia): without the benevolent aspects of adult care of children, the alternatives are children sleeping in cardboard boxes in streets, or 3-year-olds living off rubbish-heaps.

We may seem to have wandered rather far away from children's literature criticism, but in fact, as we shall see, not only does this criticism reflect broadly the structures of the society and time within which it functions, but it negotiates the same problems in detail. The ambivalences within the adult–child hierarchy express themselves on a small scale within children's literature studies as they express themselves on a large scale in society at large. Parallels can be drawn between interpretations on a socio-political level and those on the level of personal emotions and desires, closely involved as they are with the ideals of society and politics.

For all these reasons, then, children's literature criticism presents itself as a fruitful field of study: not necessarily because we can prove or disprove the importance of (children's) reading (although we will see many efforts to do so either way); not necessarily because we can prove or disprove the influence of this criticism itself; and not necessarily because children's fiction criticism has access to privileged information or knowledge, but because it exemplifies the operation of the need to establish the child as a 'reality'. The 'child' as discovery, as truth or reality, in terms of imaginative and emotional response, is fundamental to children's literature criticism. This is not to say that all critics are unaware of the constructed child: as we will see, some critics address this issue and attempt to deal with it. But the 'child's' involvement with narratives, or discourses, of, for instance, power, freedom, nature, innocence, sexuality, and hope, and the lack of success of even self-professed critical efforts to disengage from it, reveal, to me, depths of feeling and the entrenchment of the imagery.

Moreover, a comparison with a better-known and more widely discussed area of meaning-construction emphasizes the particular position of childhood: feminism has, after all, long since addressed the concept of 'woman' and 'femininity', and shares a crucial importance with 'childhood'. We also see within feminism the same debate about 'woman' as a self-evident, biologically determined category, contrasted with the view of 'woman' as a constructed discourse. But, again, this discourse can and may include considerations of a biological or physiological kind. As with childhood, arguing for the discursive nature of the concept does not mean to assert that there is no 'reality' to the notion of 'woman' or 'child', but, instead, that whatever level of 'reality' we assume or even establish, we attribute meanings to it in many different ways. With entrenched imagery, such as that of woman, it has repeatedly proved inordinately difficult to separate meaning from being. Even scientific research has problems extracting 'facts' from the web of meanings. If scientists claim to have done so, then immediately this fact *becomes* a meaning. The scientific processes of hypothesizing and experimentation do not develop in abstract space: they involve the foregrounding of elements either because they already have meaning or because the foregrounding makes them meaningful. Science, with respect to woman or the child, cannot provide us with the absolute, rock-bottom 'objective'. That this is not purely the status of science anyway is demonstrated by Thomas Kuhn's ideas about scientific paradigms, and Nelson Goodman's writing on science. How does a pattern or a 'fact' or a process become visible to a scientist? It is a complex procedure, which certainly strives to bind itself by scientific rules, such as procedures of verification and falsifiability, but nevertheless takes place *within* a larger world of meanings. Science itself has been created and endowed with meaning by humankind. This is not to question its results or achievements at all—if anything, it confirms the importance of science to our lives. As Goodman suggests:

science is no enemy of the arts. . . . Science becomes associated with unfeeling intellect, the humanities with pure emotion, thus slandering both. Intellectual effort is motivated by profound need and provides deep satisfaction; and the emotions often function also as cognitive instruments. Neither art nor science could flourish if it did not give satisfaction, or if satisfaction were the only aim. Constable urged that painting is a science, and I suggest that science is a humanity. Putting them in opposition misconceives and hurts both.[52]

The point of this argument, as with the discussion of the work of Philippe Ariès above, is to establish clearly from the outset the status of this and other discussions, which are not concerned with denying realities as such, but which, in a sense, stop striving merely to strip cultural concepts of their garments, body, and bones, to reach a kernel, a core, or a heart, and, instead, study those garments, body, and bones. And note that any heart is determined by its relation to the body and bones, and functions as part of them.

Gayatri Spivak writes, in relation to the 'reality' versus 'construction' debate, in which she was accused of remoteness or distance from urgent issues by siding with 'construction', that she felt 'obliged to stress the distinction between my position and the

[52] Nelson Goodman, *Of Mind and Other Matters* (Harvard University Press, Cambridge, Mass., 1984), 5.

position that, in a world of massive brutality, exploitation, and sexual oppression, advocates an aesthetization of life'.[53] Spivak explains that her interest does not primarily turn to questions such as 'what is the nature of the aesthetic?', or 'how indeed are we to understand life?', but towards thinking about issues such as that

1) the formulation of such questions is itself a determined and determining gesture. 2) Very generally speaking, literary people are still caught within a position where they must say: life is brute fact and outside art; the aesthetic is free and transcends art. 3) This declaration is the condition and effect of 'ideology'.[54]

Of course my argument involves my reformulation of some of the conflicts between materialist, essentialist, and realist philosophies on the one hand and idealist philosophies on the other. As Richard Rorty writes of Foucault and Habermas:

Michel Foucault is an ironist who is unwilling to be a liberal, whereas Jürgen Habermas is a liberal who is unwilling to be an ironist. Both Foucault and Habermas are, like [Isaiah] Berlin, critics of the traditional Platonic and Kantian attempts to isolate a core component of the self. Both see Nietzsche as critically important.[55]

Nietzsche himself wrote:

we have to be stable in our beliefs if we are to prosper, we have made a 'real' world a world not of change, but one of being . . . A world in a state of becoming could not, in a strict sense, be 'comprehended' or 'known'.[56]

Roland Barthes reformulated Nietzsche's view with respect not only to the interpretation of literature, but also to the 'world as literature':

knowledge of the profound self is illusory: there are only different ways of articulating it. Racine lends himself to several languages—psychoanalytic, existential, tragic, psychological . . .; none is innocent. But to acknowledge

[53] Gayatri Chakravorty Spivak, *In Other Worlds: Essays in Cultural Politics* (Routledge, London, 1988), 95.

[54] Ibid.

[55] Richard Rorty, *Contingency, Irony, and Solidarity* (Cambridge University Press, Cambridge, 1989), 61.

[56] Friedrich Nietzsche, *The Will to Power*, ed. Walter Kaufmann, new trans. Walter Kaufmann and R. J. Hollingdale (Vintage Books, New York, 1968), 281.

this incapacity to tell the truth about Racine is precisely to acknowledge, at last, the special status of literature.[57]

Barthes goes further, though I do not intend to follow his path all the way: he continues by arguing that 'in precisely this way literature . . ., by refusing to assign a "secret", an ultimate meaning, to the text (and to the world as text), liberates what may be called an anti-theological activity, an activity that is truly revolutionary, since to refuse to fix meaning is, in the end, to refuse God and his hypostases—reason, science, law'.[58] Barthes sees 'refusing God' as 'truly revolutionary', while I see it more as yet another 'belief', perhaps because Barthes strives towards not fixing meaning, and I believe we can never, despite this striving, not fix meaning at some level—in this I agree with Nietzsche. Derrida also differs from Barthes, as Spivak points out in her introduction to *Of Grammatology*: 'this [Derrida's discussion of supplementarity] might seem an attractively truant world of relativism. But the fearful pleasure of a truant world is the sense of an authority being defied. That absolute ground of authority Derrida would deny.'[59] Similarly, in locating the functioning of many of the terms of children's book criticism within its refutations of the idea of the discursive construction of childhood, I am concerned not with suggesting a new, final, essential child, but with examining the terms of discussion as they operate.

However, although readings of Derrida and like-minded theorists thus support the theoretical context and perspective of my examination of 'children' and children's fiction criticism, I am not engaged in a Derridean deconstruction of these terms. First, my aim in examining the terms is not that of a deconstructionist: I do not pursue or formulate this discussion with an eye to fulfilling what I take to be the ultimate demands of Derridean philosophy. Derrida and other philosophers and literary theorists 'write', despite their

[57] Roland Barthes, *On Racine*, trans. Richard Howard (Performing Arts Journal Publications, New York, 1983), 171.

[58] Roland Barthes, *Image, Music, Text*, essays selected and trans. Stephen Heath (Fontana, London, 1977), 147.

[59] Gayatri Chakravorty Spivak, 'Introduction', Derrida, *Of Grammatology*, pp. i–xc, lxxii.

disavowals of 'writing' (which in these terms, as Spivak explains, designates 'an entire structure of investigation, not merely . . . graphic notation or tangible material').[60] In writing, in the narrow sense, Derrida argues, we recognize and repress 'the absence of the "author" and of the "subject matter", interpretability, the deployment of a space and a time that is not "its own" ',[61] but we ignore the fact, he says, that 'everything else is also inhabited by this structure of writing in general, that "the thing itself always escapes" '.[62] Thus Derrida is the first to admit he is subject to Nietzsche's 'necessary lie' of creating a world not of becoming but of being, but this does not deter him from examining the terms of his own, and other, 'lying'.

I am selectively applying this perspective in arguing that the child is written, discursive, textual; but I am not attempting to pursue the deconstruction of all the terms of the 'closure of the game' to the full, because I am concentrating on narratives of 'children', 'adults', and 'literature'. Secondly, with respect certainly to categories as heavy with meaning as 'woman' and 'child' we do not even need to take sides with the extreme idealism of such a philosophy as deconstruction, in my view. There is enough complexity and cultural particularity involved with each of these concepts for even philosophies concerned with reality-claims and objectivity to have difficulty denying there is much ground to cover before one could reach a hypothetical 'real' child or woman. It will probably only be at the end of my argument that it will become clear how much this is the case with the child. That it is the case with 'woman' is already much more familiar. Simone de Beauvoir put forward for women similar points to the ones I have just formulated for the child. In her classic work *The Second Sex* de Beauvoir is negotiating the opposition between a determined and constructed woman:

The biological and social sciences no longer admit the existence of unchangeably fixed entities that determine given characteristics, such as those ascribed to woman, the Jew, or the Negro. . . . The fact is that every concrete human being is always a singular, separate individual. To decline

[60] Ibid. p. lxix.      [61] Ibid.      [62] Ibid.

to accept such notions as the eternal feminine, the black soul, the Jewish character, is not to deny that Jews, Negroes, women exist today—this denial does not represent a liberation for those concerned, but rather a flight from reality.[63]

De Beauvoir continues by discussing woman as 'other' to man. Man is, as she puts it, 'the positive and the neutral; . . . whereas woman represents only the negative, defined by limiting criteria, without reciprocity. . . . He is the subject, he is the Absolute—she is the Other.'[64] Self–other relationships are difficult to maintain as those of equals—'self' inherently presumes an authority, a dominance, the defining role. As with male–female self–otherness, so with the adult–child, with two crucial differences: first, whereas the female other may, through feminism, struggle towards equality with men, self-definition, and subject status, this option is not open to the child in the adult–child hierarchy, as I argued earlier. Secondly, whereas most self–other relationships are based on ostensible differentiation of self from other, every adult has, in some sense or other, been a child. An adult who defines himself by stating that he was 'never a child' or 'never able to be a child' is indicating an extraordinary situation—an exception to a very definite rule. De Beauvoir writes that 'following Hegel, we find in consciousness itself a fundamental hostility towards every other consciousness; the subject can be posed only in being opposed—he sets himself up as the essential as opposed to the other, the inessential, the object.'[65] The self defines itself largely by distancing itself from what it claims it is not—and yet the situation is never clear-cut. A woman defining herself as a woman may include in this definition elements she designates as male or masculine, yet she will rarely claim to have been a male (unless she is a transsexual, both challenging, and paradoxically complying with, the established gender-roles of society). But every adult has somehow been a child, is within himself both continuous of identity and simultaneously changed. Chris Jenks writes that 'the child is familiar to us and yet strange

[63] Simone de Beauvoir, *The Second Sex*, trans. and ed. H. M. Parshley (Penguin, Harmondsworth, 1972), 14.
[64] Ibid. 15–16.
[65] Ibid. 17.

. . . he is essentially of ourselves and yet appears to display a different order of being: his serious purpose and our intentions towards him are meant to resolve that paradox by transforming him into an adult like ourselves.'[66] The situation is quintessentially paradoxical in that adults who are no longer children are still in some sense those children. An old friend last met in childhood who is reintroduced in adulthood will simultaneously identify one as being the same person—with the same name, same ancestry—and yet a different person. Particular traits will be identified as having persisted through time, others will be said to have changed or to be totally new. Some adults claim to 'be children still', others see parts of themselves as 'the child', yet others deny having anything left of the child. Some want to 'return' to childhood, others express the wish to leave it behind for ever.

All these attitudes and emotions are expressed throughout children's literature criticism. Again, since children's fiction studies are concerned so centrally with the dynamics of the emotions and imagination, and with the emotions that pertain to what it means to be an adult or a child, they constantly negotiate these connections between the adult and the child without and the adult and the child within. Hence theories not only of identity, but also of imagination, sympathy, empathy, and memory, are implicitly or explicitly part of children's fiction criticism. As with the application of psychology and child psychotherapy, for instance, to the field of children and reading, we often find a selective application of theories of identity or memory. The very selection itself is often revealing with respect not only to the assumptions of the critic, but also with respect to the conclusions the critics wish or need to reach. Jacqueline Rose summed up these problems when she wrote that

children's fiction rests on the idea that there is a child who is simply there to be addressed and that speaking to it might be simple. It is an idea whose innocent generality covers up a multitude of sins. . . . There is no child behind the category 'children's fiction', other than the one which the category itself sets in place, the one which it needs to believe is there for its own purposes.[67]

[66] Jenks, *The Sociology of Childhood*, 10.
[67] Rose, *The Case of Peter Pan*, 1, 10.

The criticism of children's fiction reduplicates this tactic.

Children's literature criticism can be roughly divided up into different branches according to the extent to which the critics involved regard the child as a construction or a knowable reality. In the next chapter we will look more closely at the language, evidence, and logic employed by those critics who are most sure of the knowable child.

# 2

# On Knowing the Child: Stories of Origin and Hierarchical Systems

If there has been some disagreement between historians with respect to the existence of the child in history, then children's book historians have at least narrowed down the field somewhat with reference to children's books. Children's books, they say, were not around as such until the eighteenth century. F. J. Harvey Darton, that redoubtable historian of children's books in England, writes that 'children's books did not stand out by themselves as a clear but subordinate branch of English literature until the middle of the eighteenth century'.[1] Before this time we hear different stories about what children should read, or did read. With respect to Western culture those stories emerge from its twin roots: comments on education from classical antiquity, and the Christian educational practices of the church in the Middle Ages.

It is the story which is told about education which informs us of the background to the power allocated to reading, as well as to education in the wider sense. Henri-Irénée Marrou defines 'education': 'l'éducation est la technique collective par laquelle une société initie sa jeune génération aux valeurs et aux techniques qui charactérisent la vie de sa civilisation.'[2] Rather than embarking upon a traditional history of educational views on reading, however, I want to present those bits of 'history' which are most relevant to the discourse of children's literature criticism. That is, instead of presenting a history of fact, claiming it to be correct or incorrect, I

---

[1] F. J. Harvey Darton, *Children's Books in England: Five Centuries of Social Life* (first pub. Cambridge University Press 1932; 3rd edn. rev. Brian Alderson, Cambridge University Press, Cambridge, 1982), 1.

[2] Henri-Irénée Marrou, *Histoire de l'éducation dans l'antiquité* (2nd edn., Éditions du Seuil, Paris, 1950), 17.

want to attempt to present a history of reading and children as told by children's literature criticism for its own purposes.

Along the way, I hope to make visible how children's literature criticism constructs or takes on the assumptions upon which it operates. Most importantly, I would like to argue that, based on a hierarchical model of the adult–child relationship, the narratives adults attempt to convey to children are controlled and formed, implicitly and explicitly, by the didactic impulse; that the roots of allocating books (that is, criticism) to, and producing them for, children, lie in the effort to *educate*. This is in contrast to the generally accepted view that children's fiction is a category defined by, and originating from, a *move away* from didacticism, instruction, or education: that it is, in this sense, interpreted as being a liberator of children. As Alison Lurie writes, for instance:

Soon after I began going to the library, I realized that there were two sorts of books on its shelves. The first kind, the great majority, told me what grown-ups had decided I ought to know or believe about the world. . . . Along with these improving books there were also some that hoped to teach me manners or morals or both. . . . their lessons came disguised as stories. . . . But there was another sort of children's literature, I discovered. . . . These were the sacred texts of childhood, whose authors had not forgotten what it was like to be a child. To read them was to feel a shock of recognition, a rush of liberating energy.[3]

But as concepts of 'childhood' as other to 'adulthood' developed and became increasingly specific and detailed, so needs to comprehend and control this 'other' grew: the liberation through children's literature is an illusion. It is a paradoxical development of ideas, with both aspects of the paradox inextricably implicated and involved with each other. As children were beginning to be 'discovered' (or invented) they were also simultaneously, and perhaps inevitably, subject to more specific attempts to conquer and control them.

There is much importance attached to the denial of educational, or controlling, intention, however. It is often stated nowadays that didacticism in children's books has been largely removed. It is often

[3] Alison Lurie, *Don't Tell the Grown-ups: Subversive Children's Literature* (Bloomsbury, London, 1990), pp. ix–x.

regarded as heavy-handed or obvious, as we can see in Alison Lurie's comment. The children's author Joan Aiken believes 'Children have a strong natural resistance to phoney morality. They can see through the adult with some moral axe to grind almost before he opens his mouth.'[4] This attitude is part of the broader stance taken by children's literature criticism, which claims that children's books are not primarily about teaching, but about amusement, albeit with teaching through the amusement. Yet I am arguing that, even if children's books are claimed to have developed within a literary mode of narrative not dominated by the didactic impulse, they are still subordinated to the efforts of the adult world to assimilate children to its values and motives. There are continued attempts to discern and define the influence of books on children, and to select and direct books for children with the previously determined aims in mind.

Many children's book critics, then, do not tend to place much overt importance on the study of the ideas concerning education. They either take a historical perspective on children's book studies or they have an interest, as I have said, stemming from a professed love of children's books. Yet it is ideas found in writings on education which are a large component, and a powerful expression, of the creation of the category of 'childhood', and thus of 'children's books'. Education is the area above all within which explicit elements of the conventions of the adult discourse on childhood developed. Any attention, however, that critics have directed towards it has had the precise aim of distancing children's fiction from it. Attention focuses on discussing schoolbooks, texts, and primers with the principal aim of defining 'children's books' by contrasting them with, and separating them from, those overtly didactic texts. In other words, these are examinations concerned with establishing a *literary genre*. John Rowe Townsend, for instance, in his historical and critical overview *Written for Children*, draws this distinction between what he sees as purely moral and didactic treatises and schoolbooks and primers, and books intended

---

[4] Joan Aiken, 'Purely for Love', in Virginia Haviland (ed.), *Children and Literature: Views and Reviews* (The Bodley Head, London, 1973), 141–55, 149.

also, or mainly, 'to amuse'.[5] Harvey Darton also writes: 'by "children's books" I mean printed works produced ostensibly to give children spontaneous pleasure and not primarily to teach them, nor solely to make them good, nor to keep them profitably quiet.'[6] Dennis Butts writes that '[children's literature] came into existence in printed form in the eighteenth century, though religious and instructional books had appeared earlier . . .'.[7]

We find that critics draw two main distinctions in an attempt to describe their basis of literary genre traits of modern children's fiction: between books written for children and for adults, and between books written to 'educate' children and books considered as being written to 'amuse' children. These distinctions are based on principles which generate enduring problems within children's literature criticism, for both terms—to 'educate' and to 'amuse'— are descriptions of the effects of texts on readers. And as such they are the product of the link made between these texts and ontological notions of childhood. We are faced with the prevalence of reliance on the problematic acceptance of varying and changing ontologies of childhood. Or, as we put it before, we are faced with the eruption of the contradiction between the claims to knowledge of the child and the differences in, and variety of, descriptions of this child.

In order, then, to analyse better the discourse of children's books and children's book criticism, we must start 'before' the critics' 'educate' and 'amuse' divide, and examine the principles which underlie their ideas pertaining to reading in relation to concepts of childhood. A Dutch critic, J. Riemens-Reurslag, has formulated the issue which plagues those concerned with education and reading as follows:

can the transference of ideas from a book happen in such a way that it has a deep influence on the life of a child, or is a book only capable of awakening

---

[5] John Rowe Townsend, *Written for Children: An Outline of English-Language Children's Literature* (2nd rev. edn., Penguin, Harmondsworth, 1983), 18.

[6] Darton, *Children's Books in England*, 1.

[7] Dennis Butts, 'Introduction', in Butts (ed.), *Stories and Society: Children's Literature in its Social Context* (series: Insights, gen. ed., Clive Bloom) (Macmillan, London, 1992), pp. x–xvi, x.

thoughts already present in the child? And to what extent can this transference of ideas take place?[8]

It will be obvious that this question forms one small aspect of the larger debate concerning the role of 'nurture' versus 'nature' in the development of character and abilities in human beings. As Sara Goodman Zimet points out:

both personal testimony and empirical research strongly suggest that while our attitudes, values and behaviours may be influenced by what we read, when left to our own initiative we read what we are. In other words, we select our readings to support our predispositions rather than in order to change them. . . . Evidence supporting quite the opposite position [can also be] presented . . . demonstrating, in effect, that we are what we read.[9]

This is also another reflection of the 'hermeneutical circle' in perception: that not only does what we see mould our perception, but our perception also shapes what we see. The significant point to keep in mind throughout the following discussion is that these are unsolved problems. We have only to call to mind the problems of educating people in general to realize the complexity of the issue, even just on the level of rational comprehension. Children's literature criticism is interested in allying itself with a history emphasizing the effectiveness of reading in transferring cultural value and meaning to the readers, through the evocation of emotional and imaginative response.

Effectively, therefore, the roots of children's literature criticism can be located in ancient times. It was in this oral culture, we are told, that poetry became an invaluable aid to memory in dispersing 'not only the tales of the gods and famous men but also the words of hymns and prayers and the details of ritual'.[10] Carpenter describes poetry in this sense as 'a specialized idiom of communication'.[11]

[8] J. Riemens-Reurslag, *Het Jeugdboek in de Loop der Eeuwen (Children's Books through the Centuries)* (first pub. The Hague, 1949; facsimile edn. pub. Interbook International, Schiedam, 1977), p. xiii.

[9] Sara Goodman Zimet, *Print and Prejudice* (with an additional chapter by Mary Hoffman) (Hodder and Stoughton, London, 1976), 17.

[10] Frederick A. G. Beck, *Greek Education 450–350 BC* (Methuen, London, 1964), 22.

[11] Ibid. 23.

Beck quotes Rohde as saying of the Greek Homeric world that 'if anyone did possess a monopoly of teaching it was, in this age when all the highest faculties of the spirit found their expression in poetry, the poet and the singer'.[12] Beliefs and practices which were important within a culture were linked to communication through poetry and ritual. On the basis of this idea the faith both in the capacity of poetry to educate and in the importance of teaching poetry are explained: poetry encapsulated important or interesting knowledge and beliefs. Out of these terms poetry developed its traditional description: for instance Horace's well-known 'poets aim either to do good or to give pleasure—or, thirdly, to say things which are both pleasing and serviceable for life'.[13] Sir Philip Sidney famously restated this view in his 'Defense of Poesy':

> . . . I speak to show that it is not rhyming and versing that maketh a poet—no more than a long gown maketh an advocate, who though he pleaded in armour should be an advocate and no soldier. But it is that feigning notable images of virtues, vices, or what else, with that delightful teaching, which must be the right describing note to know a poet by, although indeed the senate of poets hath chosen verse as their fittest raiment . . .: not speaking (table talk fashion or like men in a dream) words as they chanceably fall from the mouth, but peizing each syllable of each word by just proportion according to the dignity of the subject.[14]

It is this idea, as James Bowen tells us, which lies at the heart of 'the *studia humanitatis*, [which] for more than two millennia, was dominant in the West, and it was within such a conceptual framework that all educational issues arose and solutions or compromises were reached'.[15]

The aims of the Greeks and Romans, as they are described, in using reading and literature are clear with respect to children and other learners: literature previously interpreted and evaluated by

---

[12] Ibid.

[13] D. A. Russell and M. Winterbottom (eds.), *Ancient Literary Criticism: The Principal Texts in New Translations* (Clarendon Press, Oxford, 1972), 288.

[14] Philip Sidney, *An Apology for Poetry or: The Defense of Poesy*, ed. Geoffrey Shepherd (Thomas Nelson and Sons, London, 1965), 103.

[15] James Bowen, *A History of Western Education*, i: *The Ancient World: Orient and Mediterranean, 2000 BC–AD 1054* (Methuen, London, 1972), p. xvi.

adults for adults was also given to children to help to inculcate in them the appropriate ideals and ideas for citizenship. Children principally memorized sections of texts, and studied the same texts repeatedly through different stages of their education. The aim was to educate young nobles for virtue, and virtue was defined by the ideals of behaviour and character for man in society. Davidson reminds us that the duties of full citizens 'were completely summed up under two heads, duties to the family and duties to the state . . . the former included the three relations of husband to wife, father to children, and master to slaves and property; the latter, three public functions, legislative, administrative, and judiciary'.[16] Plato, for instance, has Protagoras say to Socrates:

And when they send him to school they tell the teachers to pay much more attention to the child's behaviour than to their letters or their music. The teachers do that, and then when they have learned their letters and are going on to understand the written word, just as they did with speech before, they set before them at their desks the works of good poets to read, and make them learn them by heart; and they contain a lot of exhortation, and many passages praising and eulogizing good men of the past, so that the child will be fired with enthusiasm to imitate them, and filled with the desire to become a man like that . . . The people who are best able to do it—I mean, the wealthiest—do this especially . . . [17]

This passage occurs within a discussion between Protagoras and Socrates on the possibility of teaching 'excellence', on what this 'excellence' is, and on the role of this kind of teaching in the existence of the city-state. In the *Laws* Plato includes a consideration of education to help provide the citizens of his ideal state with the correct frame of mind: 'What we have in mind is education from childhood in *virtue*, a training which produces a keen desire to become a perfect citizen who knows how to rule and be ruled as justice demands.'[18]

---

[16] Thomas Davidson, *Aristotle and Ancient Educational Ideals* (William Heinemann, London, 1904), 12–13.

[17] Plato, *Protagoras*, trans. with notes by C. C. W. Taylor (Clarendon Press, Oxford, 1976), 17–18.

[18] Plato, *The Laws*, trans. with an introduction by Trevor J. Saunders (Penguin, Harmondsworth, 1970), book 1, 73.

Similarly, Aristotle's ideas on education, and so education through reading also, are shaped by his ideas about politics and the attainment of Supreme Good to which this science aspires. Aristotle also argues in the *Politics* that the aim of education must be to educate for peace and leisure, because these are noble, whereas war and business are vulgar. This view of Aristotle's explains much of the basic reasoning in favour of a 'liberal arts' education over an education consisting primarily of training in skills or technical matters. As James Bowen points out, this issue is still of fundamental relevance to modern Western education with respect to 'the rivalry between liberal and technical education with their respective antagonists considering the former a meaningless and decadent social ideal, the latter an illiberal and mindless kind of vocational training'.[19] Obviously this conflict is enmeshed in modern views on reading as an emotional and imaginative education, which yet disclaims its didactic role as such.

Other Greek educators, such as Isocrates (436–338 BC), the influential teacher of rhetoric, and Roman writers such as Cicero and Quintilian, equally concerned with oratory, also emphasize the training of character in virtue or insight (Isocrates puts more emphasis on this latter attribute) within the context of the roles noble men fulfilled in the state. Quintilian, in his *Institutio oratoriae*, sets out the education of an orator from the very beginning. Again education is explicitly moral as well as intellectual: 'We are to form, then, the perfect orator, who cannot exist unless as a good man.'[20] Quintilian recommends reading to begin with Homer and Virgil, so that 'the mind of the pupil [will] be exalted with the sublimity of the heroic verse, conceive ardour from the magnitude of the subjects, and be imbued with the noblest sentiments.'[21] In the same way he feels that, although beginners should read the best authors at once, they should choose those who are 'clearest in style and most intelligible',[22] recommending Livy,

[19] Bowen, *A History of Western Education*, i. p. xvi.

[20] Quintilian, *Institutes of Oratory or: Education of an Orator, in 12 Books*, trans. John Selby Watson (George Bell and Sons, London, 1903), i. 4.

[21] Ibid. 71.

[22] Ibid. 117.

for instance, to be read by boys rather than Sallust, who, however, 'is the greater historian, but to understand him there is need of some proficiency'.[23] Cicero is also 'agreeable even to beginners, and sufficiently intelligible'.[24]

Quintilian also considers the mechanics of learning to read with quite a detailed theory of cognitive development. He professes to be displeased with the apparently widespread practice of teaching children 'the names and order of the letters before they learn their shapes'.[25] He asserts that

this method hinders their recognition of them [letters], as, while they follow their memory that takes the lead, they do not fix their attention on the forms of the letters. . . . it will be best for children, therefore, to be taught the appearances and names of the letters at once, as they are taught those of men.[26]

Approval is also given to providing children with ivory figures to play with, and with a board with the letters cut out of it, so that the child can learn to write by tracing the grooves. The next step, in reading, is to teach the syllables, and 'not to hurry on, in order to make it continuous or quick, until the clear and certain connexion of the letters become familiar'.[27] Quintilian argues that children must have plenty of time to perfect these skills, so that the child will feel secure in reading, and have learned to read aloud while anticipating what follows.

The very detail of these Greek and Roman comments and theories on reading will be seen to be repeated and used up to the present day. There are shifts in reading materials: subjects approved of in moral and religious terms change, as do ideas about what (some) children enjoy or learn more easily, but, mostly, this type of reasoning and these assumptions appear in similar forms in many writings on 'children's books'.

Writers on education point to many changes in higher education from the time of Quintilian (first century AD) onward.[28] Bowen writes that by the sixth century Roman education, based previously

---

[23] Ibid.
[24] Ibid.
[25] Ibid. 15.

[26] Ibid.
[27] Ibid. 16.
[28] Bowen, *A History of Western Education*, i. 212.

on enquiry and discussion on the Greek model, had been reduced to the memorizing of the contents of compendia:

the educational justification advanced by Capella that the liberal arts are a complete approach to knowledge providing both the means of organization (the 'trivium' of grammar, rhetoric and philosophy) and the content into which knowledge is systematically organized (the 'quadrivium' of arithmetic, geometry, astronomy, and music) was largely lost on those who read it. . . . In effect, Roman education in the sixth century had become encyclopedic in nature and content, in the pejorative sense of the term. It was to remain so in the West for centuries to come.[29]

Christianity, carrying with it part of its Jewish roots, was seen to become the next powerful educational movement. The place of book-learning took on a central role in Christian religious education. These tremendous changes described in culture and morality, however, are not portrayed as having included profoundly changed attitudes toward the learning experience of the child through books. The children who received this type of education may be described as having belonged to different classes in society, the goals of their learning as having changed in overt content, and children as having been given different set texts to read and learn. But reading in childhood is considered as having consisted continuously of the reading and, primarily, memorizing of the same books used by adult learners beyond the acquisition of basic reading skills: the psalms, prayer-books, Latin grammars, and books of morals and manners were used. Outside formal education in monasteries, adults and children are portrayed as listening to the same stories. Ariès writes:

the Hellenistic paideia presupposed a difference and a transition between the world of children and that of adults, a transition made by means of an initiation or an education. Medieval civilization failed to perceive this difference and therefore lacked this concept of transition. The great event was therefore the revival, at the beginning of modern times, of an interest in education. This affected a certain number of churchmen, lawyers and scholars, few in numbers in the fifteenth century, but increasingly numerous and influential in the 16 and 17 centuries.[30]

[29] Ibid. 212–13.
[30] Philippe Ariès, *Centuries of Childhood* (Penguin, Harmondsworth, 1973), 396.

It was the time and thought of the Renaissance and humanism, referring back to the works of the Greeks and Romans, and of the Reformation and Counter-Reformation which are attributed with having prompted the development of 'children's books'.

Literature and reading are thus portrayed as having played an important role in ancient Greek and Roman society for all learners, regardless of age. Both adults and children read the same works to help them to learn about the ideas and behaviour appropriate to the good citizen, and to help to inspire them to achieve this ideal. Memorization of parts of texts was the method of learning in the earlier stages, particularly for children, and these same texts would then be encountered repeatedly throughout the duration of education. This is said to be even more true of Christian religious education in the Middle Ages, which was much more exclusively book-centred. The bulk of critical discussion concerned with education was aimed at defining the morals, ideals, values, or doctrine the texts could or should transfer, within the wider discussions on the structures of the ideal state, both for society and for the individual within it, which that education would conduce to bringing into existence. Texts continue to be seen as sources of great authority and influence.

The sixteenth-century educationalist Juan Luis Vives was of the opinion that

poems contain subjects of extraordinary effectiveness, and they display human passions in a wonderful and vivid manner. This is called *energia*. There breathes in them a certain great and lofty spirit so that the readers are themselves caught into it, and seem to rise above their own intellect, and even above their own nature.[31]

There are not many clearer articulations of the power ascribed to literature in the intellectual, moral, or emotional education of children. As Alastair Minnis puts it, albeit with respect to literary criticism of the time just preceding Vives:

No medieval theorist could have decried the 'intentionalist fallacy' or the 'affective fallacy', since authorial intention and the 'affective' functions of

---

[31] Juan Luis Vives, *On Education: A Translation of the De Tradendis Disciplinis of Juan Luis Vives*, introd. and trans. Foster Watson (Cambridge University Press, Cambridge, 1913), 126.

literature were of the first importance in medieval literary theory. To a considerable extent, medieval commentators derived their standards of criticism from the psychological causes of the text ('intentionalism') and from its psychological results (its 'affective' appeal to the reader). This difference of opinion should be recognized by the modern theorist and critic.[32]

Although I have already argued that this legacy of assuming the effects of reading raises all types of difficulties for children's literature criticism, it is only at this point that our 'history' enters a more overtly troubled phase: it is from the sixteenth century on, if we follow Ariès's chronology, that changes take place in ideas about children and childhood, and this brings us to the development of the ontological concept of the 'child'. Together with this development the notion arises that children could be raised and educated in a better way if the methods used somehow corresponded to, or connected with, this ontology. There now emerges a paradox with regard to books: a need, it is said, began to be felt for books which somehow corresponded to the ontology of the 'child'. But the books must still be of adult-judged quality and content, as argued by the Greek, Roman, and medieval church theorists of education. Vives formulated the paradox as follows:

although in teaching art, the most perfect and absolute parts are always to be propounded, yet in teaching, those parts of the art should be presented to the audience, which are most suited to their capacities.[33]

With the Greeks, Romans, and medieval church teachers the literary or historical texts judged to articulate and embody the greatest art were used to teach learners what was great and good. But the paradox Vives formulated created all kinds of problems in the movement to adapt this moral and emotional education to the postulated needs and capacities of 'children': how could one teach 'children'—the other to the 'adult'—with material which was simultaneously selected and created by adults? For this material must then supposedly also be 'other' to adult art and thus, to a great

---

[32] Alastair J. Minnis, 'Chaucer and Comparative Literary Theory', in Donald M. Rose (ed.), *New Perspectives in Chaucer Criticism* (Pilgrim Books, Norman, Okla., 1981), 60.

[33] Vives, *On Education*, 89.

extent, unjudgeable by adult standards. And yet, the material had to be judged as good in order to be thought able to achieve the desired effects in education. Virginia Haviland tells us that in 1844 Elizabeth Rigby (whom Haviland calls 'an advanced critic') wrote that children's books should be a 'union of the highest art with the simplest form'.[34] In this situation texts have to be good for children *and* good for adults—a difficult situation when concepts of childhood depend on differences from adulthood.

As M. W. Keatinge records, Mosellanus, Professor of Greek at Leipzig, wrote about his writing of a 'pedology' that he published in 1517 that 'the importance of my occupation [initially] made me disdain this work, doubtless useful, but humble and almost mean in appearance, and . . . not being used to it, I found it difficult to play the part suitably, since I saw that for this kind of comedy a man must become a child once more'.[35] Mosellanus is saying that the simplicity, for him, of the contents of the pedology made it more suited to being written by a child—this implies that a child would also regard it as simple. Or he means that a child should write the book because then it would reflect or convey a child's level or type of understanding accurately—but to do this the child must somehow have a previous knowledge of the contents of the pedology. What Mosellanus seems to be struggling with is the feeling that he should try to remember how he learned as a child in order to clarify or anticipate difficulties from his current position as an adult. In other words, he must be his adult and his child self at the same time, in order to tackle the pedology successfully according to his own standards.

Mosellanus's formulation is echoed throughout children's book production and criticism: the necessity and possibility of adults becoming children again are repeatedly touched on, often in terms of 'seeing through the eyes of the child'. Donna Norton's book on children's literature is actually called *Through the Eyes of a Child*.[36]

[34] Haviland, *Children and Literature*, 3.

[35] M. W. Keatinge, 'Introduction' to John Amos Comenius, *The Great Didactic*, introd. and trans. M. W. Keatinge (Adam and Charles Black, London, 1896), 122.

[36] Donna E. Norton, *Through the Eyes of a Child: An Introduction to Children's Literature* (Charles E. Merrill, Columbus, Oh., 1983).

Margaret and Michael Rustin comment, in their psychoanalytic study of modern children's fiction, that they 'have already indicated the extent to which modern children's fiction can be read through sociological eyes, as offering representations of particular social worlds from a child's eye view'.[37] Jonathan Cott describes his reaction to what he calls his 'rediscovery' of children's books:

My turning to children's books as an over-satiated adult reader induced in me the kind of 'intense attention' that, the critic Helen Vendler has suggested, the greatest literature should induce, making us enter, in her words, a state of 'receptivity and plasticity and innocence', and, in Shelley's words, purging 'from our inward sight the film of familiarity which obscures from us the wonder of our being'. . . . For children's literature reawakens in us our sense of remembering, which, in fact, is often stored in, and brought to new life by, our senses.[38]

Cott, as reader, believes he has become a child again.

Expressions of needs thus to reinhabit the child—to reclaim it after having created it—are preceded by views of a lengthy process of separation. Children's books, and the discussions surrounding children's reading, evolved further alongside and became an integral part of the creation of this cultural narrative of childhood. The story children's book critics and historians tell about the origins of children's books is that they were intended to amuse children, as opposed to educating them primarily. I have already quoted John Rowe Townsend and F. J. Harvey Darton defining children's fiction by distinguishing it from school texts and primers, or by linking books to a child readership. Central to theories of the origins of children's fiction is this linking of childhood with 'leisure' and 'amusement'. 'Childhood' began, in this sense, by being the repository for ideas about certain types of freedom: 'freedom' determined as an absence of civilizing and restrictive forces. An opposition is set up: on the one hand there are 'non-children's books', supposedly given to children earlier in history, which are said to be oppressive, dictatorial, and forces of

[37] Margaret and Michael Rustin, *Narratives of Love and Loss: Studies in Modern Children's Fiction* (Verso, London, 1987), 22.

[38] Jonathan Cott, *Pipers at the Gates of Dawn: The Wisdom of Children's Literature* (Viking, London, 1984), 18.

civilization in a negative sense with respect to children. On the other hand there are 'children's books', simply claimed not to be forces: a part, as it were, of what Rousseau would call a 'negative education', designed, as Peter Gay comments, 'to avoid the mistakes of the past and keep Émile from absorbing the vices of his culture'.[39] In this respect, the development of childhood and the roles attributed to children's fiction operate in a boundary area impinging on several concepts and aspects of freedom and liberty.

John Stuart Mill classically delineates the aspects pertaining to this boundary when he introduces his essay *On Liberty*:

The subject of this essay is not the so-called Liberty of the Will, so unfortunately opposed to the misnamed doctrine of Philosophical Necessity; but Civil or Social Liberty; the nature and limits of the power which can be legitimately exercised by society over the individual.[40]

'Childhood' represents a specialized status with regard to *both* 'Liberty of the Will' and 'Civil or Social Liberty'. As Mill writes:

Over himself, over his own body and mind, the individual is sovereign. It is, perhaps, hardly necessary to say that this doctrine is meant to apply only to human beings in the maturity of their faculties. We are not speaking of children, or of young persons below the age which the law may fix as that of manhood or womanhood. Those who are still in a state to require being taken care of by others, must be protected against their own actions as well as against external injury. . . . Despotism is a legitimate mode of government in dealing with barbarians, provided the end be their improvement, and the means justified by actually effecting that end. Liberty, as a principle, has no application to any state of things anterior to the time when mankind have become capable of being improved by free and equal discussion.[41]

Children's fiction becomes defined as being part of a liberation movement, away from didacticism, artificiality, and moralism. The notion of 'childhood', as we saw Derrida imply, is thus part of a

[39] Peter Gay, *The Enlightenment: An Interpretation*, ii: *The Science of Freedom* (Wildwood House, London, 1970, repr. 1979), 544.

[40] John Stuart Mill, *On Liberty, Representative Government, The Subjection of Woman: Three Essays*, introd. Millicent Garrett Fawcett (series: The World's Classics) (Oxford University Press, London, 1912, repr. 1969), 5.

[41] Ibid. 15–16.

developing interest, located as occurring from the Renaissance onwards, in 'nature'. The child becomes an expression of that which is 'natural': unfettered, spontaneous, unspoilt, true. It is no wonder that Rousseau's *Émile* is seen as the seminal work in relation to notions of childhood. As George Boas argues in his study of the *Cult of Childhood*:

[Rousseau] initiated the idea that childhood is something inherently different from manhood . . . since the child is, so to speak, sui generis [Rousseau says], it must be recognized that he has his own ways of seeing, thinking, feeling, and nothing is more foolish than to attempt a substitution of our ways for his.[42]

We will consider Rousseau in greater detail later, but for the time being may note that his type of linking of the child to the natural is essential to the education–amusement divide which is presented as having generated children's fiction. Desires to escape from restrictive social mores created a childhood as being everything which was *not* that which these 'adults' felt themselves to be.

The 'existence' of childhood, this presence in and of itself, is present in works of writers on education previous to Rousseau and the equally quoted (in children's literature studies) John Locke. A Dutch writer on children's literature, Anne de Vries, for instance, mentions Rousseau and Locke as the two main authors putting emphasis on the 'nature of the child'.[43] 'Education', 'freedom', 'nature', and 'the individual' are closely linked concepts related to this period of historical thought, and the 'child' is moulded by aspects of each of those redefined concepts. This is reflected in the writings of important sixteenth- and seventeenth-century theorists such as Rabelais, Vives, Erasmus, Montaigne, Luther, and Comenius. In these authors we find theories relevant to the emotional and cognitive aspects of children and their education and

[42] George Boas, *The Cult of Childhood* (Studies of the Warburg Institute 29, ed. E. H. Gombrich) (Warburg Institute, University of London, 1966), 31–2.

[43] Anne de Vries, *Wat Heten Goede Kinderboeken? De Theoretische Opvattingen over Kinderliteratuur en de Praktijk van de Boekbeoordeling in Nederland 1880–1980 (What Are Said To Be Good Children's Books? Theoretical Ideas about Children's Literature and the Practice of Judging Books in The Netherlands 1800–1980)* (Em. Querido's Uitgeverij b.v., Amsterdam, 1989), 18–19 (my translation).

reading. But, perhaps still more importantly, we find formulations of the motives and pressures which resulted in the concept of the 'child' articulated in their ideals of society, religion, morals, and values. Whereas the Greeks, Romans, and medieval church educators are presented as concentrating on defining the desired results of their endeavours, there followed a slow shift to a simultaneous consideration of the material which had to be presented to fulfil the preset goals. As Rousseau wrote in *Émile*, 'The wisest writers devote themselves to what a man ought to know, without asking what a child is capable of learning. They are always looking for the man in the child, without considering what he is before he becomes a man.'[44] Which changes were required in children to bring them to maturity, and how were they to be achieved? This question becomes pertinent to the definition required for the child.

M. W. Keatinge touches on a number of the elements involved in the developments with regard to children and education when he writes, in the introduction to John Amos Comenius's *The Great Didactic*:

The day school open to children of every rank; the large class managed by a single teacher as the only means by which such schools were economically possible; the introduction of every subject of instruction that could free the understanding from sophistic habits and teach men to look facts squarely in the face—these were the goals towards which his [Comenius's] efforts strove, and his historical antecedents are bound up with the great democratic movement of which the Reformation was the most striking manifestation, with the names of Luther, Sturm, Calvin, and Knox. The conscience had been installed by the Reformers as guide, and its counsellor, the understanding, needed education. Good schools, and nothing else, could remove monkish ignorance from the land; and this truth Luther was not slow to enunciate.[45]

Reading takes several roles within the different strands of 'the great democratic movement'. On the one hand nature, and observation and experience of the natural world and life in practice, are

---

[44] Jean-Jacques Rousseau, *Émile*, trans. Barbara Foxley (Everyman's Library, no. 518, J. M. Dent & Sons, London, 1911, repr. 1950), 3.

[45] Keatinge, introd. to Comenius, *The Great Didactic*, 125.

described as a moral force in their own right. The natural was good and true—a prelude to the pastoral and Romanticism, as well as to the Enlightenment philosophers. On the other hand reading is prescribed as the ideal medium of mass teaching. The greater availability of books through the invention of the printing press allowed for reading to be written of as an activity directed towards the construction of individuality: instead of being read aloud to, and repeating sections of text pre-interpreted by teachers, pupils could have the texts more easily available to themselves, and open to more lengthy and detailed perusal. Thus 'truth' and the values and morality of society are advocated as available through the individual's own perception of nature and books. Individuality and freedom, as ideals, must be taught in form as well as in content of teaching: a complex and self-contradictory concept.

The ideas of the child and childhood are used by these writers as a central means of dealing with the inherent paradox of teaching individuality and freedom. To do this, man-as-child, on the one hand, is described in terms of unreason and freedom; on the other hand man-as-adult is described in terms of reason and freedom. A shift from an uncontrolled, undifferentiated freedom to specific, reasoned freedoms characterizes the development postulated for the human being from 'child' to 'adult', and sanctions the education crucial to this process. This is how and why education can be allied to 'amusement', as an attempt to make it both an efficacious and a 'natural' process—an unforced process: in other words a true *liberal* arts education.

Children's fiction is presented as being the product of these ideas. Vives, for instance, writes that 'the human mind is wonderfully inclined to freedom. It allows itself to be set to work, but it will not suffer itself to be compelled. We may easily gain much by asking, but very little by extortion, and that little with difficulty.'[46] Vives also presents education through reading in terms of a natural, pleasurable process:

certain instruments, so to say, also were sought for, with which we should be more easily and pleasantly led to the paths of reason . . . Music, as a

---

[46] Vives, *On Education*, 121.

relaxation and recreation of the mind, through the harmony of sounds. Under this head, comes all poetry, which consists in the harmony of numbers. Prose oratory, however, has its rhythms, though they are not fixed by definite and constant law, like poetry.[47]

The Greek concern with harmony and balance is one of the components of the traits of Renaissance and humanist 'nature'. Vives specifies the role of books:

to books we must refer for knowledge in every subject. For without them, who could hope that he would attain the knowledge of the greater things? The direct inspiration of God teaches only very few . . . Therefore the man desirous of wisdom must make use of books, or of those men who take the place of books, viz. teachers.[48]

Montaigne equally clearly reflects this reinterpretation of education. He emphasizes that 'I wholly condemn all violence in the education of a tender mind, which one intends to bring up to honour and liberty'.[49] This Aristotelian type of statement beautifully encapsulates the paradox these thinkers are working within. Montaigne, like Vives, asserts that 'one can only tempt the appetite and affections; otherwise one only educates book-laden asses: by blows from rods one gives them a pocket full of knowledge to keep safe. Whereas if we would succeed, one must not only lodge it in their minds but espouse and wed them to it.'[50] To raise children 'to honour and liberty'—Montaigne has, as Vives did, reformulated Greek thought with new pertinence to the views of the Reformation and humanist writers on education and society. Love of learning, they argue, must be engendered henceforth as a basis and part of freedom and choice.

Although concerned with issues of freedom—both redefining the term and relating it to education—Vives and Montaigne are primarily concerned, as Rabelais and Erasmus are, with the education of the 'young gentleman'. As Keatinge points out,

[47] Ibid. 39–40.
[48] Ibid. 44.
[49] Michel Eyquem de Montaigne, *The Teacher's Montaigne*, introd. and trans. Geraldine E. Hodgson (Blackie's Library of Pedagogics) (Blackie and Son Ltd., Glasgow, 1915), 161.
[50] Ibid. 149.

Comenius, and Luther before him, were in some respects advocates of kinds of freedom different from those humanists'. Hence, they addressed educational issues from a different angle. Vives, Montaigne, Rabelais, and Erasmus and, later, Locke and Rousseau can be said to centre their educational theories—implicitly or explicitly—on 'liberty of will' in children of ruling social classes. But Luther and Comenius, as a consequence of their religious views (Comenius was a devout member of the Moravian brethren), address social and civil liberty and its relation to education. Both Luther and Comenius advocate mass education, motivated by religious zeal. Luther's views on education and freedom are important elements of his Reformation doctrines. Vives and Montaigne illustrate a concern with making education a voluntary process of enjoyment of learning, which becomes a core element in children's literature criticism. But Luther's and Comenius's propagation of reading and general literacy as a method of mass religious and moral education is another idea which persists powerfully in discussions on children's fiction.

Comenius refers back to Luther when he writes, in *The Great Didactic*:

Dr. Luther, in his exhortation to towns of the empire on behalf of the erection of schools (AD 1525), asks for these two things among others. Firstly, that schools may be founded in all cities, towns, and villages, for the instruction of all the young of both sexes . . ., so that even peasants and artisans may, for two hours daily, receive instruction in useful knowledge, in morality, and in religion. Secondly, that an easier method of instruction may be introduced, so that students, instead of developing antipathy towards learning, may be enticed by irresistible attractions, and that, as he says, boys may gain no less pleasure from study than from spending whole days in playing ball and amusing themselves. These are the views of Dr. Luther.[51]

Comenius's and Luther's interest in moral education on a large scale involves a close consideration of the nature of interpretation. The medieval Catholic Church is presented as having kept religious texts firmly to itself, for fear of dissent and divergent interpretation.

[51] Comenius, *The Great Didactic*, 228–9.

To advocate literacy on a mass scale as necessary to the open study of religious texts, as Tyndale, Luther, and Comenius do, and yet to have extremely clear views on the rights and wrongs of religious ideas indicates particular ideas about readers and reading.

The overwhelming emphasis in children's literature discussions is on views of reading as primarily for amusement, and hence they refer to these ideas as they were developed by Vives, Montaigne, Locke, and Rousseau. I would argue, however, that in fact Comenius's and Luther's discussions on the tension between individual readership and controlled interpretation are equally crucial to the common use of the concepts of childhood which characterize children's literature criticism. Children's book criticism relies on the concepts of childhood to unify and control interpretation: this is one aspect of the manifestation of the adult–child hierarchy with respect to children's reading. 'Looking through the eyes of the child' is, as I have suggested, a metaphor to be interpreted as an expression not only of concern and understanding, but also of invasion, domination, and control: 'looking through the eye of the child' also implies looking through the 'I' of the child.

Luther and Comenius, as I have read them for the purpose of discussing children's literature criticism, are concerned with mass moral education, and Vives, Montaigne, and Erasmus with the education of the 'young gentleman', as it was described by the Greeks and Romans. In fact, Luther and Erasmus wrangled over the issue of religious mass education in an exchange of writings concerned with the possibility of free will.[52] These discussions were of importance to a religious context, whereas general writings on a gentleman's education were concerned with a mixture of liberal arts and religious education for religious and civil purposes. Luther, and Erasmus in the discussion with Luther, are only discussing the teaching of Scripture, not classical texts (although Luther mentions

[52] Martin Luther and Desiderius Erasmus, *Luther and Erasmus: Free Will and Salvation* (Erasmus, *De Libero Arbitrio*, trans. and ed. E. Gordon Rupp and A. N. Marlow, 35–97; Luther, *De Servo Arbitrio*, trans. and ed. Philip S. Watson and B. Drewery, 101–332) (The Library of Christian Classics, 17, ed. John Baillie *et al.*) (SCM Press, London, 1969).

some texts of classical origin with a view to banning them). Luther's writings are pertinent to the terms of later children's literature criticism in three respects: his advocacy of mass literacy for the purpose of religious education; his description of the freedom this general literacy introduced; and his discussion of the father–child relationship between God and Christians, which parallels some aspects of the redeveloping hierarchy between earthly adults and children. Before I continue, I should emphasize that I am not concerned at this point with any 'actual' historical influence and interpretation of Luther's ideas. Instead, I am using aspects of his writings which seem to me explicitly illustrative of the constructions of ideas usually taken for granted in children's literature criticism.

First, then, Luther, in his rebellion against the corruption of the Papacy and the medieval Catholic Church, strongly advocates a return to the word of God—the Bible—as a source of authority, rather than the interpretations of the Pope. In his 'Address to the Nobility', one of the key documents of the Reformation, Luther writes:

it is a wickedly devised fable, and they cannot quote a single letter to confirm it, that it is for the Pope alone to interpret the Scriptures or to confirm the interpretation of them: they have assumed the authority of their own selves. And though they say, that this authority was given to St. Peter when the keys were given to him, it is plain enough that the keys were not given to St. Peter alone, but to the whole community.[53]

This idea is part of Luther's general idea of the liberty of Christianity. He argues Christians are all equal and free to learn the word of God themselves: 'above all, in schools of all kinds the chief and most common lesson should be the Scriptures and for young boys the Gospel . . . should not every Christian be expected by his ninth or tenth year to know all the holy Gospels, containing as they do his very name and life?'[54] To Luther, the gospel and Scriptures will reveal the word of God. Having attacked the Papacy for the

---

[53] Martin Luther, *First Principles of the Reformation or the Ninety-Five Theses and the Three Primary Works*, introd. and trans. Henry Wace and C. A. Buchheim (John Murray, London, 1883), 26.

[54] Ibid. 82–3.

misuse of the monopoly of interpretation, he seems to rely on the righteous Christian not to fall into the same error—and it is the role of the like-minded members of the community to provide correction. Luther advocates 'that no violence ought to be done to the words of God, neither by man, nor by angel, but that, as far as possible, they ought to be kept to their simplest meaning, and not to be taken, unless the circumstances manifestly compel us to do so, out of their grammatical and proper signification, that we may not give our adversaries any opportunity of evading the teaching of the whole scriptures'.[55] Thus Luther is committed, through his rebellion against what he regards as previous misinterpretation, to the self-evident meaning of the gospel when studied by all.

In the discussion between Erasmus and Luther, Erasmus questions this notion, and Luther defends his views. Erasmus addresses the problems of interpretation:

I confess that it is right that the sole authority of Holy Scripture should outweigh all the votes of all men. But the authority of the Scripture is not here in dispute . . . Our battle is about the meaning of Scripture . . . if it is so clear, why have so many outstanding men in so many centuries been blind, and in a matter of such importance?[56]

Interpretation is the crucial point in Erasmus's and Luther's dispute, as Erasmus supports free will, and Luther denies it, both basing their views on Scripture. Erasmus's argument that obscurity in Scripture has led to centuries of discussion leads to his view that these problems should not be generally aired: 'such matters might allowably have been treated in discussion by the learned world, or even in the theological schools . . . to debate such fables before the gaze of a mixed multitude seems to me to be not merely useless but even pernicious.'[57] To Erasmus Luther's resort to opening the Scriptures to public judgement and knowledge has no basis:

You [Luther] say, 'what has a miter to do with the understanding of Holy Scripture?' I reply, 'What has a sackcloth or a cowl?' You say, 'What has the knowledge of philosophy to do with the knowledge of sacred letters?' I reply, 'What has ignorance?'[58]

---

[55] Ibid. 157.
[56] Erasmus, *De Libero Arbitrio*, 43–4.
[57] Ibid. 42.
[58] Ibid. 45.

Luther defends his views again by asserting a self-evidence of meaning:

I am speaking moreover about the assertion of those things which have been divinely transmitted to us in the sacred writings. Elsewhere we have no need either of Erasmus or any other instructor to teach us that in matters which are doubtful or useless and unnecessary, assertions, disputings, and wranglings are not only foolish but impious.[59]

Luther, in this discussion with Erasmus, wants to claim that the meaning of Scripture is clear, except when obscurity is caused by 'our ignorance of their vocabulary and grammar; but these texts in no way hinder a knowledge of all the subject matter of Scripture'.[60] Finally, Luther blames any remaining obscurity on

the blindness or indolence of those who will not take the trouble to look at the very clearest truth . . . If you speak of the internal clarity, no man perceives one iota of what is in the Scriptures unless he has the Spirit of God . . . The Spirit is required for the understanding of Scripture, both as a whole and in any part of it. If, on the other hand, you speak of the external clarity, nothing at all is left obscure or ambiguous, but everything there is in the Scriptures has been brought out by the word into the most definite light, and published to all the world.[61]

Erasmus drily replies to this 'that now every Tom, Dick and Harry claims credence who testifies that he has the spirit of the gospel'.[62]

The focus of Luther's and Erasmus's discussion is analogous to children's fiction criticism in several senses. Their differences of opinion involve both acknowledgement and repression of aspects of need and purpose. Luther and Erasmus are both operating under the aegis of their absolute God and attempt to resolve the clashes between their versions of what constitutes necessary truth and the liberty required to express it, and between their varying views on the need for their truths to become other persons' truths. Their God carries the responsibility for acknowledgement and repression of purpose: accepting God as an absolute truth makes it possible to validate their motivation to have this truth accepted and known, but also implies the eternity and eventual emergence of that truth.

---

[59] Luther, *De Servo Arbitrio*, 105.          [61] Ibid. 111–12.

[60] Ibid. 110.          [62] Erasmus, *De Libero Arbitrio*, 45.

Luther's and Erasmus's discussion reflects the opposition between claims for the possibility of discovering uniform truth through knowledge (Luther's mass literacy and moral education) and the ideas of pluriform interpretation and individual meaning. The liberty of pluriform interpretation then becomes part of truth and righteousness under the limiting safety of the truth of God. René Wellek writes that

with Erasmus 'the art of criticism' ('ars critica') is applied to the Bible as a tool in the service of an ideal of toleration. Among the later humanists the term 'critic' and 'criticism' seem, however, limited specifically to the editing and correction of ancient texts.[63]

In Erasmus this ideal of toleration is limited and determined by the truth of God. This combining of tolerance and truth (which may be the compromise of 'liberal humanism', within which freedom is right) occurs in the same way in much children's literature criticism: many critics express tolerance towards, or advocate, plurality of interpretation and the use of texts for children; but the 'truth' of the 'child' limits and determines the scope and use of this interpretation for the critic. It is the child being the child which will lead to the critic being able to assert how and why and what the child reads. We see this combination of truth and tolerance in a remark made by the famous children's author E. B. White (writer of *Charlotte's Web*, *Stuart Little*, *The Trumpet of the Swan*): 'You have to write up, not down. Children are demanding. . . . They accept, almost without question, anything you present them with, as long as it is presented honestly, fearlessly, and clearly. . . . They love words that give them a hard time.'[64] The combination of truth and tolerance is also present in Lurie's description of what she calls 'the sacred texts of childhood':

These books, and others like them, recommended—even celebrated— daydreaming, disobedience, answering back, running away from home, and concealing one's private thoughts and feelings from unsympathetic

---

[63] René Wellek, *Concepts of Criticism*, introd. and ed. Stephen G. Nichols Jr. (Yale University Press, New Haven, Conn., 1963), 23.

[64] E. B. White, 'On Writing for Children', in Haviland, *Children and Literature*, 140.

grown-ups. They overturned adult pretensions and made fun of adult institutions, including school and family. In a word, they were subversive . . .[65]

In Lurie's terms, the 'true' child (author and child are merged here) is rebellious, and Lurie herself is the tolerant critic who is in on the secret.

Luther's views, too, may be said to reflect the relation between children's fiction critics and child readers, for his notion of the 'Spirit of God' in people controlling ('internal') meaning, and validating his purpose in directing meaning, is close to the role the concept of 'child' plays in controlling the meaning critics assign to texts for children. Even as Luther releases the Scriptures to public scrutiny, the Spirit of God will limit and control meaning for his purposes. Luther corresponds to the children's fiction critic who denies and represses his hierarchical role, retreating behind the 'amusement' value of children's fiction and proclaiming their freedom from overt coercion in reading and interpretation. Luther, too, rejects overt coercion or pressure in interpretation: 'I say, then, neither Pope, nor Bishop, nor any man whatever has the right of making one syllable binding on a Christian man, unless it is done with his own consent. . . . and he himself ought to teach nothing but the freest faith.'[66] The concept of the 'Spirit of God' functions in the same way as concepts of childhood do within children's literature criticism, by revealing to the adult critic, and putting within the sphere of the adult's vision, understanding, and control, the interpretation and meaning of texts for the child.

We can see, then, how Luther, in his argument, is able to reject the outright manipulation and force he sees used by the Pope and simultaneously advocate a new liberty for the Christian, and yet introduce another factor—the Spirit of God—which will offer a basis for limiting, directing, or controlling individual interpretation. The previous situation is described by Luther as an antagonistic confrontation between two forces (and the subordination of one of them): the external coercion of the Pontiff as against the internal beliefs of the individual. Under Luther's theories, these

---

[65] Lurie, *Don't Tell the Grown-Ups*, p. x.
[66] Luther, *First Principles of the Reformation*, 194–5.

dual forces become unified and internalized: man will express his own knowledge and belief, and this will be correct if the person has within himself the Spirit of God. Thus the liberty of the individual and the correct bases of belief and interpretation are reconciled. Control is now allocated to innate qualities existing in and of themselves—unless they are altogether absent, which then justifies the labelling of undesirable interpretations as invalid or incorrect.

The third term of Luther's ideas which illuminates aspects of discussions in children's literature criticism is his particular use of the common description of the relationship between God and man as a father–child relationship. This terminology has, in religious discussion in general, been one way of attempting to deal with the difficult issues of free will and predetermination. Another analogy used with respect to these problems is that of the master and servant. These doctrinal debates are fundamentally concerned with a problem many children's literature critics have cancelled out in accepting 'amusement' as a liberating force for children, functioning within the parameters of an assumed knowledge of the essence of 'child': the problem of how freedom functions with respect to the subordinate partner in a hierarchical relationship. How can humans be free with an all-knowing, all-controlling God? How can the child be free with an all-knowing, all-controlling adult? I have already claimed that this is an inevitable hierarchy, but how does it work when it claims to create freedom for children?

Religion has struggled with the problem of free will, in this sense, for centuries. As Erasmus points out: 'From the time of the apostles down to the present day, no writer has yet emerged who has totally taken away the power of freedom of choice, save only Manicheus and John Wyclif.'[67] The wish to claim the possibility of freedom of choice is indeed powerful and demands a reconciliation with a perfect God. Philip Watson explains Luther's views:

fallen man . . . retains his powers of reason and will . . . but both his reasoning and his willing are radically corrupt, being governed from the false premises dictated by Satan. . . . When the will of God runs counter to his own [man's], it seems to him arbitrary and tyrannical, and if he does not simply flout it with blind self-assertion, he complies with it in

---

[67] Erasmus, *De Libero Arbitrio*, 43.

calculating self-interest, with an eye to escaping punishment or [gaining] reward. He acts thus *of necessity*, in as much as he has no 'will of his own' over against the Evil Spirit by which he is inwardly moved; and just for that reason he acts *voluntarily*, not under coercion against his will. But he does *not* act *freely*, that is, with the spontaneity of genuine love; . . . Freedom, in the full and proper sense of the term, belongs in Luther's view only to God.[68]

It is, Watson explains, Luther's view that

it is, however, God's purpose to save man from his evil bondage, and to this end he works by means of his Word and his Spirit . . . Where and insofar as this happens, man is restored to his true and natural relationship to God, and thereby enters into the fullest freedom of which he is capable. This is the liberty of the children of God, in which men can freely cooperate with God, not for the achieving of their own salvation, but in the fulfilling of God's purposes in the world with respect both to its spiritual and temporal welfare.[69]

This is also, I would argue, the structure of the liberty of the children of man as described within much of children's literature criticism: through voluntary cooperation with the adults' word and spirit ('spirit' as in 'guiding and developing force and conscious-ness') children are seen to enter into their fullest freedom—the achievement not of their own salvation as children, but the fulfilment of the adults' purposes in the world with respect to both its spiritual and temporal welfare. Luther, with his religious conviction, *has* to formulate man's liberty within the restrictions created by the premiss of the absolute existence and perfection of a God. In doing so he provides us with an analogue of the way the liberties of the constructed subordinate child may be considered in relation to the presence of the dominant adult. Luther's theorizing on the structure of the relationship between God and man shows how the narrative of the relationship between adult and child—portrayed in children's literature criticism as being the result of the revelation of the nature of the child—in fact existed within parallel contexts of power hierarchies before the invention of this child.

We may also note that Luther's ideas, as explained by Philip

---

[68] Philip S. Watson, 'Introduction' to Luther, *De Servo Arbitrio*, 16–17.
[69] Ibid. 19.

Watson, are echoed in detail by several theories about children's responses and emotions. Compare, for instance, Vygotsky's theory of learning, where the adult is said to lend his consciousness ('zone of proximal development') to the child as a means of 'carrying' him from one stage to the next.[70] We also find an echo of the idea that children learn to comply with rules out of self-interest, in order to escape punishment and gain reward. The later attainment of the 'liberty of God' may, in this case, correspond to the achievement of higher levels of moral reasoning through the internalization of rules and regulations.

As I noted earlier, Comenius quotes Luther as an authority in discussing the need for mass education. Comenius is a prominent figure not only within the wider field of educational theory, but also specifically in connection with children's books. Comenius's further refinements of educational ideas led him to produce the *Janua linguarum*, an introduction to the study of Latin, in 1631. Though similar books had appeared before, Comenius's *Janua* became highly successful. Keatinge tells us that

it was translated into twelve European languages . . . and even travelled as far eastward as Asia . . . it is an undoubted fact that in every European country generations of children thumbed the *Janua* and no other book until they were sufficiently advanced to begin Terence or Plautus, and that for years after its publication Comenius' name was familiar in every school-room.[71]

Comenius published a number of other schoolbooks, the most important being, with a view to the development of children's fiction, the *Orbis sensualium pictus*. This was a shortened and simplified version of the *Janua*, accompanied by illustrations matched to the text. Letters, for instance, were presented with pictures of animals whose cries supposedly echoed the pronunciation of the letter. Keatinge says that

the success of this book was even more extraordinary than that of the *Janua Linguarum*. It went through numberless editions . . . the *Orbis*

---

[70] Jerome Bruner, *Actual Minds, Possible Worlds* (Harvard University Press, Cambridge, Mass., 1986), 73.
[71] Keatinge, introd. to Comenius, *The Great Didactic*, 23.

*Pictus* was the first picturebook ever written for children, and exercised a softening influence on the harshness with which . . . the first steps in learning were always associated . . . 'Apart from the *Orbis Pictus* of Amos Comenius', wrote Goethe, 'no book of this kind found its way into our hands'.[72]

Comenius is thus, for many children's book critics, one of the signposts on the way to 'amusement' and the 'liberation' of children from teaching with respect to reading and morality. The connection between children and illustration from here on becomes one of the fixed elements of children's fiction and the definition of childhood. The establishment of this connection between children and illustration is associated with attributing to children a separate and special vision and eye/I. Juliet Dusinberre, for instance, comments on Roger Fry's linking of the child-vision and Post-Impressionist painting:

Roger Fry . . . found in children a capacity to observe without interpreting, which he believed that the Post-Impressionists, and particularly Cézanne, recaptured: 'We learn to read the prophetic message, and, for the sake of economy, to neglect all else. Children have not learned it fully, and so they look at things with some passion. Even the grown man keeps something of his unbiological, disinterested vision with regard to a few things'.[73]

And, Dusinberre adds, revealing her own view of the child's eye, 'Modernist art, like Froebel's educational theory, tried to re-embody the child's unity of perception, his lack of prudery and inhibition.'[74]

Comenius, like Vives, Montaigne, and Luther, was concerned with developing a method of education which would wed children's minds to learning: instead of rebellion or resistance, they wanted to engender a love of learning and a speedy and voluntary adoption of ideals and concepts as the teacher and society wished to convey them. To devise such a method remains a powerful and coveted tool in spreading one's own beliefs and convictions through a

[72] Ibid. 78.
[73] Juliet Dusinberre, *Alice to the Lighthouse: Children's Books and Radical Experiments in Art* (Macmillan, London, 1987), 22.
[74] Ibid.

population. Keatinge informs us that Wolfgang Ratke, one of Comenius's immediate predecessors in school reform, made as great a mystery of his method as was possible. Ratke hoped, by judiciously concealing its details and advertising its merits, to sell it for a high price to some prince or noble.[75] Comenius's own aim in writing his *Great Didactic* was

to seek and to find a method of instruction, by which teachers may teach less, but learners may learn more; by which schools may be the scene of less noise, aversion, and useless labour, but of more leisure, enjoyment, and solid progress; and through which the Christian community may have less darkness, perplexity and dissension, but on the other hand more light, orderliness, peace and rest.[76]

Again, the engendering of voluntary learning as necessary to the free man—the linking of 'leisure' and 'enjoyment' with 'solid progress'—requires a postulation of those aspects of the 'child' which have to do with what it may like, love, or prefer *of itself*: its will and desires must be 'known' (meaning both 'understood' and 'possessed'). This is because these educators have come to feel that, for their purposes, certain wants and desires cannot be instilled in people at will. And, as with Luther, Comenius must construct, for the purpose of mass moral and emotional education, wants and desires which he can claim characterize as large a group of learners, 'children', as possible.

Comenius describes his methods and aims very clearly, and in so doing further explicates many of the ground rules assumed not only by later theorists and philosophers of education, but also by the discussions on children's books. Comenius, for instance, criticizes previous educational thinkers for having almost always proceeded by means of unconnected precepts, gleaned from a superficial experience, that is to say, a posteriori.[77] Comenius ventures to promise that he, on the other hand, will produce:

a Great Didactic, that is to say, the whole art of teaching all things to all men, and indeed of teaching them with certainty, so that the result cannot

---

[75] Keatinge, introd. to Comenius, *The Great Didactic*, 11.
[76] Comenius, *The Great Didactic*, 156.
[77] Ibid. 157.

fail to follow; further, of teaching them pleasantly, that is to say, without annoyance or aversion on the part of teacher or pupil, but rather with the greatest enjoyment for both; further of teaching them thoroughly, not superficially and showily, but in such a manner as to lead to true knowledge, to gentle morals, and to the deepest piety. Lastly, we wish to prove all this *a priori*, that is to say, from the unalterable nature of the matter itself . . . that we may lay the foundations of the universal art of founding universal schools.[78]

Comenius illustrates how 'amusement' starts its career as a form of claimed love and commitment to learning. Enjoyment is part of teaching thoroughly, for 'true knowledge', 'gentle morals', and 'deepest piety'. To prove his method will be able to teach 'all things to all men' Comenius turns to basing his theories on a priori logic, on 'the unalterable nature of the matter itself'. The 'unalterable nature of the child itself' is part of this thinking. We return to the connection between 'child' and 'nature': knowing a priori the traits of childhood will provide one of the bases from which to reason how to proceed further. A belief in the universal traits of the 'child', in a 'nature of childhood', provides the necessary background for believing in the possibility of devising a method for teaching 'all things to all men'. Education to Comenius is Utopian: 'the salvation of the human race is at stake', he writes, and asks:

What better or what greater service could we perform for the state than to instruct and to educate the young? Especially at the present time and in the present condition of morals, when they have sunk so low.[79]

It is the cry of educators up to the present day.

[78] Ibid.
[79] Ibid. 158.

# 3

# On Knowing the Child: Stories of Origin and the Education–Amusement Divide

I have argued that children's book criticism may be said to have been formed not, as is commonly assumed, primarily by a legacy of ideas about the ostensible possibility of liberating children from what comes to be perceived as the oppression of adults, but by a legacy of intense concern with moral and emotional education. Both education for freedom and education for and through enjoyment are subordinate elements of a moral and emotional education and are not independent goals in their own right, a liberation from moral and emotional teaching. The critic Margery Fisher exemplifies the ambivalent attitude that children's books on the one hand do not teach, and on the other hand teach through amusement and emotional appeal:

We should not *expect* children's stories to be sermons or judicial arguments or sociological pamphlets. As independent works of art they must be allowed to appeal to the imagination, the mind, the heart on their own terms . . . If a writer cannot say what he really feels, if he cannot be serious in developing a theme . . . if he has in any way to minimize . . . that approach to books for the young must eventually dilute their quality as mainstream literature.[1]

Comenius understood the concept of moral education clearly. As he said:

should there be any man who is such a pedant as to think that the reform of schools has nothing to do with the vocation of a theologian, let him know

[1] Margery Fisher, 'Rights and Wrongs', *Top of the News*, 26 (June 1970), 373–91, quoted in Virginia Haviland, 'Fiction and Realism', in Virginia Haviland (ed.), *Children and Literature: Views and Reviews* (The Bodley Head, London, 1973), 272–3, 273.

that I was myself thoroughly penetrated with this idea. But I have found that the only way in which I can be freed from it is to follow God's call, and without digression to devote myself to that work to which the divine impulse directs me.[2]

To Comenius children are characterized precisely by their susceptibility to education. He traces this trait, and its importance, to the Bible:

'Verily I say unto you, Except ye be converted, and become as little children, ye shall not enter into the kingdom of heaven.' (Matthew XVIII, 3) . . . Just consider, we elders, who consider that we alone are wise, and that you lack sense, that we are eloquent, but you speechless—we, I say, are sent to learn our lessons from you! You are set over us as masters, you are to be our models and examples. If any one should wish to deliberate why God prizes children so highly, he will find no weightier reason than this, that children are simpler and more susceptible to the remedy which the mercy of God grants to the lamentable condition of man. For this reason it is that Christ commands us elders to become as little children . . . to return to our former condition of simplicity, gentleness, modesty, purity, and obedience.[3]

At the same time, however, Comenius asserts the impossibility of adults becoming children again in this way: 'nothing is harder than to lay aside our habits, . . . there is no more difficult task than for a badly-trained man to return to his former state',[4] and concludes that, therefore, 'if the corruption of the human race is to be remedied, this must be done by means of the careful education of the young'.[5] Many of Comenius's ideas derive from theological themes concerning states of innocence and sin, redemption and damnation, many of which are traditional throughout Christian religious writing. We can see how Comenius's ideas about education and childhood are related to his theology, as with Luther. But these ideas become redefined within the context of increased pressures to develop education and literacy, and become absorbed into the structures through which people have increasingly tried to

[2] John Amos Comenius, *The Great Didactic*, introd. and trans. M. W. Keatinge (Adam and Charles Black, London, 1896), 161.
[3] Ibid. 166–7.
[4] Ibid. 167.
[5] Ibid.

observe and define 'childhood' not theologically, but as a scientific, self-evident, or natural 'reality'.

To Comenius, childhood as a theological state of innocence combines with the liberation of access to Scripture to limit access to texts in general. Increased literacy, originally advocated by theologians such as Luther and Comenius as a means of Reformation, can come increasingly under pressure from forces advocating, in their turn, restrictions on access and interpretation. We saw how this development was already present in Luther's own arguments. When children are regarded as by nature susceptible and open to moulding, if the right methods be found, it can become of increasing importance to regulate their reading: this is implied when Margaret and Michael Rustin, for instance, write that 'while [the death of] Charlotte [the spider in E. B. White's *Charlotte's Web*] provides one of the most poignant moments of children's fiction, it is also contained within a form which makes it deeply moving and integrative rather than overwhelming and destructive for its readers'.[6] Previously, writings on education recommended that the reading material of learners be selected and restricted in line with general ideas concerning blasphemy and corruption— applicable to both adults and children, if at all. But later there emerges in these authors the beginnings of an idea about increased literacy for adults as a fundamental element of 'free' reading while increased literacy for children is directed for them to an ever more limited and specific body of reading matter. Initially, most unlettered adults are represented as children under the learned clerics' or nobles' direction and guidance with regard to reading. As the democratic idea of forming one's own judgements and opinions in individual communion with a written text develops there is a shift from a hierarchy based on socio-economic class to a hierarchy based on age. Philippe Ariès remarks on this parallel between class and age:

thus the old stories which everyone listened to in the time of Colbert and Mme. de Sévigné were gradually abandoned, first by the nobility and then by the bourgeoisie, to the children and country-dwellers. The latter in

---

[6] Margaret and Michael Rustin, *Narratives of Love and Loss: Studies in Modern Children's Fiction* (Verso, London, 1987), 20–1.

their turn abandoned them when the newspaper took the place of the Bibliothèque Bleue; the children then became their last public, but not for long, for children's reading is at present undergoing the same evolution as games and manners . . . It is important to note that the old community of games was destroyed at one and the same time between children and adults, between lower class and middle class. This coincidence enables us to glimpse already a connection between the idea of childhood and the idea of class.[7]

Ariès also remarks on a move, at the end of the sixteenth century, to remove indecent books from the education of children. He suggests that

this was a very important stage, which may be regarded as marking the beginning of respect for childhood. This attitude was to be found among both Catholics and Protestants, in France and England. Until then nobody had hesitated to give children Terence to read, for he was a classic . . . They reveal a new decorum, a desire to avoid any word or expression which might be considered offensive or indecent.[8]

Ariès makes this comment with a view to contrasting medieval and (post-)Renaissance attitudes to what we now regard as children. His remark, however, covers two shifts: first a shift in moral views, and, secondly, the connection of this morality to childhood in a specific way. 'Childhood' is formed by this allocation of 'suitable' reading, behaviour, and attitudes, according to age.

Increased literacy, in Luther's and Comenius's discussions, creates a paradoxical situation in this respect: it is a freedom permitted by these theorists with a specific view in mind, to be limited when it threatens to subvert or engulf their aims. The centre of control of this freedom is placed with whoever, in a given position at a given time, is seen as holding the moral or ideological higher ground. He who can deal with knowledge and yet not be corrupted by it may teach those who would be corrupted by this selfsame knowledge (this is, ultimately, a god). Or he is seen as inevitably corrupted, but retaining the ability to transfer the knowledge without the corruption. It is this paradox of authority and teaching

[7] Philippe Ariès, *Centuries of Childhood* (Penguin, Harmondsworth, 1973), 95–7.

[8] Ibid. 106–7.

which, I have suggested, causes Jacques Derrida to disown writing
while writing, or, according to Alexander Nehamas's interpretation, Nietzsche's use of ever changing styles in his philosophical
writing. They are attempting both to acknowledge and, simultaneously, to disrupt their own authority as writers and thinkers who
are thinking about truth (even as non-truth), and who are
nevertheless moved to share their views: to express their will to
power. Nehamas writes that 'Nietzsche's effort to create an artwork
out of himself, a literary character who is a philosopher, is then also
his effort to offer a positive view without falling back into the
dogmatic tradition he so distrusted and from which he may never
have been sure he escaped.'[9] In *Beyond Good and Evil* Nietzsche
asks: 'what in us really wants "truth"? . . . *why not rather* untruth?
and uncertainty? even ignorance?'[10] As Nehamas points out: 'Yet to
ask even these questions is inevitably an effort to get matters right
concerning them, and they are therefore themselves motivated by
the very will to truth they call into question.'[11]

Nietzsche's approach to the issues raised around this will to
truth, Nehamas suggests, occur in *Beyond Good and Evil*, when
Nietzsche argues:

From the beginning we have contrived to retain our ignorance . . . in order
to enjoy life! And only on this solid, granite foundation of ignorance could
knowledge rise so far—the will to knowledge on the foundation of a far
more powerful will: the will to ignorance, to the uncertain, to the untrue!
Not as its opposite, but—as its refinement![12]

The central purpose of *Beyond Good and Evil*, Nehamas argues, is
to reject 'the fundamental faith of the metaphysicians . . . the faith
in the opposition of values'.[13] Childhood is a category which is both
one of the products of, and also a concept sustaining, these issues.
Anxiety about ignorance manifests itself in its control by the will to

   [9] Alexander Nehamas, *Nietzsche: Life as Literature* (Harvard University Press,
Cambridge, Mass., 1985), 8.
   [10] Friedrich Nietzsche, *Beyond Good and Evil: Prelude to a Philosophy of the
Future*, trans. Helen Zimmern (*The Complete Works of Friedrich Nietzsche*, vol. xii,
ed. Oscar Levy; George Allen & Unwin, London, 1923), 5.
   [11] Nehamas, *Nietzsche*, 43–4.
   [12] Ibid. 44.
   [13] Ibid.

truth, which allocates ignorance to 'safe' places of 'truth' and 'reality'. 'Childhood' constitutes such a 'safe' place: partial, limited, controlled, and *temporary*. Again, when Nehamas argues that 'Nietzsche writes that truth is created and not discovered . . . but he still believes that we must think of it as something we discover in order to go on to create it',[14] the temporal aspect within the notions of 'discovery' and 'creation' is reflected in the temporality of childhood and its resolution (or limitation) in adulthood. The concept of a will to truth as a refinement of the will to ignorance is reflected in the paradoxical views of corrupted adulthood retaining the knowledge of innocence—knowledge including the knowledge of un-knowledge—and childhood as un-knowledge in itself—un-knowledge with no knowledge of un-knowledge. Ariès's writing touches on these terms when he suggests that, in the sixteenth and seventeenth centuries, a 'different and older concept' of childhood reigned, in which 'ideas of innocence and reason were not opposed to one another'. He argues that 'the association of childhood with primitivism and irrationalism or prelogicism . . . belongs to twentieth century history'.[15] This twentieth-century position of childhood is open to both respect and protection, as being a state of innocence before the Fall, of unselfconsciousness before self-consciousness, as the ignorance supplying the truth with tolerance; it is also open to ridicule, contempt, control, and dismissal, depending on the aims and needs of the self-proclaimed knowledgeable.

The morality which Ariès defines, developing into a protection from sexuality as part of what was considered 'offensive and indecent', is an element of 'adult' paradoxical knowledge. Sexuality, in Judeo-Christian tradition, is part of knowledge and an aspect of the problematic nature of knowledge: adults dealing with the full load of ambiguous traditions regarding knowledge and sexuality can, as Comenius pointed out, attempt to redeem themselves by protecting the next generation from this corruption, and by defining their original nature in terms of their freedom from corruption. The unresolvable ideal, within this framework, is knowledge without corruption for this new generation: 'adults' as

---

[14] Ibid. 59.      [15] Ariès, *Centuries of Childhood*, 116.

'children' and 'children' as 'adults'. The ideal's paradox can never be resolved because it dismisses, within its terms, the possibility of thinking of 'children' as part of an equally constructed, but hierarchically dominant, 'adulthood'—an adulthood, moreover, which formulates 'childhood', and its needs and uses, by and of itself. 'Adult' and 'child' define each other by separation, and by comparison across the space between them as 'empty' categories. A resolution of this separation cannot be achieved because of its complicity and involvement with all the other ideas which accrue around, and define by off-setting, the 'empty' categories of 'adult' and 'child': knowledge and ignorance; sin, sexuality, and innocence; reason and madness; order and chaos; freedom and limitation or subjection.

Ariès's interest in a separation of sexuality from childhood, in games and texts from the sixteenth century onwards, involves not only a purposive construction of childhoods, but also the needs which constructed them. And, as we have noted, children's fiction can be seen not only as an expression of constriction and regulation of the child for the adults' sake, but also as an expression of a paradoxical wish to resolve the self-imposed and self-defined separations: efforts to remain in touch with, and deal with, the anxieties of ignorance and knowledge, of being and becoming, of presence and absence for their own sake. As the well-known Swedish author Astrid Lindgren (*Pippi Longstocking*) wrote: 'I don't write books for children . . . I write for the child I am myself. I write about things that are dear to me—trees and houses and nature—just to please myself.'[16] P. L. Travers, creator of *Mary Poppins*, concurs: 'You do not chop off a section of your imaginative substance and make a book for children for—if you are honest— you have, in fact, no idea where childhood ends and maturity begins. It is all endless and all one.'[17] Alison Lurie similarly asserts that

The great subversive works of children's literature . . . appeal to the imaginative, questioning, rebellious child within all of us, renew our instinctive energy, and act as a force for change. That is why such

[16] Jonathan Cott, *Pipers at the Gates of Dawn: The Wisdom of Children's Literature* (Viking, London, 1984), 155. [17] Ibid. p. xxii.

literature is worthy of our attention and will endure long after more conventional tales have been forgotten.[18]

'Amusement', then, acquires a functional definition specific to education and, as a part of moral and emotional education, to children's fiction. Amusement is not only a force of liberation and pleasure for children but also a concept applied to 'children' and 'adults' as a means for the adult to satisfy a will or need to have the knowledge and control of the child's desires, will, and consciousness through voluntary, spontaneous surrender. Thus the child comes within the adult again, not only in terms of an annihilation or suppression of the child, but also in an effort to amplify, sustain, or fulfil a living presence of the adult. In so far as children's fiction is discussed in an area created on the 'education' and 'amusement' divide it expresses its allegiance to an 'amusement' value, as defined by itself. Meanwhile, less attention has been paid to the camouflage function of this amusement. Harvey Darton shows this will towards camouflage when he writes that the first chapters of his *Children's Books in England* are

the chronicle of the English people in their capacity as parents, guardians and educators of children; with this reservation, that in these pages the child at leisure is to be considered as their preoccupation, and their care for its routine of intellectual discipline very largely (though not entirely) set aside. It is in their human aspect that I wish to see those who wrote children's books; as kind people inspired more by love and happiness than by purpose, though happiness was often enough seen as duty and duty uncompromisingly said to be happiness.[19]

Alison Lurie, likewise, having forcefully rejected books which she feels are disguised lessons in morality or good behaviour, celebrates her vision of benevolent creativity: 'It is the particular gift of some writers to remain in a sense children all their lives: to continue to see the world as boys and girls see it and *take their side* instinctively'.[20]

---

[18] Alison Lurie, *Don't Tell the Grown-Ups: Subversive Children's Literature* (Bloomsbury, London, 1990), p. xi.

[19] F. J. Harvey Darton, *Children's Books in England: Five Centuries of Social Life* (first pub. 1932, 3rd edn. rev. Brian Alderson, Cambridge University Press, Cambridge, 1982), 7.

[20] Lurie, *Don't Tell the Grown-Ups*, 14 (my emphasis).

The 'amusement' and 'education' divide allows for 'adults' as being 'kind people inspired more by love and happiness than by purpose', people 'on the side' of the child. It chooses to avoid thinking, as I am doing, of purposes which become visible and discussible when thinking of an education–amusement divide as another side of the coin of the specific formulation of amusement as a subsidiary element of the purposeful movement of education. This is why the education philosophers previous to Locke and Rousseau—commonly quoted as fathers of the 'child' and, therefore, of children's fiction—have formed the basis of the previous chapter's 'story of origin': their interests in the 'natural' and 'a priori' in liberation and liberty, and, in Luther and Comenius, in a form of democracy related to (religious) liberty, develop an emphasis on a voluntary educational process, an engendering of an enduring love of learning and selected knowledge. Education as a guiding and inspiring of spontaneous and innate growth goes together with ideas about the child and reflections on imposing—or not—from an alien position, from an 'outside'. It is also accompanied by the conception of the possibility of following and allowing a 'natural' growth by knowing it and anticipating it from the 'inside': by looking through the eye/I of this 'child'.

Locke and Rousseau follow in the footsteps of the gentleman's children educators. They focus, again, not on purely intellectual education, but on the education of the whole human as a future citizen and social being. Their interest focuses not on mass education, as with Luther and Comenius, but on the teaching of the individual. The different consequences of concentrating either on the idea of mass education or on that of one-to-one education have not been much referred to in children's literature criticism. Ideas about the child are quite different according to the needs and interests of the educators: the construction of the child is expressed partially in the efforts of educators to work with the idea of a two-way interaction rather than a one-way imposition. Children's literature criticism repeatedly intermingles assumptions and conclusions from the different methodologies and concepts of the child, derived from these different emphases on either individual or mass education. This creates one of the sources of continual problems in discussions on children and reading, as we will see.

Comenius, in promising the teaching of all things to all men, proposes a number of teaching methods and ideas which become incorporated into definitions of the child, and which recur in different forms in Locke's and Rousseau's theories of one-to-one education. As Comenius promises that the basis of his ideas are a priori he is already asserting the inevitability of his claims: 'Now that the method of teaching has been reasoned out with unerring accuracy, it will, with the assistance of God, be impossible that the desired result should not follow.'[21] Johannes Andreae wrote an introductory letter to Comenius's *Great Didactic*, and added to it, as an impressively admonitory and crucial footnote: 'It is inglorious to despair of progress, and wrong to despise the counsel of others.'[22] As with Luther, Comenius's theological convictions are echoed in his educational ideas: God-the-father and man-the-child set a precedent for his views on man-as-father and the child, besides the transference of ideas directly as the material which is actually taught. Again, the paradoxical relationship between adult and child as 'others' to each other, but articulated and devised by 'adults', is established in the theological relationship between God and man. Comenius contrasts the Greek saying 'know thyself', and the importance attached to this saying by them, with what he regards as the greater truth:

For what is the voice from heaven that resounds in the Scriptures but 'Know thyself, O man, and know me.' Me the source of eternity, of wisdom and of grace; Thyself, My creation, My likeness, My delight.[23]

Comenius's vision of man develops the idea of stages of development, and he is one of the earliest to attach importance to, and suggest a method of, grading (though he does not 'grade' strictly according to concepts of age and difficulty of teaching-matter, but primarily according to subjects to be taught at different ages.) Grading is a concept crucial to an ever more detailed

---

[21] Comenius, *The Great Didactic*, 171.
[22] Ibid. 173.
[23] Ibid. 177.

delineation of specific stages of consciousness and types of ability linked to age. Dividing people into classes on the basis of age is a consequence of the progression of these ideas. Comenius describes the progress of man through life:

What then is a man in the beginning? Nothing but an unformed mass endowed with vitality . . . Later on it begins to move and by a natural process bursts forth into the world. Gradually the eyes, ears, and other organs of sense appear. In course of time the internal sense develops . . . then the intellect comes into existence by cognising the differences between objects; while, finally, the will assumes the office of a guiding principle by displaying desire for certain objects and aversion for others. But in all these individual points of progress we find nothing but succession.[24]

This is Comenius's description of the development of earthly man at the beginning of life, but he also provides references to many notions attendant on this 'child' and 'adult' from a theological context when he explains his definition of 'nature':

By the word *nature* we mean, not the corruption which has laid hold of all men since the Fall (on which account we are naturally called the children of wrath, unable of ourselves to have any good thoughts), but our first and original condition, to which, as to a starting-point, we must be recalled. It was in this sense that Ludovicus Vives said 'What else is a Christian but a man restored to his own nature, and, as it were, brought back to the starting-point from which the devil has thrown him?' . . . In this sense, too, must we take the words of Seneca . . . 'Man is not good but becomes so, as, mindful of his origin, he strives toward equality with God. . . .' By the voice of nature we understand the universal providence of God or the influence of Divine Goodness which never ceases to work all in all things; that is to say, which continually develops each creature for the end to which it has been destined.[25]

Comenius posits two possible understandings of 'nature': the state of corruption after the Fall, or the previous state of original good and innocence. These two concepts of 'nature' relate to different 'children': as corrupted, man is the 'child of wrath', determined by its parentage and condemned by it. But there is a 'childhood' which was the 'starting-point' before the Fall—caused

[24] Ibid. 180.     [25] Ibid. 192.

by eating the apple from the tree of knowledge—a 'first and original condition' of innocence and good. A Christian—acknowledging a God the Father—can be this child again, a child 'mindful of his origin' striving to become as the Father is. Comenius's theology also provides him with the basis for assuming an innate tendency towards learning and development in man. The seeds of learning, virtue, and piety, necessary for going to heaven, are implanted within us, he says.

Comenius also quotes Aristotle's 'tabula rasa' idea, and agrees with it, thus anticipating Locke's use of the concept: virtue and aspects of character are innate to man, but ideas and concepts are (or can be) engraved on the 'tabula rasa' mind. (The 'tabula rasa', as used by Locke, is often misinterpreted as pertaining to all of man.) As long as an initial willingness to learn is seen as present in man, it can be encouraged and built upon. This idea later becomes fundamental to educationists such as Froebel and Montessori: their 'child' has an innate curiosity and desire to learn which can be either stifled or encouraged and developed. As Comenius writes: 'the seeds of knowledge, of virtue, and of piety are, as we have seen, naturally implanted in us; but the actual knowledge, virtue, and piety are not so given. These must be acquired by prayer, by education, and by action.'[26]

In this way Comenius provides the fundamentals of the reasoning he derives from his theology, which sees in 'nature' the expression of divine goodness. From this point he elaborates his theories through consistently drawing parallels between education and the growth of plants and crops, and the building of a house. He uses these examples, again, to assert his authority by claiming the self-evidence of his ideas as he shows them to occur in other areas. He finds and constructs examples to support his claims. It is important to note the expression of a need to support claims in this way: by claiming their 'naturalness'—meaning their inevitability and spontaneous, unmediated occurrence—Comenius's reasoning from a priori claims is supported. In this respect, we see in Comenius's system one of the introductions of the notion of organic

---

[26] Ibid. 204.

growth. Juliet Dusinberre deals with this concept with reference to a later period when she writes that

Much educational theory, whatever its period, starts with some form of classification. . . . Foucault argues that the late eighteenth century demonstrates a shift from taxonomy, systems of classification, to the idea of organic growth. Froebel's mentor, Pestalozzi, aimed to discover and apply what he called 'the principle of the organic'. Both men were strongly influenced by Rousseau. Froebel's original interests had been in biology.[27]

The 'child', too, becomes a part of this type of 'common sense'—as we have seen it defined by Geertz: 'religion rests its case on revelation, science on method, ideology on moral passion . . . common sense rests its on the assertion that it is not a case at all, just life in a nutshell.'[28] This type of reasoning—the constant push to establish the child, and thus education, as a discovered and not an invented 'truth'—thus provides the backbone of many writings on children and reading.

Comenius follows this path thoroughly: his principles are stated, the parallels from the natural world, building, or technology are given, and then 'deviations' from these principles are shown in education, with suggestions on how to rectify them. Having established the possibility and desirability of mass education, Comenius applies this idea to his concept of the child. Typically, unsupported assertions on the nature of children find a place amongst the buttressed statements, and this is also true for Comenius's ideas on children's (text)books:

Care must be taken to suit all these books to the children for whom they are intended; for children like whimsicality and humour, and detest pedantry and severity. Instruction, therefore, should ever be combined with amusement, that they may take pleasure in learning serious things which will be of genuine use to them later on, and that their dispositions may be, as it were, perpetually enticed to develop in the manner desired.[29]

Vives's and Montaigne's advocacy of engendering, or developing, a

[27] Juliet Dusinberre, *Alice to the Lighthouse: Children's Books and Radical Experiments in Art* (Macmillan, London, 1987), 7.

[28] Clifford Geertz, *Local Knowledge: Further Essays in Interpretive Anthropology* (Basic Books, New York, 1983), 74–5.

[29] Comenius, *The Great Didactic*, 422.

love of learning, is thus equally part of Comenius's mass education. Comenius's further details on which books should be given to children to read are, as we have seen in all the previous theorists, the consequence of his ideals and judgements concerning morality and virtue: as with Luther, (many) 'pagan' books are to be removed from schools. Children must learn from the Scriptures. Teachers who use texts by Greek or Roman authors are advocating 'a terrible abuse of Christian liberty'.[30] Children, in accordance with their eventual highest destiny, must be educated to become 'citizens of heaven'.[31] The Greeks I have discussed sought to educate the child into becoming the citizen, partaker of the liberty of democracy, while Comenius and Luther seek to educate the child to become a citizen of heaven, partaker of the liberty of Christianity.

To turn, finally, to Locke and Rousseau, we may see that they follow these patterns exactly: the 'child' is defined for their purposes, asserted as existing according to inevitable principles, and then principles of intellectual, physical, moral, and emotional education are propounded as having been reasoned from a basis of knowledge of the 'child'. A line of development is then sketched in order to produce the adult according to their preferred values or ideals. Within much of children's literature criticism little attention has been paid to Locke's and Rousseau's wider moral claims and purposes and much more to their ostensible discovery of the 'child' and their specific references to reading for this child: Dennis Butts, for instance, writes that the 'ideas of such men as John Locke . . . and Jean-Jacques Rousseau . . . helped to change European perspectives on the nature of childhood, and to suggest that it had needs and values of its own'.[32]

As with the previous theorists, Locke's and Rousseau's (reading) child cannot, and, I am arguing, should not, be abstracted and isolated from the broader moral views and beliefs of which it is the product. John and Jean Yolton (editors of the Clarendon edition of

[30] Ibid. 383.
[31] Ibid. 384.
[32] Dennis Butts, 'Introduction', in Butts (ed.), *Stories and Society: Children's Literature in its Social Context* (series: Insights, gen. ed., Clive Bloom) (Macmillan, London, 1992), pp. x–xvi, x.

Locke's writings), for instance, argue that 'Locke's political work, *Two Treatises of Government*, contains a move parallel to the child's transition from innocence to knowledge',[33] or from childhood to adulthood:

the move from pre-civil to civil society. There are in that work two components of this social maturation: [the second being] from the state of nature or the community of mankind to the civil society. This latter component is especially important for an understanding of Locke's views on education. His objective in *Two Treatises* was in part to explain political power, its nature, jurisdiction, and origin. For an understanding of its origin we must, Locke says, 'consider what state all men are naturally in, and that is, a *State of perfect Freedom* to order their Actions, and dispose of their Possessions, and Persons as they think fit, within the bounds of the Law of Nature, without asking leave, or depending upon the Will of any other Man.'[34]

The Yoltons relate these political concerns to what they see to be Locke's concerns in education:

The skill and knowledge needed to order our actions in accordance with the law of nature, to treat our possessions and persons responsibly, and *to avoid coming under the absolute control of others (a particularly frightening state for Locke in its threat to personal freedom)* are major objectives for education.[35]

Finally, the Yoltons add:

The particularity of Locke's metaphysics is echoed in his strong emphasis upon individual liberty in his political philosophy, but liberty for him is always correlative with law and order, the law and order of God's laws, of God's will . . . The child born into this world has all the equipment and potential to become a member of the community of mankind . . . Training for membership is conducted by the family; the rearing of children is guided by that objective.[36]

It can be seen, then, how Locke's wider understanding of, and strong interest in, human liberty under God may be argued to

---

[33] John W. and Jean S. Yolton, 'Introduction' to John Locke, *Some Thoughts Concerning Education*, introd. and ed. John W. and Jean S. Yolton (*The Clarendon Edition of the Works of John Locke*, gen. ed. John W. Yolton, Clarendon Press, Oxford, 1989), 1–70, 16.

[34] Ibid.     [35] Ibid. (my emphasis).     [36] Ibid.

anticipate and produce his concept of the liberty of child under adult, as with Luther.

Both Locke and Rousseau warn against over-generalizations from their work, and are aware of writing within specific contexts. These statements have been all but ignored by children's literature critics. This is because their interest lies in assimilating elements of Locke's and Rousseau's ideas on education into their a priori claims about the nature of childhood in order to satisfy their expressed interest in divining an absolute, specific relationship between the child and the book. With respect to children and reading there are within Locke's writings on education, in his *Essay Concerning Human Understanding*, and in Rousseau's *Émile*, few grounds for claiming an insight into specific, characteristic traits of children's reading in terms of moral and emotional response, other than their assertions concerning certain characteristics of a 'child' or 'children' as they postulate them for their specific purposes and uses. Locke and Rousseau, within children's fiction criticism, are often referred to, as I have pointed out earlier, as having introduced the discovery of the child and childhood. And they are attributed with having initiated an education–amusement divide for the benefit of the child, and of the adult who would eventually develop from that child. Anne de Vries is an example of referral, within writing on children's fiction, to Locke and Rousseau in this way: she writes that the division between 'adult' and 'child' occurred in the second half of the eighteenth century, and that

because of the increased interest in pedagogical theory, people slowly started to pay more attention to the needs of the child, and they started putting more emphasis on the nature of the child. In relation to this, the name of Jean-Jacques Rousseau (1712–1778) is often mentioned in the first instance. . . . The Dutch pedagogical theorists of the Enlightenment were, however, influenced primarily by John Locke's (1632–1704) ideas.[37]

Other writers and critics echo this primary view of Locke and Rousseau as initiators of an appeal for recognition of the free and

---

[37] Anne de Vries, *Wat Heten Goede Kinderboeken? De Theoretische Opvattingen over Kinderliteratuur en de Praktijk van de Boekbeoordeling in Nederland 1880–1980 (What Are Said to be Good Children's Books? Theoretical Ideas about Children's Literature and the Practice of Judging Books in The Netherlands 1880–1980)* (Em. Querido's Uitgeverij b.v., Amsterdam, 1989), 18–19.

natural 'real child', to whom specific books could and should be given which would amuse and entice the child to knowledge. Donna Norton, for instance, writes that

in sixteenth- and seventeenth-century England [children] were expected to assume adult roles early in life, [so] teaching and books were designed accordingly. Even in behavior, there was little consideration for child development, special educational needs, or literature written especially for children's interest. Much of the enlightenment that considered the child as a person has been credited to the philosophy and writings of John Locke . . . Locke believed that children who could read should be provided with easy, pleasant books suited to their capacities . . . Locke's philosophy did provide the first glimmer of hope that children should go through a period of childhood . . . this was a beginning of the realization that they might benefit from books written to encourage their reading.[38]

Rousseau's recommendation of *Robinson Crusoe* as the only reading matter initially suited to Émile's education is mentioned by Norton and many others.[39]

However, with respect to the child and reading, both Locke's and Rousseau's writing may be discussed in terms of developing further a continuing concept of amusement *as* education. 'Amusement' and 'pleasure', within their writings, achieve a high educational status as products of value systems dedicated to varying forms of liberty, social structure, or individuality. Once we view these ostensible discoverers of childhood as having instead participated in the invention of childhood, then we can trace in their writings those elements of their inventions which were subsequently used within children's literature critics' systems of discussing what they call 'children's fiction'.

Locke started *Some Thoughts Concerning Education* in 1684 as an informal letter of advice to a friend, Edward Clarke, on the education of his young son.[40] In the last of what was a regular flow of letters Locke wrote that

there are a thousand other things that may need consideration, especially if

---

[38] Donna E. Norton, *Through the Eyes of a Child: An Introduction to Children's Literature* (Charles E. Merrill, Columbus, Oh., 1983), 43–4.

[39] Ibid. 44.

[40] James L. Axtell, 'Introduction' to John Locke, *The Educational Writings: A Critical Edition* (Cambridge University Press, Cambridge, 1968), 3–97, 4.

one should take in the various tempers, different inclinations, and in particular defaults that are to be found in children, and prescribe proper remedies to each of them. But in this tumultuary draft I have made for your son, I have considered him barely as white paper, as a piece of wax, to be moulded and fashioned, and therefore have only touched those heads which I judged necessary to the breeding of a young gentleman of his condition in general.[41]

Locke's views of what this 'young gentleman' should be are as important in defining the state of the 'pre-young gentleman', and the methods required to effect the transformation, as any remarks on inherent attributes of childhood. He concludes the final version of the published essay:

Each man's mind has some peculiarity, as well as his Face, that distinguishes him from all others; and there are possibly scarce two Children, who can be conducted by exactly the same method. Besides that I think a Prince, a Nobleman, and an ordinary Gentleman's Son, should have different ways of Breeding.[42]

James Axtell, in his introduction to his edition of Locke's educational writings, argues that Locke's views, though developed for the 'young gentleman', are in fact universal rules for raising children. He is able to argue this because he takes certain views on children as definitive and self-evident: in agreeing with Locke's proposals he takes the step Locke avoids, namely that of generalizing from a particular to a universal 'childhood', despite noting that Locke advocates 'the wisdom of paying close attention to their different temperaments and rhythms of development, and thereby accommodating the educational program to the child, not the child to the program',[43] and despite acknowledging Locke's statements on different 'Breeding' for different social roles. Axtell *has* to discount these statements in order to allow for the 'discovery' of the universal child in Locke's work. Axtell's argument for universalizing Locke's claims is also bolstered by his interpretation of Locke's *Essay Concerning Human Understanding* as an attempt to

[41] Locke, *The Educational Writings*, 10.
[42] Ibid. 325.
[43] Axtell, 'Introduction', 52.

explain the grounds of universal man's understanding. These views are contradicted by John and Jean Yolton, in their introductory essay to their edition of *Some Thoughts Concerning Education*. The Yoltons, in contrast to Axtell, write:

There is one concept fundamental to Locke's general thought which is found in the *Essay* and in *Some Thoughts*: the concept of particulars. Locke accepted the principle that 'all that exists is particular'. What this expression meant within his general system was that there are no natural classes . . . Locke's commitment to particularity has many forms, including the disavowal of talk of a common human nature shared by all men . . . The centrality given by Locke to particulars in his metaphysical system is reflected in his account of persons and his work on education. Each child is to be dealt with individually . . .[44]

The differences of emphasis in Axtell's and the Yoltons' interpretations of Locke reveal the important consequences of their underlying commitments to ideas of the 'child' as essential classifying 'truths'.

Axtell also overlooks the implications of his discussion of what made Locke exceptional as a writer on education. He quotes from Locke's *The Conduct of the Understanding*:

The business of education . . . is therefore to give them this freedom, that I think they should be made to look into all sorts of knowledge . . . But I do not propose it as a variety and stock of knowledge, but a variety and freedom of thinking, as an increase of the powers and activity of the mind, not as an enlargement of its possession.[45]

Axtell sees this as Locke's innovation, that 'the emphasis of education ceased to be placed on brainstuffing and was firmly transferred to the *process* for the formation of character, of *habits*—a word always on his tongue—of mind and body.'[46] We find these ideas in the previously discussed educators, notably Montaigne, Erasmus, and Vives, those other 'young gentleman's' educators, though Axtell refers only to Vives, in a footnote.[47] He acknowledges

[44] Yolton and Yolton, 'Introduction' to Locke, *Some Thoughts Concerning Education*, 14.
[45] Axtell, 'Introduction', 58.
[46] Ibid.
[47] Ibid. 59.

that Locke's interest in educating to 'prepare the child's mental, moral, and physical capabilities to meet any situation'[48]—an interest shared, it should be added, by the other educators mentioned—is 'also the hallmark of a liberal education, and we are indebted to Locke for helping to carry that ancient, yet self-renewing tradition across the centuries from its home in classical Greece'.[49] From acknowledging Locke's link to this 'liberal education' Axtell can go on to comment that 'for long periods of time society only vaguely remembers that education means deliberately moulding human character in accordance with an ideal of human nature that changes as the values current within society change'.[50] Having said this Axtell promptly seems not to apply this idea to his own views, but assumes that somewhere beyond the changes of value there was a constant child waiting to be discovered (in other words: educational purposes are seen to be changeable, but the child not). Axtell mentions the Renaissance humanist educators as deriving their ideal of human character from early Christianity and the classical period of Greece, and grounding it 'not upon a close or sophisticated analysis of the human understanding . . . but . . . on a firm common-sense understanding of human nature and the various ways it develops from childhood'.[51] Axtell's 'common sense' is to be understood in relation to Geertz's discussion of the term, mentioned earlier: it is an assertion of a self-evident truth-discovery. To Axtell, Locke has discovered the truth about the child, education, and a universal human nature, 'based on a systematic, empirically sound philosophy of knowledge . . . on an awareness of the gradual evolution of rationality and self-discipline in a growing child'.[52] Thus 'history ends' for the child with Locke: in an evolutionary view of scientific progress towards unchangeable truth Axtell can assign to him the discovery of the true child. And Locke makes this discovery because, Axtell claims, he had the 'capacity for the detailed and quiet scrutiny of the whole human understanding . . . [the] belief in the necessity of the task . . . Locke secured an insight into human nature that was denied more impatient reformers.'[53] It is Axtell's

[48] Ibid. 58.     [50] Ibid.          [52] Ibid. 60.
[49] Ibid.        [51] Ibid. 59.      [53] Ibid. 61.

type of interpretation of Locke's child that operates most powerfully within children's fiction criticism: though there may be varying emphases on 'children as individuals', the critics' definition of texts as 'children's fiction' marks the limits of the 'individuality', or non-categorization, of the child.

Axtell's argument indicates how many writers in children's literature studies must, for their own purposes, respond to Locke and also to Rousseau: in attributing to them the origins of ideas about the child which they hold to be true, they extend Locke's and Rousseau's own claims. Even while these critics acknowledge a dependence of educational ideals on changing value systems, they combine selected claims to knowledge of particular aspects of human development—rational, moral, emotional—into one amalgamated 'child'. They are, thus, harnessing eighteenth-century comments on children's fiction, which refer to Locke's and Rousseau's influence on specific writers of what come to be called 'children's books', to a system of determinist psychology in which Locke and Rousseau provide the 'truth' about the total child. With this child they also, therefore, provide the development of the idea of a 'correct' education for it, from which children's fiction can extrapolate its 'truth' in relation to the 'child'. Darton, for instance, is one of these critics: he argues that John Newbery (commonly labelled the first commercial producer of English children's books) 'was probably acquainted with the actual texts of Locke's *Thoughts Concerning Education . . .* It might also . . . be argued plausibly that he admired and was familiar with Rousseau's writing,'[54] and notes that 'in the period immediately after Newbery's death, the works of Rousseau had a very direct effect upon English books for children. Many writers acknowledged their debt to *Émile*.'[55] These jumps are encountered repeatedly: many post-Lockian and post-Rousseauian writers on childhood, children's fiction, and education first acknowledge the dependence of concepts of childhood and education on changeable social values and morals (that is to say: there is an acknowledgement of 'history' as the formulation of

---

[54] Darton, *Children's Books in England*, 140.
[55] Ibid. 145.

changing narratives of value and meaning through time), and then jump to an almost simultaneous assertion of principles based on a knowledge of a 'real', 'true', 'eternal' child, as, it is claimed, introduced by Locke and Rousseau.

We can see reflections of this 'jump' procedure incorporated in various ways in criticism: the critic and psychologist Nicholas Tucker, for instance, reconciles his views on culture and the 'child' for the sake of his endeavour:

This gap between common intellectual strategies, and cultural or individual expectations which may differ widely from each other, obviously make it impossible to try to describe anything like a universal literary response . . . however . . . following Piaget, I shall chiefly describe the more typical ways in which children seem to approach and make sense of their stories at various ages, leaving particular details—of how individuals or whole cultures can then sometimes react to such stories quite differently—to one side.[56]

The children's author and critic Gillian Avery portrays a reading 'child' particularly suited to surviving the shifts and variations of adult definitions:

what occurs to me amid the welter of theory that has always gone on about what a child should read is the encouraging thought that you never know what he is going to make of the material with which you confront him. He has his own defence against what he doesn't like or doesn't understand in the book that is put in front of him. He ignores it, subconsciously perhaps, or he makes something different from it . . . they extract what they want from a book and no more.[57]

Tucker's 'child', Tucker hopes for the sake of his claims (he is careful to point out studies of cross-cultural differences could be carried out), exists to some extent somewhere above and beyond culture. Avery's reading 'child' is an armoured being, resisting or

[56] Nicholas Tucker, *The Child and the Book: A Psychological and Literary Exploration* (Cambridge University Press, first pub. 1981, Canto edn., Cambridge, 1990), 5–6.

[57] Gillian Avery, 'A Sense of Audience—2', in Geoff Fox *et al.* (eds.), *Writers, Critics, and Children: Articles from 'Children's Literature in Education'* (Heinemann Educational Books, London, 1976), 31–4, 33.

reforming what it does not understand: it protects itself from the exigencies of culture and history.

An invented child in Locke fulfils different functions from those of a discovered Lockian child as portrayed by children's literature critics. Locke, in formulating an image of man without, or before, civilization and education, postulates a 'non-man', whom he refers to in his *Essay Concerning Human Understanding* as 'Children *and Ideots* [*sic*]'.[58] He thus supports his idea of man born without knowledge of innate truths by providing images of non-man determined by an absence of those traits or that knowledge that he wishes to define and discuss. It should be noted, in this context, that Locke's 'tabula rasa' is subject to misunderstanding: it is often interpreted as referring to the entire child, as Anne de Vries seems to believe when she writes that 'he [Locke] regarded the child as a "tabula rasa": not nature but nurture determines how a person comes to be formed, according to Locke.'[59] However, John and Jean Yolton warn that

There is a clear genetic strain in his [Locke's] account of the human understanding. Quick was easily put off by the *tabula rasa* metaphor (as others have been too), taking that as evidence that Locke had no idea of an organism growing and developing . . . this [is an] obviously false remark . . . The *tabula rasa* doctrine was of course about ideas and propositions, not about faculties, capacities, or tempers.[60]

Locke's use of a postulated 'non-man' is analogous to Foucault's and Derrida's linking of madness and childhood, amongst other concepts, in being determinative of non-supplementarity: instead of functioning as providers of initial presence, Locke's 'Children and Ideots' constitute an absence of presence (of non-innate ideas and concepts) whereby absence and presence determine each other, but are subjected to the need to determine a presence for the sake of the argument Locke wishes to put forward. Removed from the

---

[58] John Locke, *An Essay Concerning Human Understanding* (*The Clarendon Edition of the Works of John Locke*, gen. ed. P. H. Nidditch *et al.*, Clarendon Press, Oxford, 1975, repr. with corrections, 1979), 49, my emphasis.

[59] De Vries, *Wat Heten Goede Kinderboeken?*, 18–19.

[60] Yolton and Yolton, 'Introduction', 38.

defined and defining presence of Locke's 'human understanding', Locke's 'child' can only lead an independent life as a category-concept, which can be linked to any other writer's postulated arguments and purposes. 'Children's fiction' is based on a denial of 'childhood' as not only an 'empty' category in Locke, and every other writer we have looked at who involved this notion in discussions, but as a space outlined by *purpose* at every level. This is inevitable in its hierarchical involvement with the 'adulthood' which it helps to determine, and which determines it. To discuss children's fiction as the refinement of a 'non-force' from the force of education—that is, as the eventual amusement split off from the education Locke wanted it to be part of—Locke's child needs to be presented as a presence in and of itself, which would exist, which could 'be', independent of context. Only as a presence as such can it function as the free and unforced (and, within the concept, even individualized) consumer of children's fiction: a child amused for itself, not a child for whom amusement is a force in its own right (inevitable or not).

Locke wrote, then, of the inappropriateness of giving books to children to read which demanded a knowledge of the concepts and facts which, he argued, need to be acquired because they are not innate. He also, in his model of a development of human understanding, argues against books for children which would require a fluency of reading skills. Locke seems to have been familiar with Comenius's *Janua* or *Orbis sensualium pictus*, and hence with the idea of translating ideas about specific states of consciousness, or cognitive and developmental interests, into books. He elaborates on this idea, and advocates the further development of these books. For Locke, as for the other educators discussed, whether primarily interested in the gentleman's liberal arts education or in democratic mass education for literacy, 'amusement' is in the service of the promotion of cognitive and moral education. Thus, amusement, as *less* force, is employed by Locke in reaction to his perception of existing duress and loss of liberty in the teaching and learning situation. Therefore, as with the other educators discussed, Locke discusses amusement and education in an attempt to resolve 'education as force' (teaching as limiting liberty) in its clash with liberty and virtue. Locke's amusement cannot be separated from his education, as children's fiction tends to assume. It is necessary to hold them together to allow for the statement that, ultimately, causes much liberal debate: that 'liberty' is right.

Locke's education and amusement are as constitutive of each other as his 'child and idiot' and 'man': alleviating an oppression of children *in* education, removing discipline and force, constitutes an education which Locke advocates as being gentle towards the child, and respectful. Locke's concern, in this way, with cognitive and intellectual, and moral and emotional, education involves him in the attempt to present an education which benefits from the child he postulates. That is to say: however much many critics believe in, and admit their belief in, the capacity of children's fiction to engender knowledge or value in the child, the presence of the child which, they claim, was revealed by Locke and Rousseau helps to limit its fears for its own powers. Children's fiction is seen as a means for the maximum facilitation of cognitive and intellectual development with minimum use of overt force, or is seen as a reflection and expression of a maximum understanding on the part of the adult author and critic of the child as child—of the liberty of child as self-constituted presence. Both are views determined by a concern to maintain narratives of altruistic relations with the non-self.

To Locke '*Vertue* [sic] . . . [is] the first and most necessary of those Endowments, that belong to a Man or a Gentleman.'[61] Children's fiction writers agree, and allocate to reading a role in establishing this 'vertue'. Michele Landsberg writes that 'the books I read as a child transformed me, gave meaning and perspective to my experiences, and helped to mold whatever imaginative, intellectual, or creative strengths I can lay claim to now. No doll or game had that impact on me; no pair of new jeans ever changed my life.'[62] Another kind of 'vertue' required in relation to children's texts is that described by the Austrian writer Maria Lypp. She

---

[61] Locke, *The Educational Writings*, 241.
[62] Michele Landsberg, *Reading for the Love of It: Best Books for Young Readers* (Prentice Hall, New York, 1987), 7.

regards children's fiction as a form of communication depending on an 'asymmetrical' relationship between adult author and child reader. The adaptations the adult author introduces for the child reader form, Lypp says, the 'code of children's fiction'.[63] But, she argues, there is an 'ideal of *symmetrical* communication'.[64] To Lypp 'symmetrical communication' implies 'wahre Verständigung' (true understanding)[65] between author and reader: this concept now becomes a prescriptive criterion for 'good children's fiction'. Maria Lypp wants to see a striving toward 'symmetrical communication' expressed in the children's text to make it 'good' or 'literature'. She argues for the appreciation of 'the child's vision' as something inherently valuable and worth preserving and using. Hence, in Locke, Landsberg, and Lypp, and many other writers on children's literature, their ideals of personal and social 'vertue' operate strongly to determine their arguments concerning the relationships—as they see them—between 'adult' author and 'child' reader. The 'vertue' they advocate may be an exponent of theological, social, political or cultural narratives of value.

Children's fiction, then, operates within the parameters of a discussion on liberal arts education, or moral education as part of this. To educationists such as Locke, Montaigne, Vives, and Luther, moral virtue must be instilled in the child through and through, and yet they attempt to combine this with their strong interests in forms of human liberty. Rousseau discusses this same process, in his terms, in *Émile*. As with Locke, Rousseau's 'child' (particularized as Émile) is defined in the areas of interaction between concepts of innocence and sin, knowledge and ignorance, reason and chaos, freedom and nature, and nature and civilization. In Rousseau, even more strongly than in Locke, we see how the

---

[63] Harry Bekkering, 'Van Poesie tot Poezie—Het Kindervers' ('From Verse to Poetry—Children's Verse'), in Nettie Heimeriks and Willem van Toorn (eds.), *De Hele Bibelebontse Berg: De Geschiedenis van het Kinderboek in Nederland en Vlaanderen van de Middeleeuwen tot Heden (The Whole 'Bibelebonts' Mountain: The History of Children's Books in The Netherlands and Flanders from the Middle Ages to the Present Day)* (Em. Querido's Uitgeverij b.v., Amsterdam, 1989), 341–91, 370–1.
[64] Ibid. 372.
[65] Ibid.

'child' is the product of the paradox of *teaching liberty*. Peter Gay writes that Rousseau 'like his favorite philosopher, Plato, ... sought to discover and produce the moral man who would make the moral society, and a moral society that would foster the moral man'.[66] And, Gay adds,

Rousseau often insisted on the critical importance of education. Throughout Émile he scatters hints that education and life and, in particular, education and politics, belong together ... [Rousseau] lays it down that 'we must study society through individuals, and individuals through society: those who want to treat politics and morals separately will never understand anything of either'.... Occasional diversions apart, Rousseau's work stands under the sign of civil education—paideia.[67]

Gay also argues that

Rousseau was not a totalitarian; he was not even a collectivist. If he was anything, he was, with his fervor for freedom, what his earliest readers called him: an individualist. But, then, none of these names reach the heart of Rousseau, for looking beyond politics Rousseau was above all a moralist, and, as a moralist, an educator.[68]

Rousseau himself said of all his writings, late in life, that within them he saw

the development of his great principle that nature has made man happy and good but that society depraves him and makes him miserable. *Émile* in particular, that book that has been so much read, so little understood, and so poorly appreciated, is nothing but a treatise on the original goodness of man.[69]

*Émile*, Rousseau stressed, was a theoretical treatise of this original goodness of man, and is strongly linked to his political ideas as he developed them in his *Social Contract*.[70] As with Luther, Rousseau's child–adult hierarchy—with the child being allocated a

[66] Peter Gay, *The Enlightenment: An Interpretation*, ii: *The Science of Freedom* (Wildwood House, London, 1970, repr. 1979), 535.
[67] Ibid.
[68] Ibid. 534.
[69] Ibid. 538.
[70] Jean-Jacques Rousseau, *The Social Contract and Discourses*, trans. and introd. G. D. H. Cole (Everyman's Library, J. M. Dent & Sons, London, repr. 1968).

freedom beneath, or within, adult culture and society—is the result of his views on the possibility of liberty *within* restriction, as commensurate with his ideas in the *Social Contract*. Rousseau is, in moral and political terms, concerned with resolving the conflict between his intense interest in freedom and his concern for a better society. Gay writes that Rousseau's 'solution is modern, and inextricably intertwined with his educational program. The society that makes obedience lawful, and lawful obedience practicable, is a society of Émiles.'[71] Rousseau formulates the problem as follows: 'To find a form of association which will defend and protect with the whole common force the person and goods of each associate, and in which each, uniting himself with all, may still obey himself alone, and remain as free as before.'[72] Rousseau's solution, Gay sums up, 'is the social contract, by which each surrenders all his powers to the general will; but since each is the general will, he has lost nothing essential and rather gained what he needs most: civic freedom'.[73]

It is within the context of the paradox of civil freedom to which Rousseau suggests a solution that Émile's education is formulated. *Émile* is in this sense, as with Locke's educational and cognitive studies, not devoted to a simple advocacy, as children's literature criticism would have it, of giving children amusement, or of making their education amusing: both Locke's and Rousseau's 'child' is the product of their views on the attributes of 'adult' cognitive processes or the moral rights and wrongs of society 'negatived' or 'subtracted'. And, as with the humanist and democratic educators, the 'child' functions as part of their suggested solutions to resolving the conflict between liberty and the demands of a just society or just God. In *Émile* Rousseau considers intensely the possibility of liberty for the child. Liberty does not, to Rousseau, mean leaving the child totally to its own devices, just as he does not advocate the return of man to the savage, but argues for this development to a higher civilization in order to become free. Rousseau asks: 'Do you know the surest way to make your child miserable? Let him have

[71] Gay, *The Enlightenment*, 549.
[72] Rousseau, *The Social Contract*, 12.
[73] Gay, *The Enlightenment*, 549.

everything he wants; for as his wants increase in proportion to the ease with which they are satisfied, you will be compelled, sooner or later, to refuse his demands, and this unlooked-for refusal will hurt him more than the lack of what he wants.'[74] Rousseau realizes that the adult–child hierarchy is inevitable within the construction of society: adults cannot withdraw from it even by withdrawing themselves or their rules from the presence of the child; even that constitutes a presence or rule, and sooner or later the child encounters limits. Rousseau asks: 'Do you not see how cruel it is to increase this servitude by obedience to our caprices, by depriving them of such liberty as they have? A liberty which they can scarcely abuse, a liberty the loss of which will do so little good to them or us.'[75] The child's liberty is a specialized liberty, particular to childhood, and is part of Rousseau's argument for the specialized concept of 'child' as a whole. It is a *liberty without power* that Rousseau sees for the child:

So there is only one of the child's desires which should never be complied with, the desire for power. Hence, whenever they ask for anything we must pay special attention to their motive in asking. As far as possible give them everything they ask for, provided it can really give them pleasure; refuse everything they demand from mere caprice or love of power.[76]

Rousseau's reference to understanding the child's motives points to his invention in *Émile* of the teacher (the 'adult', or himself as teacher), simultaneous with his invention of Émile the child. This teacher has an insight, understanding, and anticipation of Émile's thoughts, feelings, motives, will, and development, and, through this far-reaching understanding and insight, a control of those thoughts, feelings, motives, will, and development. A reading of Émile reveals the dominant presence, not of the child Émile, but of the teacher Rousseau. Émile has a child's liberty 'such as they have'; the teacher has the power. For Rousseau, disagreeing with Locke, the child is strongly defined by its lack of reason and judgement, and therefore

---

[74] Jean-Jacques Rousseau, *Émile*, trans. Barbara Foxley (Everyman's Library no. 518) (J. M. Dent & Sons, London, first pub. in this edn. 1911, repr. 1950), 51.
[75] Ibid. 52.                                                   [76] Ibid. 53.

Use force with children and reasoning with men; this is the natural order; the wise man needs no laws. Treat your scholar according to his age. Put him in his place from the first, and keep him in it, so that he no longer tries to leave it. Then before he knows what goodness is, he will be practising its chief lesson . . . Let him only know that he is weak and you are strong, that his condition and yours puts him at your mercy.[77]

An education for Rousseau's purposes consists of 'well-regulated liberty'.[78] And, like Locke, Rousseau clearly states that

there is another point to be considered which confirms the suitability of this method: it is the child's individual bent, which must be thoroughly known before we can choose the fittest moral training. Every mind has its own form, in accordance with which it must be controlled . . . Oh, wise man, take time to observe nature . . .[79]

In line with this, Rousseau wishes that 'some trustworthy person would give us a treatise on the art of child-study. This art is well worth studying, but neither parents nor teachers have mastered its elements.'[80] Rousseau's child is firmly and wholly within the hierarchy, even as a free individual, just as his adult is a free individual within Rousseau's society. As Rousseau sums up:

Take the opposite course with your pupil: let him always think he is master while you are really master. There is no subjection so complete as that which preserves the forms of freedom; it is thus that the will itself is taken captive. Is not this poor child, without knowledge, strength, or wisdom, entirely at your mercy? Are you not master of his whole environment so far as it affects him? Cannot you make of him what you please? His work and play, his pleasure and pain, are they not unknown to him, under your control? . . . He ought to do nothing but what you want him to do. He should never take a step you have not foreseen, nor utter a word you could not foretell.[81]

Children's literature criticism and production almost wholly ignores this context: it isolates loose elements of a concept of the 'child' and a postulated origin of an 'education–amusement' divide of which children's fiction is supposed to be the product. Because of this, it does not identify any need to examine or resolve the

---

[77] Ibid. 55.      [79] Ibid. 58.      [81] Ibid. 84–6.
[78] Ibid. 56.      [80] Ibid. 162.

problems of freedom within restriction—the possibility of moral and emotional liberty of response for any actual child reader (as opposed to all the 'child' readers constructed by adults). It is this ignored issue—drowned by the claims that children's fiction is simply the ultimate liberator of the fantasy and emotional lives of children—that recurs, in various guises, again and again in discussions on children's books. It is these claims of children's literature studies as they stand that we will review in detail in the next chapter.

# 4

# On Knowing the Child: The Terms of Children's Literature Criticism

Children's literature criticism views itself as split between critics who are quite sure that they have a knowledge of the child sufficient for their purposes, and critics who claim they cannot predict the way children read. This division can be quite acrimonious: Jan Needle, for instance, criticizes Michele Landsberg's *Reading for the Love of It*[1] for its 'total lack of doubt' about its correctness in picking books for children, according to what he calls their 'respectability factor'. Needle adds that 'the fact that Landsberg's book is now being used in colleges of Education in Canada filled me with despair'.[2] Needle argues that adult critics cannot predict the uses to which a child will put a book. Like Needle, the author Nina Bawden protests against what she sees as many reviewers' and critics' habit of treating the child as 'an object in a sociological survey, an unformed creature without will or thought of his own, to be tamed, educated, never learned from—forced into their way of thinking'.[3] But critics like Landsberg are passionate in their defence of the need, if not to censor, at least to present the child with good books, because they are convinced that these good books, the right books, will affect the child in important ways. Bernard Lonsdale and Helen Mackintosh argue that they 'are convinced that literature experiences can make a significant contribution to personality development and the enrichment of children's lives'.[4]

[1] Michele Landsberg, *Reading for the Love of It: Best Books for Young Readers* (Prentice Hall, New York, 1987).

[2] Jan Needle, 'Personal View', *Sunday Times* (31 July 1988), 'Book Section', G4.

[3] Nina Bawden, 'The Imprisoned Child', in Edward Blishen (ed.), *The Thorny Paradise: Writers on Writing for Children* (Kestrel Books, Harmondsworth, 1975), 62–4, 64.

[4] Bernard J. Lonsdale and Helen K. Mackintosh, *Children Experience Literature* (Random House, New York, 1973), p. v.

Nicholas Tucker, likewise, claims that 'children . . . sometimes need stimulation in their literature to help them to move away from certain lazy, immature ways of thinking'.[5] John Rowe Townsend describes this split as running between 'book people' (among whom he includes authors, publishers, reviewers, public librarians) and 'child people' (parents, teachers, school librarians).[6] These terms are still widely used, although, as Townsend pointed out when he coined them, there are many overlaps between the groups.

In order to understand further the purposes at work in children's literature criticism, I will be studying, in this chapter, the writings of critics who base their work on a declared knowledge of the child and, following my previous arguments, shall suggest that the division between 'book people' and 'child people' is of a different order from the way in which it is usually portrayed. We will be considering this argument further in the next chapter, where we will be looking at critics who tend to reflect more on the principles of an 'adult' literary criticism on which they attempt to base their work. But to return to the topic of this chapter: the 'child people' accuse the 'book people' of a lack of concern for the needs of the child. The 'book people' accuse the 'child people' both of a lack of respect for the individuality of children and of a lack of sophistication in their discussions. John Rowe Townsend has suggested that

most disputes over standards are fruitless because the antagonists suppose their criteria to be mutually exclusive; if one is right the other must be wrong. This is not necessarily so. Different kinds of assessment are valid for different purposes . . . I would only remark that the viewpoints of psychologists, sociologists, and educationists of various descriptions have rather little in common with each other or with those whose approach is mainly literary.[7]

Townsend focuses here on the differing views which are the product of needs to see 'children' in various ways. But he does not

[5] Nicholas Tucker, *The Child and the Book: A Psychological and Literary Exploration* (Cambridge University Press, first pub. 1981, Canto edn., Cambridge, 1990), 2.

[6] John Rowe Townsend, 'Standards of Criticism for Children's Literature', in Nancy Chambers (ed.), *The Signal Approach to Children's Books* (Kestrel Books, London, 1980), 193–207, 199.     [7] Ibid. 193–207.

turn his attention to studying how enmeshed the various views actually are in terms of the degree to which they are based on the same system of relying on the existing, known 'child'. Townsend's terms are confusing because they implicitly propagate the idea that there are critics who can get away from the 'child' by concentrating on the book, or by concentrating on children as individuals. But, as we have seen in our 'stories of origin', it is one of the illusions of children's literature criticism that it can divest itself of the child by concentrating on individuality. The term 'book people' further implies that a text can be divested of the child through some sort of purified concentration on the book as a book, and we will see how this vision predominates within children's literature criticism, although it often has but a tenuous relation to adult literary theory. It is, therefore, more relevant to children's literature criticism that both 'book people' and 'child people' are 'child people', ultimately unable to escape relying on the existence of the 'real' child.

To avoid the confusion Townsend's terms introduce into our analysis, then, I am going to rename 'book people' 'pluralists', and 'child people' 'educationalists'. These new terms redefine and relocate the principal source of disagreement between the two groups as being not primarily their concentration on the 'child' or on the book, but a difference of emphasis on the importance of the type of lesson literature is believed to teach. We will see later how the collapse of Townsend's distinction between 'book people' and 'child people' includes the invalidation of his suggestion that 'different kinds of assessment are valid for different purposes'. There is another consequence to the move away from Townsend's division of critics to my view, as I have argued it through the previous chapters, that very nearly all children's literature criticism, no matter how sophisticated or 'purist' (children's literature criticism's term for critics who preoccupy themselves with the literary, and do not—ostensibly—discuss child readers) it deems itself to be, is united in its basis in a 'knowledge' of the 'child': this shift forms a further reason why we will be going over ground which many critics would regard as well covered. We will be going back to the drawing-board, to an extent, in including in our examination books such as educational guides on children's literature. In going over this ground again we will be re-examining the relation between the educational guides and 'literary' children's literature criticism, and not taking for granted that there is the separation between them that children's literature criticism makes so much use of.

We will see the values and purposes of the 'stories of origin' reflected in, and threaded through, the terms that children's criticism uses. Most importantly we will see that the 'educationalist' critics and the 'pluralist' critics are separated not primarily through the former's claimed purchase on the 'child' and the latter's denial of this, but by an emphasis on mass education and individual learning: this is not so much a divide as a difference of emphasis. Educationalists emphasize the need for mass teaching of morality and values through literature, while pluralists emphasize the teaching of individuality. Of course, since individuality is itself an exponent of systems of value and morality, this is another reason why it is more helpful to speak of a difference of emphasis between educationalists and pluralists, rather than of an actual divide between their views and aims. Educationalists do incorporate the attempted construction of individuality within mass education in their writing, just as the pluralists have all sorts of implications for mass education in their concern for the individual. Obviously the narratives of liberal humanism and freedom, as I have read them in the previous chapters, form one level of the following discussion. The political and personal ideologies of Western democracy, individuality of thought and emotion, and the possibilities of self-determination, interact with each other within the debates on children's literature criticism. The other level of the discussion, interacting with that of socio-political ideology, involves the different formulations of the depths of the child's emotional response to the book. As we have seen, emotional involvement with the book is not just postulated, it is essential to the educative function of the book within children's literature criticism. Finally, education and emotion meet within both the educationalists' and the pluralists' arguments concerning their definitions and uses of 'literature'.

The first point to note is that any divergence between the approaches of the educationalists and the pluralists is much more apparent in their theory than in their critical practice. For the purposes of theory the educationalists try to stabilize the child reader with the help of psychological theories of cognitive and emotional development: they follow James Axtell in his discussion of Locke by attempting to link their invention of the child reader to ideas of a scientific and empirical 'discovery' of the nature of the child. The pluralists stabilize their child reader through its individuality *within its child status*. The pluralists' child is seldom an individual 'beyond' childhood. Having stabilized and determined their reading 'child', however, their practical criticism does not necessarily differ, although critics from either camp may differ substantially amongst themselves in their critical writing styles and judgements. The situation *is* a complicated one: critics are having to cope, as John Rowe Townsend has also remarked,[8] with a variety of areas of expertise, such as psychology, education, and literary criticism and literary theory, not all of which they may feel comfortable with.

One consequence of having to cope with all these different fields is that the purposes of the children's literature critics become clear not only from reading 'beyond' their ostensible claims, but also from observing that much of their psychology or literary criticism, within the discourses of these fields themselves, is applied in limited, vague, or incorrect ways. Because of this, purpose easily overwhelms the ostensible restrictions or camouflage of appropriated scientific claims. This becomes clear quite quickly if we look at the educationalists' use of psychology. Donna Norton characterizes the strategy of the educationalists when she explains her 'model for evaluating and selecting books based upon literary and artistic characteristics which readers can then use themselves. The importance of child development in this process is also stressed.'[9] The educationalists believe that good books, which they call 'literature', effect the desirable developments in children, as all the educationalists we have looked at also believe, from the Greeks onward. Michele Landsberg is echoing Juan Luis Vives's descrip-

8 Ibid. 195.
9 Donna E. Norton, *Through the Eyes of a Child: An Introduction to Children's Literature* (Charles E. Merrill, Columbus, Oh., 1983), p. ix.

tion of poetic 'energia' some three hundred years later when she argues that

good books can do so much for children. At their best, they expand horizons and instill in children a sense of the wonderful complexity of life . . . No other pastime available to children is so conducive to empathy and the enlargement of human sympathies. No other pleasure can so richly furnish a child's mind with the symbols, patterns, depths, and possibilities of civilisation.[10]

Norton agrees: 'literature and literature-related activities nurture child development'.[11]

Norton slips a term into this sentence which indicates many of the difficulties of the theoretical basis the educationalists claim in psychology: her reference to 'literature-related activities' in addition to 'literature' relates to the methodological problem in psychology of isolating effects of literature from increased attention to children on the part of teachers or parents, from generally increased or better focused use of language, or from improvements in the teaching situation due to the attention of researchers, and so on. Charlotte Huck, like Norton, refers to this problem without letting it divert her from her purposes: in her section on 'Language Development' she mentions studies which suggest the positive effects of classroom work combining reading with discussion, drama, art, and music. Huck also refers to a study by Cazden which, she says, 'points out the value of reading to the young child in a review of her study'.[12] Huck then quotes Cazden's conclusion: 'Reading to an individual child may be a potent form of language stimulation for two reasons. First, the physical contact with the child and second, such reading seems inevitably to stimulate interpolated conversation about the pictures which both adult and child are attending to.'[13]

The evasion of the problem of the causes of these effects relates to the ignoring of much of the problem of *how* teachers can learn from

[10] Landsberg, *Reading for the Love of It*, 34.
[11] Norton, *Through the Eyes of a Child*, 5.
[12] Charlotte S. Huck, *Children's Literature in the Elementary School* (Holt, Rinehart and Winston, 3rd edn., 1976), 25.
[13] Ibid.

or observe children, which I mentioned in the first chapter. Many educationalists accept that the influences of work with children and books effect results and this satisfies them. In itself this would not be an unreasonable proposition, especially since many books discuss 'literature-related activities' at some length (examples are Norton, Huck, Myra and David Sadker's *Now Upon A Time*,[14] James Smith and Dorothy Park's *Word Music and Word Magic*,[15] Joan Glazer and Gurney Williams III's *Introduction to Children's Literature*,[16] and Bernard Lonsdale and Helen Mackintosh's *Children Experience Literature*[17]), were it not for the fact that these writers constantly revert to an emphasis on the effect of the good book, even within these activities. A book such as Nicholas Tucker's *The Child and the Book*[18] also implies, though on a much more limited scale, the role of 'literature-related activities'. The crucial point is that any distinction between learning in general and learning from the book is wholly blurred. The argument the children's literature critics use to prove the power of the good book is flawed in this way from the start. The outcome of this strategy, in any case, is that the critics appear to have a knowledge, and therefore a control, of learning from books. The book represents a conveniently packaged and carefully controllable portion of reality for teaching.

This blurring of the distinction between the effects of a book and those of learning in general riddles these educationalists' writings, and reappears frequently in other critics' work as well. Educationalists bolster their claims further, however. Their sources are practically identical: Jean Piaget is their mainstay. Piaget's theory of sequential stages in the development of cognitive faculties is a godsend to these critics: even if the stages are argued to take place at varying ages, their sequential nature ensures, for the critic, that they will come along at some point at least. Lawrence Kohlberg's

---

[14] Myra Pollack Sadker and David Miller Sadker, *Now upon a Time: A Contemporary View of Children's Literature* (Harper and Row, New York, 1977).

[15] James A. Smith and Dorothy M. Park, *Word Music and Word Magic: Children's Literature Methods* (Allyn and Bacon, Boston, Mass., 1977).

[16] Joan I. Glazer and Gurney Williams III, *Introduction to Children's Literature* (McGraw-Hill, New York, 1979).

[17] See above, n. 4.

[18] See above, n. 5.

theory of stages of moral development is popular for the same reason: the stages may occur earlier in some children than in others, but some day they will happen. Maslow and Erikson, Walter Loban, and Mussen, Conger, and Kagan share this trait of suggesting developmental stages in emotional and cognitive development. Donna Norton writes that

research in child development has shown that there are recognizable stages in language and social development. Children do not progress through these stages at the same rate, but there is an order through which they mature. The characteristics of children demonstrated during each stage provide clues that can be used in selecting appropriate literature; this literature can benefit them during that stage of development, helping them progress to the next stage.[19]

Theories of sequential growth and learning, in this context, function in precisely the same way as Comenius's substantiation of the 'a priori' knowledge of children that he draws from his analogies with the growing of plants and the building of houses: the aim is to find a way of externalizing and schematizing innate growth to gain a priori knowledge of the 'child'.

Of course, the researchers mentioned are mostly eminent developmental psychologists and their work is grounded in perfectly respectable research. The problem is that their theories and work are not necessarily appropriate to the determination of individual children's emotional attachment to books, or even to the simple determination of which books will make sense to children: Barry Wadsworth points out that Piaget himself did very little research into reading as such, and that when he was once asked about reading at a conference he apparently replied he had no opinion on it.[20] Jerome Bruner, one of Piaget's most eminent successors, rejects, as we have seen, the invocation of 'psychological processes or mechanisms that operate in "real life"' to 'discover how and in what ways the text affects the reader',[21] arguing that 'such proposals explain so much that they explain very little. They

[19] Norton, *Through the Eyes of a Child*, 6.
[20] Barry J. Wadsworth, *Piaget for the Classroom Teacher* (Longman, London, 1978), 133.
[21] Jerome Bruner, *Actual Minds, Possible Worlds* (Harvard University Press, Cambridge, Mass., 1986), 4.

fail to tell why some stories succeed and some fail to engage the reader . . . And above all, they fail to provide an account of the processes of reading and of entering a story.'[22] Gordon Bower and Ernest Hilgard also warn in their *Theories of Learning* that

To move from [learning] theory to [educational] practice is not all that easy. The naive view is that the basic researcher stocks a kind of medicine cabinet with aids to solve the problems of the teacher. When a problem arises, the teacher can take a psychological principle from the cabinet and apply it like a bandage or ointment to solve the educational problem.[23]

If any one theory would qualify as providing guidance concerning the possible establishment of emotional response to a book, it would be Freud's psychoanalysis. However, Freud argues the following:

But at this point we become aware of a state of things which also confronts us in many other instances in which light has been thrown by psychoanalysis on a mental process. So long as we trace the development from its final outcome backwards, the chain of events appears continuous, and we feel we have gained an insight which is completely satisfactory or even exhaustive. But if we proceed the reverse way, if we start from the premises inferred from the analysis and try to follow these up to the final result, then we no longer get the impression of an inevitable sequence of events which could not have been otherwise determined. We notice at once that there might have been another result, and that we might have been just as well able to understand and explain the latter. The synthesis is thus not so satisfactory as the analysis; in other words, from a knowledge of the premises we could not have foretold the nature of the result.[24]

The very generality of the educationalists' claims, and their lack of consideration of the complexities of translating theories of psychological stages into attempts to connect books to children, further bring to the fore the fact that the most important function that the mention of these theories has is to 'prove' that the values and ideologies of liberal humanism are scientific, and therefore

[22] Ibid.

[23] Ibid.

[24] Sigmund Freud, 'The Psychogenesis of a Case of Homosexuality in a Woman', *Case Histories II*, trans. James Strachey, compiled and ed. Angela Richards (The Penguin Freud Library, 9, ed. James Strachey and Angela Richards) (Penguin, Harmondsworth, 1990), 367–400, 395.

correct and true. Scientific discourse about 'reality' and about 'facts' which can be tested and reduplicated assures educationalists of the safest 'knowledge'. The psychological theories provide them with reassurance concerning the value of their work with 'literature'. If one looks at the writings of the educationalists listed above, the following statements are supplied to form the basis of their literary criticism and teaching advice:

1. Literature helps children to progress from one developmental stage to the next.
2. Literature encourages language development in pre-school children.
3. Literature provides a model for language, and stimulates oral and written activity.
4. Children can relate to a literary character's experience and enjoy using their imagination.
5. Cognitive processes are necessary to understanding literature and cognitive processes can be stimulated by carefully selected literature.
6. Literature can encourage the oral exchange of ideas and the development of thought processes.
7. Books can play an important part in children's personality development.
8. Literature can help to understand feelings.
9. Children can identify with characters in a book who experience similar feelings.
10. Literature can help children to become sensitive to the feelings of others.
11. Literature can help to combat sexism, and non-sexist books provide models and stimuli for discussion.
12. Literature can help to make children aware of different views.

The very generality, tautology, and vagueness of these claims seems to be tacitly acknowledged by the educationalists, however: mostly they emphasize that these effects 'may' take place, or may be 'helped' to take place. In short, the educationalists are sure that stimulation through reading aloud, reading in silence, and discussion of reading is in general a good thing . . . provided the book is right; and they will judge which book is right.

In effect, the problematic way psychological theories are applied to reading is a surface symptom of the problem that children's literature critics simultaneously rely on a division between 'reality' and the book (books offer specific benefits because they are not 'real') and on an implicit view of the world as text (the books are good if they are 'real' and 'true', and if we respond to them as if to 'reality'). We can isolate one element which is given most weight in explaining the psychological process of 'entering a text', and which reflects the paradox most strongly: 'identification'. It will be clear that this term is extremely closely entangled with the 'child': 'identification' is based on identity, and 'child' is a definition of identity. Norton describes identification as a 'process [which] requires emotional ties with the model; children believe they are like these models and their thoughts, feelings, and characteristics become similar to them'.[25] Judith Thompson and Gloria Woodard use 'identification' in attempting to grasp the dynamics of reading:

One limitation to most of these books, however, is their emphasis on, identification with, and relevance only to middle class children. For too many black children, they depict an environment removed from their immediate experience . . . Identification for the young black reader rests in the central character's intimate knowledge of the black subculture.[26]

Dorothy Broderick adds that 'reading [has] to do with the readers' search for self-identification and their need to learn about persons different from themselves'.[27] Robert Leeson partially agrees with these views when he concludes that

it is argued that the working-class child does not want 'only to read about itself' and likes to escape into a different world in its reading. This is true, but only half the truth. For a full range of reading experience, the reader

    [25] Norton, *Through the Eyes of a Child*, 20.
    [26] Judith Thompson and Gloria Woodard, 'Black Perspective in Books for Children', in Donnarae MacCann and Gloria Woodard (eds.), *The Black American in Books for Children: Readings in Racism* (Scarecrow Press, Metuchen, NJ, 1972), 14–28, 23.
    [27] Dorothy M. Broderick, *Image of the Black in Children's Fiction* (R. R. Bowker, New York, 1973), 6.

needs to identify, to recognise himself or herself, as well as to escape and have vicarious pleasure and thrills.[28]

Margaret and Michael Rustin also write: 'good writing for children both describes complex mental life, and invites its readers to share in it by identification, the narratives themselves providing material for reflection'.[29]

Gloria Mattera discusses the possible dynamics of bibliotherapy. To do this she defines three processes in reading: 'identification' (which she defines, following Russell and Shrodes, as 'real or imagined affiliation of one's self with a character or group in the story read');[30] 'catharsis' (defined after Spache as the Aristotelian 'feeling of purgation following identification with a character's motivations and conflicts');[31] and 'insight' (defined after Spache as 'achieving awareness of one's own motivations, needs and problems, and considering a course of action, which like that of the book character, may lead to successful solutions').[32] All three of Mattera's reading processes are based on, or derived from, initial 'identification'. The duality of functions reading fulfils in relation to the child, as far as these writers are concerned, is again reflected in these statements: reading is a learning experience through emotional response, as well as emotionally rewarding and enjoyable in itself. The process of reading is regarded as having to do with a specific mode of recognition of the 'self' in the 'other', as well as learning about that which is different from the 'self'. Epstein suggests that

the appreciation of literature resembles the process of growing up in that they both involve the discovery of distinctions between the self and the world: the aim of both is differentiation, concreteness and the

[28] Robert Leeson, *Children's Books and Class Society: Past and Present*, ed. Children's Rights Workshop (Papers on Children's Literature no. 3) (Writers and Reading Co-operative, London, 1977), 43.

[29] Margaret and Michael Rustin, *Narratives of Love and Loss: Studies in Modern Children's Fiction* (Verso, London, 1987), 253–4.

[30] Gloria Mattera, 'Bibliotherapy in a Sixth Grade' (Ed.D., The Pennsylvania State University, 1961, microfilm-xerography by University Microfilms International, Ann Arbor, Mich., 1978), 10.

[31] Ibid.

[32] Ibid. 10–11.

development of a character of one's own. This is why literature is exciting and why it is, finally, inseparable from life.[33]

'Identification' is extensively used throughout children's literature criticism. Both the supposed ability of the child to recognize itself in the text, and the child's supposed dependence on this ability to understand and emotionally respond to a text, explain to the adult critic the nature of children's reading and the differences between adult literature and children's literature. Identity, reading as a process, and the effects of reading are now firmly tied together: children's literature is legitimized as being necessarily somehow different from adult books, if children's reading is indeed based primarily on 'identification', for then the children's books need to provide the grounds for 'identification' by providing the discovered 'essential child'. Or at least children's literature will be defined by providing a child-image which will offer possibilities for 'identification' to as many 'real child' readers as possible. This is how we find the child in the book. In the educationalists' practical criticism the child is quite literally spoken of as being in the book: Charlotte Huck, for instance, provides extensive schemes where a stage of child development ('characteristics') is listed alongside the type of book therefore suitable for the child ('implications'), and alongside this we find listed books which are said to contain or reflect each stage of child development.[34] Virginia Haviland approaches the child in the book from the creative angle:

another creative force which produces convincing and honest children's books is found in an identification with childhood, or, at least, in an instinctive understanding of childhood. The obvious identification with childhood that was so notable in the success of Hans Christian Andersen and Beatrix Potter is to be found, although with vastly different expression, in the writing of Laura Ingalls Wilder, Meindert DeJong, William Mayne, and Maurice Sendak.[35]

[33] J. Epstein, '"Good Bunnies Always Obey": Books for American Children', in Sheila Egoff, G. T. Stubbs, and L. F. Ashley (eds.), *Only Connect: Readings on Children's Literature* (Oxford University Press, Toronto, 1969), 70–90, 86.

[34] Huck, *Children's Literature in the Elementary School*, 31.

[35] Virginia Haviland, 'A Second Golden Age? In a Time of Flood?', in Virginia Haviland (ed.), *Children and Literature: Views and Reviews* (The Bodley Head, London, 1973), 88–97, 89.

'Identification' is an inherently problematic concept throughout the discussion of reading and meaning: it raises as many questions as it answers. In any case it leads children's literature critics constantly back to the problem of the lack of consensus on the 'child'. Anthony Storr writes that

reading which produces an emotional effect rather than conveying information does not put things into the mind, but rather objectifies contents which are already present. If this were not so, we should be unable to react emotionally to a book at all. There has to be a lock within us which the key of the book can fit, and if it does not fit, the book is meaningless to us.[36]

'Identification' thus seems to refer to that key fitting into that lock, that moment of understanding in which the reader supposedly feels or thinks something like: 'yes! I have felt/thought/seen/heard that myself and so I know what this means or what this feels like'. 'Identification', then, is nothing other than a cover term for the possibility any reader has of comprehending any text (or another person or culture) from within the confines of his own experience. And, as Bruner points out, this explains so much that it explains very little. It does not explain how people, as readers or in general, can ever come to understand anything different or new, or how and why persons look for and recognize themselves in what is not themselves.

'Identification' is as problematic a term in adult literary criticism as in children's literature criticism: as a basis for the dynamics of reading it limits critics to some sort of image of the child (or reader) perpetually reading himself or herself. There are critics who are interested in this concept, but it offers no solutions to the issues in children's literature criticism. D. W. Harding has written that

Popular borrowings from psychology have made great play with the ideas of identification and vicarious satisfaction as basic processes in the reader's response . . . if they are not taken literally—and in this context [reading] they never are—they are nothing but fancy labels for much more familiar and ordinary processes, chiefly for imaginative insight into what another

---

[36] Anthony Storr, 'The Child and the Book', in Egoff *et al.*, *Only Connect: Readings on Children's Literature*, 91–96, 94.

person may be feeling, and the contemplation of possible human experiences which we are not at the moment going through ourselves.[37]

Harding, instead, suggests that 'what is spoken of as "identification" with a character in a novel or play is a high degree of empathy with his supposed experience and an intensely interested contemplation of the events he takes part in'.[38]

The notion that children's reading is based on identification is closely linked with the widely accepted idea that children who enjoy a book become immersed in it far more than adults, seeing the book as reality and no longer responding to events around them: this 'child' constitutes the image of a Romantic and innocent reader. This attitude is illuminated by the article 'The Reading of Fictional Texts' by the adult literary critic Karlheinz Stierle.[39] Stierle is interested in examining the relations, as he sees them, between 'fictional' texts, 'pragmatic referential' texts, illusion, and reality. He reveals his vested interest in literary theory: towards the middle of the article he argues that 'the popular novel, in particular, is a form of fiction that presupposes a quasi-pragmatic reception. Here the act is only a means to an end: illusion building.'[40] Stierle does not approve of this 'illusion building', which he describes also as 'an act of non-reading'.[41] He claims that

*Competent* reading of fiction has to pass from quasi-pragmatic reception to *higher* forms of reception, which alone can do justice to the specific status of fiction. Only if the reader is aware of the great variety of activities entailed in 'reading' does he have a chance to perform the skills demanded by the text, and to approach it with the *right attitude*.[42]

To Stierle 'such a reading can only be achieved if the act of reading is accompanied by theoretical reflection',[43] and 'thus literary theory can provide us with new ways of reading which, in turn, could give reading a new place in society . . . The communicative function of

<hr/>

[37] D. W. Harding, 'Considered Experience: The Invitation of the Novel', *English in Education*, 2/1 (1967), 3–14, 7.
[38] Ibid.
[39] Karlheinz Stierle, 'The Reading of Fictional Texts', in S. R. Suleiman and Inge Crosman (eds.), *The Reader in the Text: Essays on Audience and Interpretation* (Princeton University Press, Princeton, NJ, 1980), 83–105.
[40] Ibid. 87.     [41] Ibid.     [42] Ibid. (my emphases).     [43] Ibid.

literature is to be preserved.'[44] This theory is supposed to transcend collections of historical and sociological accounts of how actual readers read specific texts, for 'the fixed accounts of how a specific literary work has been read are always merely partial accounts whose particularity never entirely reflects the complex experience of reception. They are marked by contemporary concepts, conventions, and prejudices, as well as by the particular interests of the critic.'[45]

Stierle is concerned, then, with the problem of accounting for variable responses to texts, and wishes to promulgate theories which will encourage a high-level and complex reading of fiction. His argument is supported by the inclusion in the article of a discussion of the 'child' as reader, in which his somewhat derogatory reference to the 'quasi-pragmatic' reading of 'trivial literature', which leads to 'illusion building', is granted one exception:

the reading of fiction in terms of mimetic illusion is an elementary form of reception that has a relative right of its own. Depending on the vividness of the illusion, the reader may be compelled to identify with fictional roles. Take, for example, the child's experience of the imaginary, which is the purest and least restricted form of this type of reception.[46]

What is regarded as an unsatisfactory, low-level, 'wrong' way of reading for Stierle's adult reader becomes, allocated to a postulated child reader, 'the purest and least restricted form of this type of reception'.[47] The choice of the positive terms 'purest' and 'least restricted' indicates a temporary approval of such reading—'naive reading' Stierle also calls it—which must, however, be transcended through maturity.[48] For the child, Stierle further asserts, 'the imaginary world of the fairy tale is real presence, its verbal mediation is skill unperceived. That is why the imaginary, though fixed in language, may have such a powerful impact on the child.'[49] Also, 'the child's pleasure in repetition reveals his desire to gain control over . . . preconceptual forms of experience like fear, hope, happiness, unhappiness, wonder, and horror'.[50] Stierle refers, in

[44] Ibid. 88.        [46] Ibid. 84–5.        [48] Ibid.        [50] Ibid.
[45] Ibid.          [47] Ibid. 85.          [49] Ibid.

this context, to Sartre's *The Words*, which 'strikingly illustrates how he, as a child, experienced without reservation an imaginary world verbally created and how, at the same time, by experiencing this illusory world, he acquired a consciousness of language and its power to produce illusion'.[51] Finally, 'though the child can still ignore this relationship between illusion and conceptual coherence, its recognition is a prerequisite to aesthetic experience once the referential illusion has seriously been questioned. Only illusion that is sustained by fiction can turn into aesthetic experience that lasts and does not spend itself with illusion.'[52]

Stierle's child reader is confidently identified and characterized, but is, in fact, only one of several versions. This child reader is necessary to conceal the intense prescriptive morality of his argument: his child reader has allocated to it those modes of reading Stierle perceives, and disapproves of, in adults. In the 'child' it is 'pure', in the 'adult' it pertains to 'trivial literature'. The path to developing the correct ways of reading includes the experience, but subsequent discarding, of 'naïve reading'. Allocated to childhood, the type of reading Stierle has constructed as being dysfunctional within his view of society can be relegated to the realms of both nostalgic reminiscence and temporary primitivism.

In Stierle's criticism the child reader becomes a safe carrier of aspects of reading that Stierle feels he must acknowledge, but which he wishes to confine and contain. Thus certain types of reading may be discriminated against by being allocated to different social classes, levels of education, and cultural background. The rejected reading processes are necessary to the description and definition of the correct or desirable ways of reading. In this way 'illusion building', 'naïve reading', and 'quasi-pragmatic' reading, for instance, are marginalized by Stierle as belonging to 'trivial literature' or 'children'.

Stierle's child reader is thus characterized by a trait often identified with child readers by adult critics and authors of children's literature: the child's claimed ability to become immersed in a book, unaware of textual mediation or a distinction

[51] Ibid.
[52] Ibid.

between 'fact' and 'fiction', or 'text' and 'reality'. It is a trait which these 'adults', as they are described in Stierle's article and similarly elsewhere, regard with ambivalence: it is often described as a longed-for capacity, one that adults are unable to recapture, and yet is often simultaneously derided as 'naïve' or as resulting in an undesirable 'illusion'. The tension within discourses which separate the world into 'fact' and 'fiction', 'objective' and 'subjective', or 'reality' and 'text', is revealed here: we noted earlier how Derrida, for instance, refers to the desire to overcome these separations. Presumably, Tucker's 'lazy reading', from which children need to be moved onward, constitutes something like 'escapism', which is another reference to the fact–fiction divide: escapism is characterized as being both necessary to life, and in this sense beneficial or harmless, and also facile, cowardly, or corrosive. The Rustins also refer to immersion in fiction when they argue that 'children display intense feelings about fictional characters—they are loved/hated and often identified with in a total way, whereas the sophisticated adult reader holds him- or herself at much greater distance'.[53] The Rustins emphasize the idyllic character of this type of reading:

Children are also able to re-evoke in adults their own capacity for intensity of feeling. For these reasons, and because its primary subject matter is a life-stage so important to both children and the adults in touch with them, fiction for children has been able to achieve a particular distinction and, at moments, perfection. . . . For children, the boundary between internal and external reality is more fragile and permeable than it is for most adults. This creates a propensity for make-believe, and for the investing of imaginary creations with strong feelings and self-identifications. The child reader is thus, potentially at least, unusually open to the pleasures and imaginative power of fiction.[54]

Another aspect of this image of the immersed reader is the critics' widespread use of 'dreaming' and 'wonder'. The 'child's' supposed capacity for wonder, hoping, and dreaming—one of its most Romantic manifestations—is constantly invoked. Typically, these words are made to work hardest in the writings of the North

---

[53] Rustin and Rustin, *Narratives of Love and Loss*, 4.
[54] Ibid. 4, 18.

American educationalists: the 'child' takes its place within the discourse of the American Dream, allied to the images of the pioneer and the immigrant. Thus the 'child', in this guise, joins that now practically empty invocation of the American Dream which has become almost parodied by its role in American advertising: the 'child' mingles there with 'tradition', 'wonder', 'dream', 'delight', and 'cherish'. Charlotte Huck, for instance, claims that 'good writing, or effective use of language . . . will help the reader to experience the delight of beauty, wonder, and humor . . . He will be challenged to dream dreams, to ponder, and to ask questions to himself.'[55] Huck amplifies this view of the wide-eyed little traveller into the future when she describes the limitations of the 'child's' understanding:

> . . . the feeling of nostalgia is an adult emotion that is foreign to most boys and girls. . . . Cynicism and despair are not childlike emotions. . . . Few children have known despair. They may have endured pain, sorrow, or horror; they may be in what we would consider hopeless situations, but they are not without hope. . . . Children see beauty where there is ugliness . . .[56]

This type of writing provokes much irritable response from critics (such as Jan Needle's response to Michele Landsberg) where the problems of differing visions of the child as reader are expressed through, and exacerbated by, the disparity between commitment to this hopeful vision and the 'realists'' concern for *their* 'real child', who is seen as feeling rage and despair, and being faced perhaps with indifference, brutality, or poverty.

This irritation surfaces continually between the educationalists and the pluralists, as I pointed out at the start of this chapter. I think it is fair to say, however, that the irritation is directed more from the pluralists towards the educationalists than vice versa. The educationalists, despite their quoting of psychology, mostly advocate that the teacher, librarian, or parent learn to understand the individuality of each child, although, again, they do not explain how this is to be done: they seem to assume this is something most

---

[55] Huck, *Children's Literature in the Elementary School*, 4.
[56] Ibid. 5.

adults with good intentions towards children are capable of to some degree or other. Glazer and Williams, for example, discuss the psychologists, but conclude:

Piaget, Bruner, and Gagné agree on one central point: each child is unique. And no one can know a child's learning ability or mental maturity simply from knowing how old the child is. . . . The studies by Cohen, Piaget, Kohlberg, Smith, and others are not the last word on who the child is. These experts cannot tell you how one boy or girl thinks. Your own curiosity and sensitivity may be more useful than studies in exploring the mystery of a child you want to know. But research can sharpen common sense, and give some ideas on where to start in answering questions about young readers. Common sense alone is often wrong. . . . The point is, adult intuitions about children cannot always be trusted.[57]

Within the liberal humanist discourse in which the educationalists participate the issue of individuality is important in itself. But the educationalists' uncomfortable combination of defined 'children' and individuality, and their lack of attention to the complexity of using psychology in interpretations and judgements of books, provoke the ire of quite a few pluralist critics. The question of how to learn from children—what it means for the adult to use what Glazer and Williams refer to as 'curiosity and sensitivity . . . common sense . . . adult intuitions'—does not seem to elicit an equal level of response from the pluralists. Few children's literature critics discuss this issue anyway—presumably leaving it to the psychologists or to 'common sense'—but those who do do not appear to identify it as an area of disagreement between the camps of children's literature. But the crucial difference between the educationalists and the pluralists hinges on the issue of generalization, on the one hand, and individualization, on the other, and not on knowing or not knowing the 'child', as pluralists often claim. In making this claim the pluralists view themselves as not knowing the 'child', or not forcing definitions on it. The pluralists are ideologically and emotionally committed to the individuality and non-predictability of children's responses to books and literature. And yet they have largely found it impossible to deal with the

[57] Glazer and Williams, *Introduction to Children's Literature*, 13, 19.

presence of some 'child' in connection with the field of children's books. They, too, often assign a powerful function and influence to reading for 'children'. Just as the educationalists' stabilized 'child' is partly undermined by their simultaneous belief in children's individuality, the pluralists' individualized 'child' is partly undermined by the difficulty of avoiding any definition of childhood at all.

The pluralists, then, formulate their criticism of the educationalists mainly in two ways: first, they emphasize that, in their view, 'children' seem to make significantly different uses and interpretations of books. Secondly, they observe that the educationalists disagree amongst themselves in the claims they make for the influences particular books may have. In other words, the pluralists observe that the educationalists all claim to know the 'child', but that these 'children' differ. Therefore, the problem of actual varying interpretations made by the educationalists on behalf of 'children' is unsolvable: assuming different child readers leads to the use of different criteria, which leads to different interpretations. It has to be said that, to a great extent, this does undermine the educationalists' practical criticism of children's books, with respect to the aims they set themselves. Important social issues such as racism, for instance, have led educationalists with the same strongly anti-racist views to differ utterly in their judgement of a book: Bob Dixon praises Paula Fox's *The Slave Dancer* as being 'a novel of great horror and as great humanity . . . [approaching] perfection as a work of art',[58] while Sharon Bell Mathis calls it 'an insult to black children',[59] and Binnie Tate claims that it 'perpetuates racism . . . [with] constantly repeated racist implications and negative illusions [*sic*]'.[60] Donna Norton mentions Mark Twain's *Huckleberry Finn*, amongst others, as being at the centre of similar controversies.[61]

[58] Bob Dixon, *Catching Them Young*, i: *Sex, Race and Class in Children's Fiction* (Pluto Press, London, 1977), 125.

[59] Sharon Bell Mathis, '*The Slave Dancer* is an Insult to Black Children', in Donnarae MacCann and Gloria Woodard (eds.), *Cultural Conformity in Books for Children: Further Readings in Racism* (Scarecrow Press, Metuchen, NJ, 1977), 146–9, 146.

[60] Binnie Tate, 'Racism and Distortion Pervade *The Slave Dancer*', ibid. 149–53, 149, 152–3.

[61] Norton, *Through the Eyes of a Child*, 56.

The fundamental assumption that books influence children makes these issues crucial: does, or can, *The Slave Dancer* perpetuate racism or does it counteract it (or does it do neither)?

As in my previous discussion of the use of psychology to attempt to stabilize the 'child', I should point out in this context that research on whether books can have this specific type of influence on children is generally inconclusive for the same reasons: the difficulty of separating the influence of books from other variables, and the question of how differences of view are measured, cause many obscurities. Sara Goodman Zimet attributes the difficulties of research in this area to the problem that '. . . there are so many other factors operating at the same time. Peer pressure, family and community values, religious beliefs and so on—all impinge on the individual to create his or her particular value system.'[62] Some brief examples may suffice to indicate what has happened in much of this type of research: Zimet mentions personal testimony as one proof of the influence of books, and singles out Smith's 1948 research[63] among over 500 fourth-, fifth-, and sixth-grade students, Shirley's 1969 study of a group of 240 secondary pupils,[64] and Lind (1936) and Weingarten (1954),[65] who worked with college students. In all four cases, the members of the target groups were asked how they were influenced by reading. (With reference to the dates of these studies it should be noted that, as Zimet also remarks, research is not often done in this area because of the acknowledged complexity.) Zimet reports that

all four groups indicated that their attitudes, ideas and behaviour were affected [but] the similarity within groups and between groups ended here. On the one hand, there was tremendous variability among individuals as to how they thought their attitudes, values and behaviour were influenced. On the other hand, not all books affected all individuals in the same way. Thus, the intent of an author either to persuade, to inform or to entertain may produce a response in the reader that had not been anticipated.[66]

---

[62] Sara Goodman Zimet, *Print and Prejudice* (Hodder and Stoughton, London, 1976), 15.
[63] Ibid.        [64] Ibid.        [65] Ibid. 16.        [66] Ibid.

In analysing research specifically concerned with the effects of reading on children as regards their attitudes towards minority groups, Zimet writes that

all four investigators [Jackson, 1944; Fisher, 1965; Tauran, 1965; Litcher and Johnson, 1967] reported significant changes. When characters belonging to minority groups were presented in a favourable light the attitudes of the readers moved in a positive direction . . . when characters belonging to minority groups were presented in an unfavourable light, attitudes of readers moved in a negative direction.[67]

However, Zimet then emphasizes that the studies do not make clear whether the students were not simply conforming to the wishes of the teacher, rather than responding to their reading, and 'there is therefore some room for doubt about the extent to which attitudes were genuinely influenced'.[68] In any case, she adds, Jackson's study found possible changes of attitude to have become undetectable only two weeks after the initial experiment.[69] This whole issue is not of direct relevance to our present discussion, as interpretation of books, as we have seen, is quite different from determining whether the books have any influence at all. But the question is so important, and so many strong beliefs are held with regard to the influence that not only books, but also television and films, have on children, that I wanted to devote some attention to this subject. The fact that these questions have still not been resolved, and that assertions are still made and strong beliefs held, is strongly related to the entire discussion concerning purpose in children's literature criticism.

Returning to the controversy between the educationalists and the pluralists concerning interpretation, we can see how the 'child's' individuality is established and used: Elaine Moss and Peter Dickinson, for instance, argue that children may have a need for, or may make use of, books some adults consider to be rubbish. Elaine Moss explains in her article 'The "Peppermint" Lesson' how her daughter, Alison, appeared to become attached to a book (*Peppermint*) about an unwanted kitten that is finally given to a little

[67] Ibid. 19.
[68] Ibid.
[69] Ibid.

girl, who loves it and wins first prize in the cat show with it.[70] Moss describes the book:

Like the words, the pictures are totally without distinction. Comic-style kids and cats, blobby colours, accentuated sashes and splashes. Totally expendable, one would have thought: a watered-down, vulgarized 'Ugly Duckling'.[71]

Moss then goes on to explain what later occurred to her as being the reason for Alison's attachment to the book: 'Alison is an adopted child . . . she was taken home, like Peppermint, to be loved and cared for and treasured.'[72] She adds that a 'technically efficient and typographically superior'[73] book explaining adoption to pre-school children, which she had provided her daughter with, did not seem to inspire the same reaction as *Peppermint*. Moss concludes that this type of 'artistically worthless book—hack-written and poorly illustrated'[74] may therefore 'be more important to that child's development than all the Kate Greenaway Medal-winning books put together'.[75]

Peter Dickinson, in his 'Defence of Rubbish', argues along similar lines that it may sometimes be those books that he defines as 'rubbish . . . all forms of reading matter which contain to the adult eye no visible value either aesthetic or educational',[76] which children may put to some use, or enjoy. To sum up the reasons Dickinson suggests for this: children might use 'rubbish' to learn about aspects of a culture, to feel they are part of a group, or to discover for themselves what they enjoy reading or might come to prefer; 'easy' reading might provide a psychological sense of security, comfort, or reassurance; people in general might be better

---

[70] Elaine Moss, 'The "Peppermint" Lesson', in Margaret Meek, Aidan Warlow, and Griselda Barton (eds.), *The Cool Web: The Pattern Of Children's Reading* (The Bodley Head, London, 1977), 140–2.

[71] Ibid. 141.

[72] Ibid.

[73] Ibid. 142.

[74] Ibid.

[75] Ibid.

[76] Peter Dickinson, 'A Defence of Rubbish', in Geoff Fox *et al.* (eds.), *Writers, Critics, and Children: Articles from 'Children's Literature in Education'* (Heinemann Educational Press, London, 1976), 73–6.

off with a mixture of 'good' and 'bad' reading (Dickinson feels this is a 'more nebulous' point);[77] and, finally, as Dickinson puts it, 'the innocence—I suppose there is no other word—of the child's eye can take or leave in a way that I feel an adult cannot, and can acquire valuable stimuli from things which appear otherwise overgrown with a mass of weeds and nonsense'.[78] D. W. Harding supports the usefulness of 'rubbish' when he speculates that 'children have to make delayed discoveries of what they have in some sense known a long time—whether about Santa Claus or sex or religion. From this angle there may be a thoroughly valid defence of novels that offer an improbably sweetened taste of experience.'[79]

What is characteristic is that in Moss's, Dickinson's, and Harding's statements we again see expressed defining views of 'children' and their reading: even in pleading for the freedom to choose to read 'rubbish', Moss, Dickinson, and Harding use arguments based on what is 'good' for the 'child'. They only actually differ in defining which books are appropriate to their 'child's' development or needs. Moss and Dickinson include 'rubbish', and Harding 'improbably sweetened' novels, as appropriate, in the sense of fulfilling constructive functions in children's growth. The result of views such as those of Needle, Avery, Moss, Dickinson, and Harding are the same: they suggest the subversion of the educationalists' self-assigned role as the selector of books for children on the basis of some type of assigned response. It is an important difference between educationalists and pluralists, but it is also deceptive: of the critics I have just listed, Needle, Avery, Moss, and Dickinson are still contributors to children's literature criticism. Their definitions of the 'child' may not include limiting their reading, but they still do produce children's literature criticism, and their 'child' still pervades their practical criticism: the critics' involvement with children's literature criticism as it stands provides the boundaries of their 'children's' existence.

But the attempts to use psychology to stabilize the 'child', and therefore the child in the book, are only one of the tactics employed

---

[77] Ibid. 74.
[78] Ibid. 74–6.
[79] Harding, 'Considered Experience', 10.

by critics. Both educationalists and pluralists involve themselves with the theory of literary criticism. Principles from adult literary criticism and, more recently, from literary theory are adopted in various ways to stabilize the text from another angle: that is, to prove it to be a good text for the child. The educationalists and the pluralists here again differ with respect to emphasis: the educationalists need the good book to influence the 'child' in the right way; the pluralists employ arguments which refer to the value of art and literature in general. The pluralists therefore seem detached from the 'child', but in fact are only camouflaging their position: art and literature are supposed to be good for *someone*, unless one clings tenaciously to the view that they exist in abstract perfection. In this instance, that someone is still the 'child'.

The 'literary' position is applied in various ways. Let us look first at the 'literary' approach which accepts more or less as given a stable, unified method of literary criticism. This position, as with the psychological theories, reveals its paradoxes and confusions quite easily: I mentioned Lillian Smith earlier as a critic who wishes to 'consider children's books as literature, and discover some of the standards by which they can be so judged . . . They are a portion of universal literature and must be subjected to the same standards of criticism.'[80] Smith then promptly introduces the following type of comments: 'children may not consciously recognize their search for lasting truth in their indiscriminate reading of fairy tales . . . and all the variety of literature that brings delight and rouses a warm response in their minds';[81] and 'there is much in *Gulliver's Travels* that children cannot understand. They take what they like from it; and what they like best is the inexhaustible imagination that pictured and peopled the Lilliputian world . . . To them it is a story as alive today as when it first appeared in 1726.'[82] Another self-styled 'literary' critic is Dorothy Neal White, who writes that

adults out of touch with children's books frequently infer that the bad book can have only two vices, immorality and bad grammar. If a book is

[80] Lillian H. Smith, *The Unreluctant Years: A Critical Approach to Children's Literature* (American Library Association, Chicago, 1953), 7.
[81] Ibid. 16.
[82] Ibid. 23.

not littered with split infinitives, and does not incite its reader to arson or robbery with violence, it is assumed to be harmless . . . The worst fault in present-day children's books is not any flagrant departure from formal grammar, but the colourless, dull, passionless use of language which ultimately ruins for a child his sense of the resources and vitality of the English tongue.[83]

Just a few lines down, Dorothy White is condemning books on the grounds of 'snobbery'[84] and the 'mishandling of personal relationships'.[85] These 'literary' critics are still reading on behalf of their vision of the 'child reader'; they are still inhabiting their 'child' mind.

The reliance on the education–amusement divide as constituting the establishment of children's fiction as an educational non-force leads to these repeated attempts to establish stabilizing 'literary' criteria for children's fiction. And these 'literary' criteria are asserted to function in the same way as 'adult' literary criticism: in this way the 'literary' children's literature critics attempt to move from the 'child' to 'literature'. But, as with Lillian Smith and Dorothy White, the child readers' supposed feelings, responses, preferences, and needs pervade their criticism. Thus children's literature criticism, overwhelmingly, cannot rid itself of all these child readers in this way either: the construction of literary criteria which are supposed to be absolute, child-independent qualities of text cannot vanquish the power of the 'child' on the critics.

Children's literature criticism focuses its attention on changing, correcting, replacing, or attempting to shake off the 'child'. It never fully realizes, however, that its problems arise from its remaining directed and controlled by the unacknowledged power of the liberal arts educational ideals. Children's literature criticism remains one of the last moral outposts of these ideals: it keeps faith with the fundamental assumption that literature (as opposed to books as a whole) will affect and, therefore, influence—and, with a bit of luck, influence in desirable ways. This is the case with all children's

---

[83] Dorothy Neal White, *About Books for Children* (Oxford University Press, New York, 1949), 9–10.

[84] Ibid. 10.

[85] Ibid.

literature critics. The belief in the redemptive role of art is the mainstay of their work.

The educationalists, in employing their 'literary' criticism, select views from the wide gamut of adult literary criticism which fit in with their needs. If the psychological theories the educationalists mention are appropriated and moulded for their purposes, this is no less true of adult literary criticism. In this respect, we might extend Jacqueline Rose's statement that 'children's fiction . . . sets in place . . . the [child] which it needs to believe is there for its own purposes' [86] by saying that this implies setting in place psychologies and literary criticisms which it needs to believe are there for its own purposes.

In exactly the same way that the educationalists struggle mightily to discuss the child's 'childness' and 'individuality' simultaneously, so they attempt to discuss 'literature' with *and* without the 'child' at the same time. We find Glazer and Williams, for instance, writing themselves into the following corner: first they claim that 'good' children's books have to do with 'strong materials—good plots, rich settings, well-developed characters, important themes, and artistic styles . . . bold and imaginative language',[87] and that this 'freshness . . . comes from the author. And in the author it begins with an understanding of who the child is.'[88] Then they continue by arguing that even if children do not like these 'good' books, they may still be 'good literature . . . built of strong materials . . . the likes and dislikes of children do not determine the quality of literature . . . Books must be judged as literature on their own merits. And children should be given excellent literature.' [89] The paradoxality of these statements hinges on the question of whether the attraction of a book, for child readers, does indeed depend on the critics' 'child' being in the book. If this were the case, then children would love books that critics claim are good because of their identification of this child in the book. In practice, of course, this is what critics are

---

[86] Jacqueline Rose, *The Case of Peter Pan or: The Impossibility of Children's Fiction* (series: Language, Discourse, Society, ed. Stephen Heath and Colin MacCabe) (Macmillan, London, 1984), 10.

[87] Glazer and Williams, *Introduction to Children's Literature*, 34, 19.

[88] Ibid. 22.

[89] Ibid. 34.

doing continually: asserting their ability to identify the child in the book, and then linking it with their child reader, on this child reader's behalf. But if children do not appear to like books in which the critics discern their child, then the adult critics cease to have any function for their child reader: they have no basis on which to link the child to the book.

Lonsdale and Mackintosh, like Glazer and Williams, seem to believe in the possibility—and necessity—of establishing a distinction between 'literary' qualities and child reader suitability. They then, similarly, almost simultaneously undermine their own position by referring back to the child as a measure of these 'literary' qualities: Lonsdale and Mackintosh, like all educationalists, advocate that teachers should guide children through literature by, first, knowing what children 'are like at [various] years of age; what their reading interests are; what [their] reading skills; what their attitudes are towards reading',[90] and, secondly, by knowing 'what literature is—what makes a book a good book; what authors and illustrators are contributing to a rich body of literature for boys and girls; how are the stories geared to the needs, interests, and abilities of children.'[91] Donna Norton, similarly, writes that

the criteria usually used to evaluate children's fiction include elements of plot, characterization, setting, theme, style, and point of view. Also, it is necessary to be concerned with other characteristics: relevance, suitability, potential popularity, and the development of nonstereotypes in the literature.[92]

There is no separation possible of the type John Rowe Townsend suggested between educationalists' criteria and 'literary' criteria: children's literature criticism does not consist of various parallel views which can be applied at will for various purposes. These views are, on the contrary, mutually enmeshed and derive from convoluted reformulations of bits of other disciplines. Much children's literature criticism stumbles on its assumption that discourse appropriated from other disciplines, such as science or 'literary criticism', exists to some extent as an abstract entity, which

[90] Lonsdale and Mackintosh, *Children Experience Literature*, p. v.
[91] Ibid.
[92] Norton, *Through the Eyes of a Child*, 78.

will maintain its shape in every context. A belief in independence of the 'literary' is strongly reflected in, and connected with, these children's literature critics' refusal to focus on the construction of the 'child': these critics maintain their discourse of 'truth' and 'reality' on many levels. Michele Landsberg defines literary merit as deriving from the following issues:

Is the language original, fresh, and interesting? Are the characters wooden, or do they live and breathe on the page? Do they speak in individual voices, so you can tell who's talking just by the characteristic speech patterns? . . . If it's a fantasy, does the author create a believable world, no matter how strange, and abide by the rules of that world so that your belief in it is never shaken, or do you come thudding back to the banal commonplace with maddening regularity? If the story is an adventure, does it convince you?[93]

Landsberg adds that 'the point of developing such [critical expertise] . . . is that good books can do so much for children.'[94] The children's author Leon Garfield amplifies, as many other authors and critics do, the 'reality' issue: 'words must live for [children]; so must people. That is what really matters, and it entails believing entirely in what one writes and having a real urgency to convince the reader that it is absolutely, utterly true.'[95] We may note that this 'reality' of the book is a part of the idea that the 'child' becomes immersed in the book, and also that it forms part of the paradoxical maintenance of both the merger between and a strong separation of 'reality' and texts. Charlotte Huck's 'literary' criteria are also based on this 'truth' and 'reality' terminology: a plot should be 'organic and interrelated. . . . [grow] logically and naturally . . . [it] should be credible and ring true';[96] a setting 'should be authentic and true';[97] a theme 'should be . . . based upon justice and integrity';[98] and, finally, characterization 'should be . . . as convincingly real and lifelike as our next-door neighbours'.[99]

[93] Landsberg, *Reading for the Love of It*, 33.
[94] Ibid. 34.
[95] Haviland, *Children and Literature: Views and Reviews*, 132.
[96] Huck, *Children's Literature in the Elementary School*, 7.
[97] Ibid.     [98] Ibid. 8.     [99] Ibid. 9.

Who decides what is 'real' and 'true'? Who says which book contains these qualities? These are not trivial or pretentious questions, designed to develop sophistical discussions: they lie at the core of the problem of literary criticism and of all interpretative activity as a whole. It is not the case even that the critics quoted above, who appear to share the same 'literary' criteria to such a great extent, produce the same judgements of books. Some children's literature critics are aware of these problems within children's literature. They have attempted to resolve them by turning to the literary theory of adult literary criticism. Unlike critics such as Norton, Huck, Landsberg, Smith, or White, these children's literature critics have become involved with the discussions and problems of adult literary theory and criticism. Some have also suggested that children's literature criticism might contribute to, rather than only benefit from, the thinking concerning issues of adult literature criticism. Do these critics finally escape the paradoxes and confusions of children's literature criticism as we have viewed them up till now? This is what we will be considering in the next chapter.

## 5

# On Not Knowing the Child: Children's Literature Criticism and Adult Literary Theory

Some of the educationalist and pluralist critics we have looked at found themselves attempting to disassociate their 'literary' judgements from what they perceived to be children's tastes or preferences, despite ultimately referring the origin of this literary quality back to versions of the 'child'. However, there are critics who elaborate the disassociation between their judgements of the literary values of children's books and the 'child'. We saw in Lillian Smith's and Dorothy White's writing an effort to transfer (part of) their faith from 'children's literature' to 'literature'. Their views of children as readers still provided the basis for their views. But because children's literature criticism is under pressure from its own views of freedom, it feels the need to attempt to free the 'child' as reader. Therefore, some critics attempt to move further away still from the 'child' and transfer their faith not only to 'literature', but also to 'adults' as readers. These critics defend themselves from criticism of their supposed child neglect by returning to the claim, shared by educationalist and pluralist critics, that it is precisely literary value which provides benefit to children. In other words, while these critics attempt to remove the separate child reader as the standard for critical evaluation and judgement, they still maintain the extra-textual reading child as their ultimate goal and reference-point.

John Rowe Townsend is one of the critics who emphasize literary values. He writes:

I believe that children's books must be judged as part of literature in general, and therefore by much the same standards as 'adult' books. A good children's book must not only be pleasing to children. It must be a good book in its own right.[1]

Townsend seems to echo Lillian Smith with this statement. But he adds that 'children are not a separate form of life from people; no more than children's books are a separate form of literature from just books'.[2] There are other supporters of this argument that 'children reading' should be considered as part of 'people reading', and 'children's books' as part of books in general, and that, among these books in general, they may qualify for inclusion amongst a qualitatively based selection of 'good' books or 'literature'. The author Meindert DeJong, for instance, argues that 'creative books for children are the nearest thing to that purest of all literary forms, the lyric poem'.[3] C. S. Lewis remarked that 'no book is really worth reading at the age of ten which is not equally (and often far more) worth reading at the age of 50'.[4] Paula Fox, like Townsend, DeJong, and Lewis, a children's book author, writes that 'what applies to good writing is, I think, absolute, whether for children or grown-ups or the blind or the deaf or the thin or the fat'.[5]

This type of criticism relies on the view that 'literature' provides a privileged mode of meaning, learning, or experience. And this is inevitable in so far as the entire thrust of their undertaking operates—in its various ways—to secure the good for the child. The emotive quality of much children's literature criticism we have considered reveals its high moral and emotional stakes: to these critics children's fiction matters. Therefore these critics use a type of critical view which may be compared to that of the literary critic I. A. Richards. Of course, many of these literary critical views have been formulated extensively throughout the history of literary

[1] John Rowe Townsend, *Written for Children: An Outline of English-Language Children's Literature* (2nd rev. edn., Penguin, Harmondsworth, 1983), 11.

[2] John Rowe Townsend, 'Standards of Criticism for Children's Literature', in Nancy Chambers (ed.), *The Signal Approach to Children's Books* (Kestrel Books, Harmondsworth, 1980), 193–207, 197.

[3] Meindert DeJong, 'The Cry and the Creation', in Virginia Haviland (ed.), *Children and Literature: Views and Reviews* (The Bodley Head, London, 1973), 160–9, 164.

[4] Fred Inglis, *The Promise of Happiness: Value and Meaning in Children's Literature* (Cambridge University Press, Cambridge, 1981), 102.

[5] Haviland, *Children and Literature: Views and Reviews*, 131–2.

criticism. We have observed how children's literature criticism developed alongside, and made use of, these views in the 'stories of origin'. But children's literature criticism has undergone a concentrated burst of development in the twentieth century, and it clearly assumes the terminology of several twentieth-century critics. Richards wrote on literature and its functions in educating and engaging emotions and aesthetic sensitivities. The liberal arts tradition that I have discussed thus not only provides many of the assumptions children's literature criticism relies on, but also allies children's literature criticism with those adult literary critical views which also base themselves on the liberal arts terminology. I. A. Richards sums up this basis when he writes that

the arts, if rightly approached, supply the best data available for deciding what experiences are more valuable than others . . . The enlargement of the mind, the widening of the sphere of human sensibility, is brought about through poetry . . . the age-long controversy as to whether the business of poetry is to please or to instruct shows this well . . . [but] neither term is appropriate to the greater forms of art . . . Tragedy is still the form under which the mind may most clearly and freely contemplate the human situation, its issues unclouded, its possibilities revealed.[6]

Children's literature criticism on behalf of the 'child' is bound to Richards's critical motivation and terms of discussion through their joint commitment to the basic tenets of the liberal arts education: note Richards's reference to the issue of separating 'pleasure' from 'instruction'. Ironically, however, it is also Richardian criticism and its ideologies which exclude children's fiction from the literary canon that children's literature critics such as Townsend, Fox, and DeJong believe it should be part of.

Thus, children's literature critics such as Townsend (I will refer to them as 'literary pluralist' critics) are involved in a number of problems: first, they are attempting to work with what they take to be the terms of an adult literary criticism which excludes their field; and, secondly, they reformulate adult literary criticism as a unified, stable critical methodology. In fact, adult literary criticism is itself a compilation of different theoretical and practical perspectives, some

[6] I. A. Richards, *Principles of Literary Criticism* (Routledge and Kegan Paul, London, 1928), 33, 68–9.

of which are anathema to each other. Finally, the literary pluralist critics must also still account for their extra-textual 'child'.

We can see these topics reflected in Robert Leeson's response to Townsend's suggestions for criticism:

Townsend's critical system would be book-centred rather than child-centred . . . Well, let's agree . . . Let's further agree that there is great disagreement over criteria in children's literature . . . If the criteria are jumbled, it is because children's literature is in a state of expansion and change greater than at any time in its history. To bring together these disparate elements into a comprehensive (let alone unified) critical theory will take time and effort . . . It will happen, I think, through a process of synthesis, not by the rejection of non-literary criteria . . . Even less will it be done by a retreat into an aestheticism developed in the field of adult literature . . . How pure are the purists? How influenced by non-literary criteria in a world where the events of the 1940's and 1950's upset the stable judgments of the 1920's and 1930's? [7]

Leeson apparently presupposes a 'comprehensive' critical theory in 'adult' 'book-centred' literary criticism, formed by 'literary criteria' which have prompted 'a retreat into aestheticism' by 'purists'. In suggesting aims for a children's literature criticism Leeson includes a critique of an adult literary criticism as he perceives it.

In emphasizing the literary aspects of some children's fiction these 'book-centred' critics are in effect also relying on a reformulation of Northrop Frye's ideas about readers, texts, and reading. Leeson certainly seems to be referring to a Frye type of New Criticism, or 'close reading', in his sketch of an adult literary theory. Lillian Smith and Dorothy Neal White also seemed to have New Criticism's ideas in mind. In Townsend and Leeson's terms children's literature criticism was in the 1970s, and largely still is, in the position that Frye was formulating in his *Anatomy of Criticism*[8] when he wrote that his essays were a contribution to remedying a problem he discerned: namely, that

there is as yet no way of distinguishing what is genuine criticism, and

[7] Robert Leeson, 'To the Toyland Frontier', in Chambers, *The Signal Approach to Children's Books*, 208–16, 209–10.

[8] Northrop Frye, *Anatomy of Criticism: Four Essays* (Princeton University Press, Princeton, NJ, 1957).

therefore progresses toward making the whole of literature intelligible, from what belongs only to the history of taste, and therefore follows the vacillations of fashionable prejudice . . . We have no real standards to distinguish a verbal structure that is literary from one that is not.[9]

The consequence of this, Frye argued, was that a 'determinist fallacy' operated. He defined this as the attempt 'not to find a conceptual framework for criticism within literature, but to attach criticism to one of a miscellany of frameworks outside it . . . whether Marxist, Thomist, liberal-humanist, neo-classical, Freudian, Jungian, or existentialist'.[10] Frye wanted critics 'to make an inductive survey of [their] own field and let [their] critical principles shape themselves solely out of [their] knowledge of that field'.[11] Compare this with Townsend's similarly oriented description of his ideal children's book critic:

He should, I believe, approach a book with an open mind and respond to it as freshly and honestly as he is able; then he should go away, let his thoughts and feelings about it mature, turn them over from time to time, consider the book in relation to others by the same author and by the author's predecessors and contemporaries. If the book is for children he should not let his mind be dominated by the fact; but neither, I think, should he attempt to ignore it.[12]

And, echoing Frye's definition of the 'determinist fallacy', Townsend argues that

it is perfectly possible to judge books for children by non-literary standards. It is legitimate to consider the social or moral or psychological or educational impact of a book; to consider how many children, and what kind of children, will like it. But it is dangerous to do this and call it criticism.[13]

Frye and Townsend, on the basis of their liberal arts beliefs, also comment similarly on the need for 'good' criticism. Besides viewing this criticism, as F. R. Leavis does, as the result of the critics'

[9] Ibid. 9, 13.
[10] Ibid. 6–7.
[11] Ibid. 7.
[12] John Rowe Townsend, *A Sense of Story: Essays on Contemporary Writers for Children* (Longman, London, 1971), 15.
[13] Ibid. 14.

engagement with, and judgement of, literature, Townsend quotes Henry S. Canby: 'Unless there is somewhere an intelligent critical attitude against which the writer can measure himself . . . one of the chief requirements for good literature is wanting . . . the author degenerates.'[14] Frye, in the same way, argues that the literary critic is 'for better or worse, the pioneer of education and the shaper of cultural tradition. Whatever popularity Shakespeare and Keats have now is equally the result of the publicity of criticism'[15] and 'a public that tries to do without criticism, and asserts that it knows what it wants or likes, brutalizes the arts and loses its cultural memory'.[16] The literary pluralist critics, in the service of the 'child', are asking for attention to the literariness of some children's fiction beyond a strictly determinist interest in educational, psychological, or sociological aspects of children's reading and childhood. They act for a 'real child' reader, but not necessarily for the child in the book, and are therefore ever more committed to sustaining a division between textual and non-textual narrative, or, as Frank Lentricchia puts it, between that 'romantic mystique of a unique literary discourse and unique literary values' and an 'objectively knowable lump of thereness . . . reality'.[17]

Wayne Booth summarizes some of the terminology critics have used to discuss 'unique literary values' within this 'unique literary discourse'. Their terms of discussion, like those of many of the child- and book-centred children's fiction critics, are based on a distinction between literary discourse and extra-textual 'reality' or 'life', and involve references to the interrelations between these two worlds. Booth writes, in considering 'general qualities on the basis of which critics since Flaubert have judged fiction',[18] that

some critics would require the novel to do justice to reality, to be true to life, to be natural, or real, or intensely alive. Others would cleanse it of impurities, of the inartistic, of the all-too-human. On the one hand, the

[14] Ibid.
[15] Frye, *Anatomy of Criticism*, 4.
[16] Ibid. 5.
[17] Frank Lentricchia, *After the New Criticism* (Athlone Press, London, 1980), 25, 33.
[18] Wayne Clayton Booth, *The Rhetoric of Fiction* (University of Chicago Press, Chicago, fifth impression, 1965), 37.

request is for 'dramatic vividness', 'conviction', 'sincerity', 'genuineness', 'an air of reality', 'a full realization of the subject', 'intensity of illusion'; on the other, for 'dispassionateness', 'impersonality', 'poetic purity', 'pure form'.[19]

The use of certain of these criteria characterizes literary movements, such as Romanticism, naturalism, and realism, and we have seen all of these kinds of terms used by various children's literary critics with respect to their perception of the correspondence or divergence between the 'literary child' ('the child in the book') and the 'real child': the 'child', too, is a text subject to reinterpretation within different contexts, several of which are strongly connected to literary movements. To give one more example of cross-referral between artistic visions and images of how childhood operates: Roger Duvoisin explains that 'one of the reasons for making a page which is well designed is to tell the story with more simplicity, more verve, clarity, and impact; to give importance to what is important; to eliminate what destroys the freshness, the originality of the page; in other words, to make a page which will be more easily read by the child.'[20]

The book-centred literary pluralist critics are knocking on the door of a Leavisite 'literature' of which Leavis wrote that 'we accept the field [of literature] to be more or less strictly delimited in accordance with the conception of literature as a matter of memorable works'.[21] Children's fiction, excluding some up-graded books such as the 'Alices', are usually not included in this canon. Frances Mulhern describes the 'adult' reader and critic prevalent in the criticism of F. R. Leavis:

the values implicit in 'literary criticism' were drawn from [Leavis's] 'sense' of a community that he and his collaborators could neither identify in the real nor define in thought—except as part of a circle of meanings whose interdependence was exclusive and absolute. The perimeter of the

---

[19] Ibid. 37–8.
[20] Roger Duvoisin, 'Children's Book Illustration: The Pleasures and Problems', in Haviland, *Children and Literature: Views and Reviews*, 177–88, 178.
[21] F. R. Leavis, *Anna Karenina and Other Essays* (Chatto and Windus, London, 1967), 139.

circle marked the limits of persuasion: what 'Scrutiny's' audience did not 'know already' it could not be told.[22]

Children's literature criticism such as Townsend advocates tries to envisage just such a community of adult critics and readers for children's books, which will gain the books an entrance to literary prestige and canonization.

We can draw a parallel between Townsend's effort, and Elaine Showalter's suggestion that feminist literary criticism is concerned 'with the way in which the hypothesis of a female reader changes our apprehension of a given text, awakening us to the significance of its sexual codes'.[23] Her interest, in other words, lies in analysing the assumptions guiding accepted interpretations of texts based on a 'male' reader. Literary pluralist critics are postulating an 'adult' reader to take the place of their 'child' reader, in order to reveal the works' 'literary' aspects. In this context, the literary pluralist critics' previous 'child' reader is also similar to Heilbrun's[24] view on male/female readers, which Jonathan Culler explains as entailing the suggestion that reading as a woman is not necessarily what occurs when a woman reads: women, Heilbrun argues, can, and have, read as men. Literary pluralist critics see critics as previously having solely read children's fiction 'as children', and they want critics also to read this fiction as 'adults' for the literary purposes which are ultimately to benefit the (child) reader.

Children's literature criticism has been compared to feminist criticism in other ways. I am using Showalter and Heilbrun's comments for the purposes of analogy, but Lissa Paul, for instance, has argued that children's fiction and women's writing share a common base:

children, like women, are lumped together as helpless and dependent; creatures to be kept away from the scene of the action, and who otherwise ought not to be seen or heard. But women make up more than half of the population of the world—and all of us once were children. It is almost

[22] Francis Mulhern, *The Moment of 'Scrutiny'* (New Left Books, London, 1979), 175.

[23] Jonathan Culler, *On Deconstruction: Theory and Criticism after Structuralism* (Cornell University Press, Ithaca, NY, 1982), 50.

[24] Ibid.

inconceivable that women and children have been invisible and voiceless for so long.[25]

As I have indicated before, I do not believe this comparison is justified. There are two main points I would make: the first is that women *have* been able to become writers, to find voices, whereas most children's fiction is not written by children. It is relevant to note that Paul discusses children's fiction as if it were written by children, just as she writes about books written by women. Much of Paul's argument rests on this assumption: she writes that

as long as the signs and language of women's literature and children's literature are foreign, other, to male-order critics, it is almost impossible to play with meaning. So one of the primary problems feminist critics and children's literature critics have is how to recognize, define, and accord value to otherness.[26]

Paul overlooks the fact that much children's literature is written by these very 'male-order critics', unless she is assuming, as so many critics do, that writing children's fiction constitutes having become a child again. Paul herself runs into the paradoxes this issue generates, when she comments, for instance, that the 'separation [between adults and children] is no longer possible'.[27] She then expresses discomfort with respect to Peter Hunt's suggestion of a 'childist' criticism, feeling that 'it maintains them-and-us distinctions'.[28] Subsequently, we find references to 'the freshness of child vision',[29] and the quoting with approval of Aidan Chambers's view that in *Huckleberry Finn* Mark Twain 'stays true to the adolescent self he once openly was and still secretly is'.[30] Secondly, I question, as I have argued throughout this book, that the 'child' as an embedded subordinated discourse in Western culture can be part of a liberation movement comparable to feminism. Is there a

[25] Lissa Paul, 'Enigma Variations: What Feminist Theory Knows About Children's Literature', in Peter Hunt (ed.), *Children's Literature: The Development of Criticism* (Routledge, London, 1990), 148–66, 150.
[26] Ibid. 155.
[27] Ibid.
[28] Ibid. 156.
[29] Ibid.
[30] Ibid. 157.

freedom appropriate to the 'child'? What type of freedom would this be? Is a protective stance always repressive? Is the withdrawal of protection always a liberation? And if 'childhood' is defined as a state of protection, of freedom within limitation, as defined by Rousseau, then of what type should that protection be?

The attempt to read children's fiction as an adult involves a self-created paradox we have already encountered in several guises: this criticism claims to remove the 'child reader' from its writings without removing an extra-textual 'real' child. But it cannot be done: relying on a distinction between textual and non-textual narratives—between 'fact' or 'reality' and 'fiction'—seems to allow a separation of 'child' and 'adult' reader/critic to leave only an 'adult'. But the 'child' stays, albeit under cover of being a 'real' child outside the 'adult' critic, rather than the 'adult' critic being the 'child' by seeing through the eye/I of the child. Children's fiction criticism still cannot do without some 'child'.

We can see this reflected in attempts, on the part of literary pluralist critics, to describe the grounds for introducing some children's fiction into the literary canon. They try to formulate this too in terms which leave the 'child' aside. We saw earlier some of the problems this raised in efforts to deal jointly with the 'child' and 'literary' qualities, such as in the educationalist critics' works. Townsend and Alice Jordan offer the suggestion that 'literature' encompasses the books that stand the test of time. Townsend writes that 'where the works of the past are concerned, I have much faith in the sifting process of time—"time" being shorthand for the collective wisdom of a great many people over a long period'.[31] Jordan claims that 'until a book has weathered at least one generation and is accepted in the next, it can hardly be given the rank of a classic and no two people are likely to be in full agreement as to what should be included in a list of them'.[32] Jordan also attempts further descriptive and prescriptive criteria in which we can see the 'child' creeping back in, if we had not already suspected it of maintaining a hidden presence within 'time' in the 'test of time'

---

[31] Townsend, *Written for Children*, 11.

[32] Alice M. Jordan, 'Children's Classics', in Haviland, *Children and Literature: Views and Reviews*, 38–44, 39.

formulations. She writes, for instance, that 'some of the books written for children have a charm of style that insures their acceptance as literature in the best sense of the word . . . simplicity and sincerity are important factors'.[33]

The literary pluralist critics are giving an affirmative response to Julia Briggs's question whether children's books should be critically considered by the same methods as adult books. To do this they follow specific elements of specific adult methods, and, because for their purposes they choose methods which allow reference to 'real adult' readers, they include references to 'real child' readers. Ironically, this option is a sword that cuts two ways, for it is this sustained presence of the 'real child' which still forms one of the primary bases for adult literary criticisms which work with 'literature' and 'literary canons' to exclude children's fiction. Dutch critics Karel Eykman and Aukje Holtrop, for instance, use their 'real' child and its supposed needs to free children's fiction from needing to qualify for the literary canon. They argue, in discussing children's poetry, that 'there is no need to involve such things and verses with such weighty issues'.[34] And they assume that the children's poetry they discuss would not 'pass' the literary theoretical test they apply, namely Wellek's and Warren's concepts of 'unity', 'complexity', and 'density', but also that this is not relevant for child readers anyway.[35] Another Dutch critic, Jan Blokker, takes much the same view. He claims that children's fiction has never developed any new or original genres, themes, or literary points of view, but only used those which had already been developed in adult literature.[36] Blokker, however, also sees this as being unimportant to his 'child' readers: 'objections on literary aesthetic grounds seem to me to be irrelevant—one of the nice

---

[33] Ibid.

[34] Harry Bekkering, 'Van Poesie tot Poezie—Het Kindervers' ('From Verse to Poetry—Children's Verse'), in Nettie Heimeriks and Willem van Toorn (eds.) *De Hele Bibelebontse Berg: De Geschiedenis van het Kinderboek in Nederland en Vlaanderen van de Middeleeuwen tot Heden (The Whole 'Bibelebonts' Mountain: The History of Children's Books in The Netherlands and Flanders from the Middle Ages to the Present Day)* (Em. Querido's Uitgeverij b.v., Amsterdam, 1989), 341–91, 345 (translations from the Dutch are my own).

[35] Ibid.                                      [36] Ibid. 295.

things about kids is that they have no taste in our adult sense of the word, and do not adopt our somewhat perverted tendency to differentiate between Kitsch and Art until they are halfway through puberty'.[37]

Relying on adult criticism which operates around a literary canon, therefore, offers as much danger as opportunity to children's literature criticism, depending on the 'child' used. But all these critics—whether their child readers need literature or not—rely on a 'child' to validate their argument, even if only to create or shore up an 'adult' critical view to oppose it. In order to preserve 'children's fiction' and 'children's literature', and 'adult fiction' and 'adult literature', as concepts and values there must be real 'adult' and 'child' readers. Townsend himself sets up a child reader who is close to, but not the same as, his adult reader: 'an author can—as I have said elsewhere—expect as much intelligence, as much imagination, as from the grown-up, and a good deal more readiness to enter into things and live the story.'[38] Jonathan Cott is another literary pluralist critic who reveals a typical allegiance to an adult literary criticism which supports 'literature' as a privileged mode of meaning and experience. In Cott's descriptions, which I have quoted earlier, we find involved all the factors I have discussed: the reliance on the power of literature, the separation between child and adult which is simultaneously sustained and claimed to be overcome (Cott describes himself as an 'adult' reader, but the power of literature makes him a 'child' again), and the designation of qualities and characteristics to the child and adult which direct and explain Cott's interest and purpose as a children's fiction reader and critic.

In short, many self-proclaimed book-centred critics of children's fiction retain as their guiding star the 'real child', based on their reliance on a distinct literary discourse determined by adult readers and critics, whom they select. However, there are some critics who explore, in one way or another, the borders of the systems of knowledge of the 'child'. In approaching these borders, they also address the basis of those discourses of adult literary criticism

---

[37] Ibid.
[38] Townsend, *A Sense of Story*, 13.

which share the conviction of the redemptive value of literature, and its connections with knowable readers. Going beyond critics such as I. A. Richards and F. R. Leavis, with their reliance on the effects of the text, and the New Critics' advocacy of the autonomy of the text, we now must turn to the children's literature critics who attempt to participate in the adult literary criticism of narratology, reader-response criticism, and deconstruction.

In order to consider these ideas, we will be concentrating primarily on writings on children's literature criticism by Barbara Wall, Peter Hunt, and Jacqueline Rose. All three are prominent critics who have been involved with the most recent debates within children's literature criticism. The dates of publication of the three works I will be focusing on primarily (Barbara Wall's *The Narrator's Voice*, 1991;[39] Peter Hunt's *Criticism, Theory, and Children's Literature*, 1991,[40] and Jacqueline Rose's *The Case of Peter Pan*, 1984[41]) reveal that part of the difference in the use of adult literary theory is due to chronology: earlier criticism, such as that of Smith and White, and even that of Townsend, Leeson, and Chambers, was responding to the literary theory of earlier adult critics—as they perceived it for their purposes. A tension arises because the developments in adult literary theory have to do with challenges posed to the liberal arts ideals: feminist and multi-cultural writing and criticism challenge the assumptions of homogeneous readership, the effects of reading are questioned along with these shifts, hierarchical structures in society and the separation between 'reality' and textuality are explored. Do these developments introduce solutions to the problems of children's literature criticism? Or will they prove to be vulnerable to similar paradoxes and assumptions to those we have repeatedly encountered?

Barbara Wall bases her examination of children's literature

[39] Barbara Wall, *The Narrator's Voice: The Dilemma of Children's Fiction* (Macmillan, London, 1991).

[40] Peter Hunt, *Criticism, Theory, and Children's Literature* (Basil Blackwell, Oxford, 1991).

[41] Jacqueline Rose, *The Case of Peter Pan or: The Impossibility of Children's Fiction* (series: Language, Discourse, Society, ed. Stephen Heath and Colin MacCabe) (Macmillan, London, 1984).

criticism on narratological theory, which concentrates on articulating relations between narrator (the voice which tells the story in the
text), text, and narratee (the listener to whom the story is addressed
within the text). Wall establishes her starting-point clearly: she
claims to be writing about books written *for* children up to the age of
12 or 13 years. It will be clear from our discussion so far that this
statement already presupposes a number of factors, and Wall
confirms this:

My conclusions are founded on the conviction that adults . . . speak
differently in fiction when they are aware that they are addressing
children. In life, overhearing a conversation in the next room, we readily
deduce from the kinds of information and explanations being given, that
an adult is talking to a child. And even if the words are inaudible we might
still make the same deduction because we recognise some almost
indefinable adjustments in pitch and tone. These difficulties, when adult
speaks to child, translated, sometimes subtly, sometimes obviously, into
the narrator's voice, can be observed in fiction for children. Such
subtleties of address define a children's book . . . Since in fiction for
children the age difference between addresser and addressee is inescapable
and crucial, the manner of the communication takes on a special
significance.[42]

Wall assumes without further explanation that, first, 'adults' use
different pitches and tones when addressing 'children'; and,
secondly, that these 'almost indefinable adjustments in pitch and
tone' translate into written language, and can be recognized, if not
defined, in writing.

　　Wall quickly runs into all kinds of difficulties. The most
interesting one, for our purposes, is that she seems to contradict
herself with respect to the idea of the 'real reader'.[43] Early on in her
book, she argues that this

real reader is the child who holds that text and reads those words . . .
These are the physical parties in the transaction, whose existence cannot
be legislated away by theories of narration, for without them there would
be no transaction, nor any reason for the transaction—but they are not the
parties to be found within the pages of the book.[44]

　　[42] Wall, *The Narrator's Voice*, 2–3.　　　[43] Ibid. 4.　　　[44] Ibid.

Just before this, she had commented that the 'real author' 'is under threat from deconstructionists who see authors not as individuals but as constructs of their times'.[45] We might question whether Wall's brief statement gives us a fruitful impression of deconstruction: the New Critics had already dispensed with the author under the 'intentionalist fallacy' (the idea that the authors' intentions determine the meaning of the text), and deconstruction would not allow that the 'individual' was any less a construction than a 'real author'. In any case, Wall seems to be aware of theories relating to constructions of identity and definition, although she rejects them, but does not even consider applying the 'construction' concept to the 'real reader . . . child'. This suggests again how unquestionably the 'child' exists for most children's literature critics.

The 'real child' certainly proves to be central to Wall's work, for she goes on to argue that children's fiction can, and should, fulfil the 'real child' reader's needs. However, somewhat later in the book, a most surprising passage occurs: Wall writes that

. . . the child narrators and narratees created by the writers of children's fiction are as much fiction as the stories which they tell or which are told to them. Real children, as I know from my own experience as a child writer and as a teacher, are as likely to be writing of little understood adult experiences as they are to be writing the kind of story which adults think suitable for them. . ... Child narrators and child narratees . . . are . . . constructed by writers for children from profound ignorance of what goes on in children's minds, or at least in some children's minds. . ... As a critic, I must accept that any adult writer's perception of children as readers and writers may bear little relation to the reality. There is no question, however, that a great number of children have enjoyed what has been written for them by adults, have indeed welcomed it. In confining my attention to what takes place within the pages of a text, I accept that I am dealing with a complex nest of fictions. I do not confuse these fictions with reality.[46]

Wall thinks she has driven her 'real' child right to the fringes of her discussion, well out of the texts' way. She admits the constructed nature of the 'child' *in* the text, but always maintains the 'real' child.

[45] Ibid.
[46] Ibid. 88–9.

Yet her statement is one of the most remarkable examples of self-contradiction we have encountered: at one and the same time she states that she, as a child writer and teacher, knows children, but that writers construct children 'from profound ignorance of what goes on in children's minds'; she also claims that the 'adult writer's perception of children as readers . . . may bear little relation to the reality', but that she does not confuse the resulting 'nest of fictions . . . with reality'. Wall is tangled up in the assumption of knowledge of the 'real' child.

The idea that Wall conveys in her passage, probably unintentionally, is that she is better able to judge what goes in children's minds than the other adults and writers she refers to: although fictional child narratees are constructed wrongly by authors, out of ignorance, Wall can know who the 'real child' is. Of course, this is in fact the inevitable implication of all the writing of children's literature critics. Wall's attempt to concentrate on a fictional child in the text, while skirting a 'real' child, fails. Her writing and criticism is based on her confidently expressed judgements of the needs and characteristics of 'children': of irony, for instance, she writes that the 'irony of Mark Twain may not be for children, but that of E. Nesbit, Beatrix Potter and Mary Norton undoubtedly is';[47] of C. S. Lewis and Roald Dahl, that they 'are popular authors. Many child readers respond favourably to the sense of security given to them by the familiar voice of the explaining, rather patronising, narrator';[48] of Barrie's *Peter Pan*, that 'it is the difficulties which such sophistication and detachment in the narrator present to children of an age to be entertained by the events of the story that have caused the numerous rewritings' and that '[Barrie's] preoccupation with the nature of children, his deep seated resentment at their self-sufficiency, his recognition of their selfishness, their heartlessness, and their ability to wipe out the past and to lose themselves entirely in the activities of the moment, prevented him from addressing the child reader within his book with continuing friendliness and respect.'[49] And these are examples only of overt statements.

[47] Ibid. 2.          [48] Ibid. 18.          [49] Ibid. 26–7, 28.

Wall openly reveals her strong interest in the 'good' for the 'child', like the educationalist critics do: she argues that 'writing down' to the child should not primarily be a pejorative term, but that it can be an acknowledgement of authors' attempts to meet the needs of the child, which is what children's literature is about—about writing for the child. Therefore, her criticism of the books she discusses is the expression of her judgements of, first, the needs of the child and, secondly, the ways in which narrators do or do not fulfil those needs. Wall's ideas about the right way to treat 'children', interestingly, produce a strongly evolutionary description of the history of children's books: she views those authors as 'good' who produce the least patronizing or condescending narrators—and she decides which narrators are condescending or patronizing. Inevitably, given the conventions of nineteenth-century narration, Wall's good narrators are those who anticipate the development of less overtly omniscient narrators or who are the product of that development. The net result is a children's literature which improves through time, as its narrators, according to Wall, become less condescending or moralizing, and more friendly and need-fulfilling (although modern narrators may fail for Wall by being, for instance, cold or detached).[50]

The judgements produced by Wall's narratological criticism are identical in type to those of the educationalist critics. Wall writes about Arthur Ransome's books, for instance, that

[Ransome] was not uncomfortable, nor self-conscious, in addressing children, because he so loved what he was doing—that is recreating his childhood . . . He simply put himself in the place of the children he was writing about and described what they saw and did, felt and thought. He has no viewpoint apart from theirs. . . . The voice of the narrator is unobtrusive, undogmatic, uncondescending, but distinctly adult too, in its unwavering intention to make absolutely clear what is described [a passage from *Swallows and Amazons* is quoted] . . . All readers, young and old, know when reading these words that this passage with its carefully and simply explained detail is addressed to children.[51]

[50] Ibid. 240.
[51] Ibid. 30–1.

The needs of Wall's 'real child' pervade and direct her writing, although she initially attempted to remove him from the text and maintained she was speaking only of 'children' constructed within texts as narratees. As Peter Hunt remarks: 'Narrative theory cannot escape the problem of audience. Perception/reception controls what the text is seen to be and, consequently, how it is described.'[52] Wall's interpretative strategies are no more stabilized through narratology than those of the educationalist critics were stabilized by their psychology, or those of the pluralist critics by their adult literary criticism. Her disagreements with other critics, even critics whom she otherwise much admires, reveal that Wall's intended narratological 'proofs' are only critical assertions amongst other critical assertions:

Aidan Chambers . . . and Charles Sarland . . . have both charged [William] Mayne with exhibiting a cold detachment in his attitude to his readers. Sarland accuses Mayne of using a technique of 'alienation' . . . implying indeed that he employs a subversive, even unfriendly, narrator. Chambers notes that Sarland 'brilliantly uncovered' the fact that Mayne creates 'an implied author who is an observer of children and the narrative; a watcher rather than an ally' . . . Both Chambers and Sarland assert that Mayne deliberately sets out to obstruct emotional involvement in his stories. . . . I believe the contrary to be true. Far from being a 'watcher rather than an ally' Mayne's narrator is constantly and benignly close to his characters and his narratee; it is closeness—familiarity—rather than distance which causes difficulties for some readers. It is the very special kind of 'ally' which Mayne's narrator is . . . that may deter readers . . . who do not wish to move slowly, to attend closely, to be immersed in the experience of the moment for its own sake. . . . And [Mayne] deals with children's feelings in the way children perceive them.[53]

Peter Hunt is a children's literature critic who has actively engaged adult literary theory in the discussions around children's literature criticism. He has also followed Aidan Chambers in suggesting that adult literary theory can be illuminated and explained through the issues of children's literature criticism: 'This book uses critical theory and practice to help readers to deal with

---

[52] Hunt, *Criticism, Theory, and Children's Literature*, 120.
[53] Wall, *The Narrator's Voice*, 207.

children's literature, and children's literature to help readers to deal with literary theory.'[54] Hunt's style reveals his concern to address many possible audiences: he does not wish to alienate readers by using the jargon and intentional complexity of some adult literary theory, which allies itself more with philosophy than with the tradition of liberal arts literary criticism, but he also does not wish to blanket the difficulty of the issues raised by relating children's literature criticism to adult literary theory. This attitude is revealing: it constitutes a challenge to the convolutions of some adult literary theory, and seems to substantiate the view that children's literature criticism presents the concerns of adult literary theory—such as the processes of interpretation, the position of the reader, and the status of texts—in a relevant and concrete context. As Hunt argues:

Theory is an uncomfortable and uncomforting thing, for by seeking to explain what we might otherwise have thought was obvious, it draws attention to hidden problems. We usually get along quite well by assuming things to be true that we really know to be quite untrue; for example, that we know how people read, and what happens when they do; that the perceptions and reactions of children and adults are much the same; that we know how and why stories work. Theory may not solve any of those problems directly, but it forces us to confront them. Having said that, criticism has a great deal to answer for in positively restricting the pleasure derived from texts.[55]

Although Hunt touches on several approaches in adult literary theory, he too is restricted by the context of children's literature criticism. He writes:

Both the children who read the books and most of the adults who deal with them either know nothing of decontextualised reading or literary value systems or cannot understand the point of them, seeing them as illogical or threatening. But criticism is changing. It has many valuable elements which can help us to understand how we understand; help us to work with texts and with people.[56]

---

[54] Hunt, *Criticism, Theory, and Children's Literature*, 5.
[55] Ibid. 1.
[56] Ibid. 2.

Hunt is also, willingly or unwillingly, steered by the purpose of children's literature criticism to 'help us to work with texts and with people'. The difficulty is that some of the adult literary theory Hunt engages with questions the very ideas necessary to children's literature criticism: selection or canonization of books, the assumptions surrounding the influence books have, the generalization of reader response, and the notion of readers as audience. These theories are not necessarily interested in helping people to work with texts, or to help them in the ways that children's literature criticism needs. Hunt, therefore, although he opens the field to an exploration of many problems from many angles in his articles and books, skews his argument from the start for the benefit of children's literature criticism, in the same way that all children's literature critics do. And again, this may seem a legitimate procedure: after all, Hunt *is* a children's literature critic, and children's literature criticism is his concern. But, as with other critics, his appropriation of the terms of adult literary theory generates similar problems to those we encountered with Barbara Wall. Wall and Hunt cannot solve the problems they themselves want to solve, any more than those critics we have already examined. Hunt states, for instance, that

'criticism' is perhaps an unfortunate term: it has, in the past, been applied to everything from analysis to prescription, and it commonly carries a pejorative overtone. That is not what we are about here. We are concerned with understanding what happens when we read, and how we can perceive and talk about a book or make a reasoned selective judgement. (And we are talking about how *real* readers read—not students or critics or others who deliberately read in a deviant way.)[57]

Hunt has moved from an acknowledgement of ignorance with regard to knowing how reading works to defining a *real* reader and a deliberately deviant reading.

A 'real reader' is now established as both the object and recipient of Hunt's work; Hunt has committed himself to a division between a 'real' world and 'fiction' or 'text'. Moreover, Hunt's statement implies that the 'real reader' is a common-sense sort of person. The

---

[57] Ibid. 3.

'real reader' as an individual is also the beneficiary of Hunt's work: he concludes his introduction by writing that 'this book is about theory in the sense that it tries to give the individual an understanding of ways of reading texts, so that she or he can then evaluate or use a text in whatever way seems most useful or valid'.[58] Hunt has extended the concern for the individual child reader displayed by all children's literature critics to the individual adult reader of children's literature criticism.

Hunt's concern with the reader determines his discussion and formulation of the 'literary', as with the other critics we have been discussing in this chapter. Hunt is quite happy to disrupt the idea of the canon as a group of texts with any specific claim to primacy of effect or affect. He strongly seems to individualize the reader and his choices and tastes. He argues that the idea of the canon is part of political and cultural power structures which impinge particularly on the 'child'. In this way he appears to align himself with critics such as Dickinson, Harding, and Moss, who argue that non-literary books may have beneficial effects. Hunt now states that the reason for studying children's literature is that 'it is important, and because it is fun'.[59] And it is important because it has 'great social and educational influence; they [children's books] are important both politically and commercially'.[60] The release of children's literature criticism from canons and value judgements, the assertion of the individuality of readers' responses, and the assertion of the importance of children's literature as a social and educational influence sit together uncomfortably: the influence of children's literature is generalized and becomes that of any book, in any situation. Hunt does not supply us with specific types of child readers who will benefit from reading 'rubbish', as Harding, Moss, and Dickinson do. How does he justify discussing books at all in this diffuse context?

It might be of use at this point to remind ourselves of the uses adult literary theory may make of the study of literature and reading under these circumstances. Adult literary theories which challenge

---

[58] Ibid. 4.
[59] Ibid. 17.
[60] Ibid.

the possibilities of adult literary canons as anything other than the exercise of political and cultural power, and which deny the possibility of generalized or consistent reader response, generally are allied with deconstructionist criticism, of which I drew a thumb-nail sketch in the first chapter. Peter Hunt has been influenced by deconstruction, and by critics who contributed to the development of deconstruction (as well as by other literary theorists). But, as I have argued, deconstruction does not allow for the maintenance of a consistent, unconstructed 'real reader'. The study of reading, to deconstructionists, is not a study: it is participation in the play of meaning. This 'play' is not a fictional, non-essential 'game': it is the inevitable flux and movement of meaning, which cannot be stabilized or stopped. Deconstruction dissolves the polarity of subject and object: the critic is not an objective observer or analyst of the object, but a participant, who is read as much by the text as the text is read by him. The deconstructionist does not view himself as a subject exterior to an object. Text and critic mutually and continually construct one another. As Gayatri Spivak, for instance, writes: 'everyone reads life and the world like a book . . . The world actually writes itself with the many-levelled, unfixable intricacy and openness of a work of literature.'[61] The 'child' in this view functions as do texts reinvented and reinterpreted by readers.

If the pluralist critics try to allow for individual children's interpretations and uses of their books, deconstructionist critics dissolve the separation between 'text' and 'reality' and, therefore, subvert the 'real child' on whom children's literature critics rely. The reasons why this type of critic participates in literary theory are described in many ways: in terms of experiencing the joy of working with the text, in terms of illustrating the processes of the 'play' of meaning, or as a means of participating in the demonstration of a philosophical position. These reasons may be connected with the 'good' of the reader at some level—some deconstructionists have allied themselves, for instance, with the ultimate subversion of the

---

[61] Gayatri Chakravorty Spivak, *In Other Worlds: Essays in Cultural Politics* (Routledge, London, 1988), 95.

illusion of fixity of meaning which supports ideas of 'truth'. Because of this, some have also employed deconstruction in the service of political ideals. However, this does not constitute the claim that reading itself is of necessity influential or to the good of the reader. Hunt therefore may admit to being influenced by deconstruction, but he does not subscribe to its beliefs: as with all children's literary critics, his 'real child', part of a 'real' world, prevails.

It becomes clear, then, that, although Hunt attempts to loosen the bonds of canons and generalized readers for the purposes of discussion, he soon gets caught up in them again. His 'real reader' forces this to happen. For instance, he first rejects attempts to substantiate the importance of children's literature by merging adult and children's literature canons as vulnerable to 'a quagmire of unproductive status and value arguments'.[62] He then rejects arguments that the quality and inventiveness of children's literature are superior to those of contemporary adult literature.[63] Hunt concludes that 'it is perhaps easier to avoid literary arguments and to consider the use to which the texts are put. . . . children's literature has much to contribute to the acquisition of cultural values, and it [is important to] literary education'.[64] The study of children's books is shifted to their usage as cultural and historical artefacts. However, on the next page, Hunt scorns 'a major British award-giving committee [which] actually questioned whether "literary" standards were at all relevant in choosing a "good" children's book'.[65] And he argues against views such as

the unexamined assumption that what is written for children must necessarily be simple . . . The assumption that children's literature is necessarily inferior to other kinds . . . is linguistically, as well as philosophically, untenable. It also assumes a homogeneity of text and authorial approach that is improbable, a view of the relationship of reader and text that is naive, and a total lack of understanding both of the child-reader's abilities and of the ways that texts operate. The second assumption is that most of the texts are trivial . . . there is a confusion between text features which are characteristic of children's literature and text features of low-level, or 'bad', adult literature. Obviously, a large

---

[62] Hunt, *Criticism, Theory, and Children's Literature*, 19.
[63] Ibid.    [64] Ibid.    [65] Ibid. 20.

proportion of books for children is of negligible worth by almost any 'literary' yardstick; but it is not clear to me whether this proportion is any higher than that for so-called 'adult' literature.[66]

Hunt's 'real child' and his 'literature' thus make a come-back, although they remain under discussion. Hunt attempts to appease the demands he perceives on the part of literary theory to surrender the liberal arts ideals, but he cannot be brought to abandon his 'child' in practice. This creates a considerable tension in the formulation of his arguments. Often he pushes his explorations right to the limit of sustaining a 'real child', but he always retreats at the last moment, motivated by his obvious attachment to children's literature itself, as well as to his 'child' reader. It is relevant to note in this context that Hunt is himself also an author of children's fiction.

Hunt's open style in exploring issues conceals to an extent the way that his feelings steer his argument. This becomes clearer if we examine how he explores the notion of the constructed child: for instance, in discussing ways adults might read children's texts, he suggests that adults can '*surrender to the book on its own terms*. This is as close as we can get to *reading as a child*; but this is a very long way from reading as a child does. . . . it is difficult to replicate [children's] encounters with texts.'[67] And he writes in a section on 'defining the child' that

. . . the adult community . . . create[s] or allow[s] different kinds of childhood—which, socially, might best be defined as a period of lack of responsibility, as well as one merely of incomplete development. . . . In short, childhood is not now (if it ever has been) a stable concept. The literature defined by it, therefore cannot be expected to be a stable entity.[68]

Hunt situates himself in this most 'open' position, but then reinstates some notion of the 'child' by concluding, 'on the whole, then, that a particular text was written expressly for children who are recognizably children, with a childhood recognizable today, must be part of the definition'.[69] And, having said this, he can back up and complete this section on 'defining children's literature' by

---

[66] Ibid. 21.         [68] Ibid. 58–9, 60.
[67] Ibid. 48.         [69] Ibid. 62.

claiming that 'despite the flux of childhood, the children's book can be defined in terms of the implied reader. It will be clear, from a careful reading, who a book is designed for: whether it is for the developing child, or whether it is aiming somewhere over the child's head.'[70]

Hunt thus extends Wall's tactic of acknowledging 'childhood' to be a 'nest of fictions' and then returning to his own 'fictions', which he feels he has stabilized: Wall stabilizes through the narrator's voice, and Hunt by limiting his 'child' to an entity recognizable only within a certain time and space. Wall claims that one can 'hear' whether a narrator is addressing a 'child' narratee, while Hunt suggests that one can identify whether a 'child' is the 'implied reader'.[71] We have noted Ariès's view that 'childhood' is diachronically unstable—that it changes through history—but Hunt implies that it is synchronically stable. We have already seen that this is not the case: this is the very conundrum of children's literature criticism. It might also be suggested that Ariès's view of diachronic instability reflects a perception of synchronic instability.

However, Hunt's negotiation of the difficulties of the field continues with this pattern of questioning all the terms of discussion and then retreating to a position which reaffirms the terms. Hunt's 'child' reader is retrieved increasingly as his discussion progresses: 'children' are cast as constituting a (sub)culture that is 'primarily oral . . . The oral mind-set has a "spectacular" influence on narrative and plot'.[72] There is also, Hunt suggests,

the child's natural tendency towards performance, 'easy access to metaphor', and an ability to handle complex narrative acts . . . [which make] it clear that we are dealing not with lesser ability, but with a different kind of ability, one that seems likely to view narrative . . . in a way not accounted for in a conventional theory. Further, the text may actually seem to symbolize an alien culture, and as such may be perceived perversely or subversively.[73]

The child, for Hunt, is a 'developing reader',[74] and in order to

---

[70] Ibid. 64.     [72] Ibid. 75–6.     [74] Ibid. 87.
[71] Ibid.        [73] Ibid. 76.

define this child he employs strategies familiar to us from John Locke in the 'stories of origin'. Hunt wants to distinguish between adult reading and child reading 'by trying to find out what children . . . *can't* do';[75] and this is to be achieved by examining 'the way in which a "skilled" reader reads—how *we* as adults make meaning— [in order to] be able to see what a developing reader lacks'.[76]

Locke, I argued above, articulated 'human understanding' partly by sketching a process of development from 'children and idiots', who are defined by their lack of this understanding, to the 'adult', who acquires this understanding. Hunt's strategy demands the same construction of an 'adult', who now bears part of the burden of stabilizing the 'child': if '*we* as adults' exist and know what *we* are, then the 'developing' child reader is defined as that which the '*we* adults' are *not*. The outcome is not that children are allied with 'idiots', as in Locke, but with 'deconstructors', as Hunt perceives them.[77] These 'deconstructors', lacking the knowledge of cultural and literary codes, may be 'ready to read "against" texts, to use them as a basis for extravagant readings, free of tiresome constraints of understanding, and hence free to misread . . .'.[78] As Hunt further comments, 'unskilled readers must find *all* texts "unconventional"'.[79] (The logic of this type of argument has always escaped me: why should these children necessarily find language or experience 'fresh', 'original', or 'unconventional', as so many critics argue, because they have had fewer encounters with these things? Surely 'freshness', 'originality', and 'unconventionality' are values derived from *comparison*, not abstract qualities which adhere to objects. This type of thinking is again the product, not of knowing the 'child', but of attempting to construct the 'non-adult' by trying to 'unthink' knowledge or facts. Thus, the statements seem to result from the following argument: 'I, as an adult, know about such and such. Now, I try and imagine that I do not know this. Wouldn't I find it all wondrous when I learned about it?' This translates into the artistic strategy of *alienation*, but does not constitute a return to ignorance. We can compare this to Mosellanus's comments about his pedology in the 'stories of origin'.)

---

[75] Ibid. 90.     [77] Ibid. 97.     [79] Ibid. 132.
[76] Ibid.     [78] Ibid.

Hunt attempts to be self-aware and self-critical throughout his book. This is part of his pattern of challenge and retreat that I have described, and which is also in evidence in his mode of presentation of his final conclusion. Throughout his discussion, Hunt has retreated from prescriptive statements with regard to his child reader. In relation to this he best displays the tension within his argument himself when he admits that 'I *would* do good for others, but I can never be sure of *what* is good for the others.'[80] I have analysed this tension as the result of his initial, almost by-the-way establishment of the 'real reader'. His position demonstrates the self-contradictions generated by the education–amusement divide stretched to breaking-point. Hunt wants to free the 'child' (and 'adult') reader to the maximum of his ability, and yet he simultaneously retains a belief that 'many of us will want to hold on to the book as a liberating influence, the repository of freedom and correct thinking'.[81]

Hunt's proffered compromise is to 'recognize, at least in the interim, a distinctive kind of criticism, one that I have called "childist" . . . [and to] propose a radical rethinking of the ends of criticism . . .'.[82] He describes his 'childist' criticism:

Simply to invite adults to read as children is scarcely novel, and it is likely not only to revive old prejudices, but, as we have seen, to prove remarkably difficult. Rather, we have to challenge all our assumptions, question every reaction, and ask what reading as a child actually means, given the complexities of the cultural interaction.[83]

But, despite this carefulness, Hunt's reformulation of the 'childist' stance a few pages later echoes the educationalist critics' proposals surprisingly clearly, however much he may hope that it will be read differently within his context: 'reading, as far as possible, from a child's point of view, taking into account personal, sub-cultural, experiential, and psychological differences between children and adults—in short, allowing the reader precedence over the book'.[84] This, again, starkly reveals the restrictions children's literature criticism has imposed on itself. Peter Hunt, despite his scrupulous

---

[80] Ibid. 172.  [82] Ibid. 189.  [84] Ibid. 198.
[81] Ibid. 153.  [83] Ibid. 191.

examination of children's literature criticism, steps back from the abyss of losing the 'child' and, therefore, children's literature criticism as we know it. A final quote concerning 'childist' criticism indicates Hunt's own sense of difficulty—which he cannot resolve:

> childist criticism is something that we have seen in practice. It is based on possibilities and probabilities, not in the absence of empirical data, but in the face of the immense difficulty of dealing with that data. It is thus no different from adult criticism, except that in adult criticism it is rarely, if ever, admitted that there *is* a problem with the data.[85]

Hunt has shown us how difficult it is to say anything about the 'child' as reader, but, given his 'real reader', he cannot do other than plead for a move from what he perceives as a crassly prescriptive criticism to one that is more modest and self-reflective (on the part of the adult critic).

Adult criticism may not admit that there is 'a problem with the data', according to Hunt, but nor does it need to: as I indicated in my sketches of deconstruction, for instance, adult criticism may, if it chooses, ignore the liberal arts belief in bettering culture and the reader. This may lead to a form of solipsism deplored by other adult critics, but it is not a forbidden enterprise. Deconstruction, and related adult approaches to literature, re-format adult literary criticism, sometimes to the extent of making critics question whether they constitute 'literary criticism' at all—hence terms such as 'literary theory' and 'critical theory', which indicate the lapsing of boundaries between disciplines such as literary criticism, philosophy, and psychology. This has led to interdisciplinary studies of meaning-construction. The point is that adult literary criticism, theoretically, has options outside *itself*, it can close itself down or reformulate itself within new contexts (although this is a difficult enterprise). But children's literature criticism, based, as I have argued, on the premiss of the 'real child', collapses with the abandonment of this 'real child'. It does not have any options. Without the 'real child' it has no reason to exist.

Jacqueline Rose is one of the few theorists who confronts this option: in *The Case of Peter Pan or: The Impossibility of Children's*

[85] Ibid. 194.

*Fiction*, she closes down the field of children's fiction and therefore, by implication, children's literature criticism, by questioning the status of the 'existence' of the child. (There are a few other critics who discuss children as constructions, such as Adrienne Kertzer.)[86] Rose is not (therefore) strictly speaking a children's literature critic, as the other thinkers we have looked at so far are. She writes, for instance, 'I would . . . want to distinguish myself from Hunt's overall project which seems to be, along with that of a number of children's book critics, to establish the literary "value" and credentials of children's writers and children's book criticism (the ultimate fantasy, perhaps, of children's book criticism that it should come of age and do what the adults (that is adult critics) have been doing all along) . . .'.[87] But the implications of Rose's argument for children's fiction and children's fiction criticism are crucial. I have already referred to and quoted her argument that children's fiction constructs the 'child' it needs to believe is there for its own purposes; indeed, her formulation provided the starting-point for my own thinking on the subject. Rose's overall intention, in *The Case of Peter Pan*, is to contribute to the wider issue of the 'dismantling of what I see as the ongoing sexual and political mystification of the child'.[88]

Children's fiction, Rose argues, exemplifies the construction of a 'child' who is innocent, and who is connected to ideas about an innocence of language and perception:

children's fiction has never completely severed its links with a philosophy which sets up the child as a pure point of origin in relation to language, sexuality and the state. . . . children's writers took from Locke the idea of an education based on the child's direct and unproblematic access to objects of the real world . . . children's fiction emerges, therefore, out of a conception of both the child and the world as knowable in a direct and unmediated way, a conception which places the innocence of the child and a primary state of language and/or culture in a close and mutually dependent relation.[89]

[86] Adrienne E. Kertzer, 'Inventing the Child Reader: How We Read Children's Books', *Children's Literature in Education*, 15/1 (Spring 1984), 12–21.
[87] Rose, *The Case of Peter Pan*, 154.
[88] Ibid. 11.
[89] Ibid. 8, 9.

Rose's influence on my own thinking is very clear here. But she is discussing the issues on a different level and, interestingly, does after all construct a 'child' for *her* own use and purposes: a Freudian *unconscious* 'child'.

Rose refers to Townsend's type of claim that 'what is best about writing for children is that the writer can count absolutely on the child's willingness to enter into the book, and *live* the story',[90] as 'to describe children's fiction, quite deliberately, as something of a soliciting, a chase, or even a seduction'.[91] This identification of children's fiction as a form of seduction of a 'child' is based on Sigmund Freud's psychoanalysis. For Rose, the 'adult' and the 'child' operate within this context, and it is a relationship which corrupts the concept of 'children's fiction':

children's fiction is impossible, not in the sense that it cannot be written (that would be nonsense), but in that it hangs on an impossibility, one of which it rarely ventures to speak. This is the impossible relation between adult and child. Children's fiction is clearly about that relation, but it has the remarkable characteristic of being about something which it hardly ever talks of.[92]

Rose discusses *Peter Pan* (all 'Peter Pans', not necessarily one of J. M. Barrie's versions or any other) as exemplifying the inherently problematic concept of children's fiction. 'Peter Pan' combines in form and content the theme of what Rose describes as 'the adult's desire for the child'.[93] She warns us that she is not using 'desire' here 'in the sense of an act which is sought after or which must actually take place',[94] but 'to refer to a form of investment by the adult in the child, and to the demand made by the adult on the child as the effect of that investment, a demand which fixes the child and then holds it in place'.[95] Rose locates this 'desire' as originating from 'the whole problem of what sexuality is, or can be', and the child is used 'to hold that problem at bay'.[96] The dynamics of children's fiction, for Rose, reside in Freud's concept of the child's sexuality as being bisexual, polymorphous, and perverse. (She warns that '[Freud's] real challenge [in arguing this child's sexuality] is easily

[90] Ibid. 2.      [92] Ibid. 1.      [94] Ibid.      [96] Ibid. 4.

[91] Ibid.      [93] Ibid. 3.      [95] Ibid. 3–4.

lost if we see in the child merely a miniature version of what our sexuality eventually comes to be'.[97] I would add to Rose's warning by emphasizing that Freud's discussions of sexuality remain widely and persistently misunderstood. His child's sexuality is *not* the same as an adult's *conscious* genital sexuality. The Freudian child's bisexuality and perversity and what is commonly perceived as some adults' bisexuality or perversity are *not*—usually—expressed in the same ways.) This child's sexuality is never fully removed from, or resolved in, the unconscious of the adult. Therefore the adult is, unconsciously, threatened by this child sexuality, and attempts to control it.

Rose's child, then, exists as a Freudian unconscious child sexuality. This child need not exist outside the unconscious of the 'adult' at all. Rose's arguments can be construed as applying to the relationship between a 'real' adult and a 'real' child, or to dynamics within the unconscious and conscious of the 'adult'. Where other critics we have looked at hold various views about the possibility or impossibility of (fully) becoming the 'child' again, this 'child' is always somewhere within the unconscious of the 'adult'. This is possible because, for Freud, the unconscious is timeless, and therefore, as Rose puts it, 'the most crucial aspect of psychoanalysis for discussing children's fiction is its insistence that childhood is something in which we continue to be implicated and which is never simply left behind. Childhood persists . . .'.[98] Freud, Rose writes, made it possible to ask

why, in terms of our own relationship to language and sexuality, we attempt to construct an image of the child at all. What we constantly see in discussion of children's fiction is how the child can be used to hold off panic, a threat to our assumption that language is something which can simply be organised and cohered, and that sexuality, while it cannot be removed, will eventually take on forms in which we prefer to recognise and acknowledge each other. Childhood also serves as a term of universal social reference which conceals all the historical divisions and difficulties of which children, no less than ourselves, form a part.[99]

[97] Ibid.
[98] Ibid. 12.
[99] Ibid. 10.

Therefore, Rose sees 'these purposes [as] often perverse and mostly dishonest, not wilfully, but of necessity, given that addressing the child must touch on all of these difficulties, none of which it dares speak'.[100]

Rose's discussion of the Freudian child disrupts many of the 'child' constructions we have observed other critics using. The Freudian child, in allowing Rose to analyse the situation of children's fiction and children's fiction criticism as inherently unsolvable, breaks the tension we see building up as critics increasingly try to release or free the 'child', while maintaining the 'real' child, separate and knowable (even if knowable only to the basic extent of being able to maintain its 'being there'). And yet Rose does not escape language (she would not expect to be able to) and has also established a 'child' for her purposes, even if this 'child' represents a level of sexuality which the 'adult' cannot afford to acknowledge within himself. Rose's establishment of her child has two important consequences: the first is that she deals much more with the image of the Romantic type of innocent child than with images of bad, corrupted, or amoral children. The construction of innocent children clearly supports her argument concerning the suppression and denial of Freudian child sexuality in its initial bisexual and polymorphous stage. The selection of *Peter Pan* as the example *par excellence* of the dynamics of children's fiction, for Rose, also concentrates on the overt presentation of innocence to suppress and deny the presence of sexuality. The second consequence is that Rose, having based her argument on the impossibility of the relationship between her adult and her child, not only cannot do otherwise than close down children's fiction and children's fiction criticism, but also does not seem to leave space to discuss the continuing negotiations between 'adults' and 'children' (internal or external 'children'). In other words, she cannot close down the ongoing constructions of meaning relating to 'children' and 'adults'.

We have now come full circle since the beginning of this book, having examined children's literature criticism from its 'stories of

[100] Ibid.

origin' to its death. I wrote in the first chapter that I intended to explore the operation of need with respect to the 'child', and particularly its expression in maintaining the existence of a 'real child'. I hope I have made clear how this 'reality' is a text, which is continually (re)constructed in children's literature criticism. Children's literature criticism powerfully reflects Rose's point that 'children's fiction emerges . . . out of a conception of both the child and the world as knowable in a direct and unmediated way'.[101] We can say that what the examination of the claims to knowledge reveals is the camouflage of ignorance—a camouflage born of the power of the need to believe that knowledge *is* present. Or, if we follow the Freudian terms of Rose's argument, we can say that the various strategies to maintain the 'real child' that I have analysed are the expression of the unconscious 'desire' Rose describes. This desire of the 'adult' to master and control 'child' sexuality can be seen as the source of what I have discussed as 'need' and 'purpose'. In discussing need and purpose as they reveal themselves in the paradoxes and problems of children's literature criticism, I have, therefore, ended up in the same position as Rose: if children's literature criticism depends on, and is defined by, its claim to the existence of the 'real child', *a claim which it undermines itself*, then it is indeed dead. As Peter Hunt remarks, under the pressure of a glimpse of this death from which he subsequently retreats (note especially his resort to 'common sense'), '. . . we have to assume a certain congruence between what you see and what I see and what a child-reader sees; otherwise the whole business of making books (and, especially, talking about them) becomes a nonsense. There must be a middle ground of common-sense agreement about what meaning is.'[102] As children's literature criticism operates at present, I can only conclude it makes non-statements, for its own purposes. In making judgements and criticisms on behalf of a 'real child' who does not exist, its writings are useless to the fulfilment of its own professed aims.

Where do we go from here? Do we simply bury children's literature criticism, with due respect? We still are left with the

---

[101] Ibid. 9.
[102] Hunt, *Criticism, Theory, and Children's Literature*, 89.

continuing powerful (re)constructions of 'adults' and 'children' within society on other levels. It is possible to reject children's fiction criticism as it stands, but this does not solve the problems of the continuing (re)constructions of adult and child on other levels, and within other disciplines. In my first chapter, I referred to the problems of professionals dealing with child abuse and neglect as an emblem to be kept in mind in this discussion. I suggested that perhaps it was more relevant for people working with children to know more about themselves than to keep constructing 'children'. In other words, as I have argued throughout (and as Rose also argues), children's literature criticism is only a sub-plot of wider problems with 'knowing' the 'child' and, most specifically, the emotions of the 'child'. And the 'knowing' of the 'child' is in turn a sub-plot of the problem of 'knowing' any other person's meanings and emotions. The disciplines which confront most directly the emotions and meanings of humans are psychoanalysis and psychotherapy. Within these fields, we find discussions relating to 'knowing' and 'not knowing' the patient, and how knowledge and meaning operate within the negotiations between therapist and patient. I would like to examine some of these discussions with two aims in mind: first, to confirm the extent to which children's literature criticism makes 'non-statements' with reference to the 'child'; and, secondly, to see if we can move onwards from the impossibility of children's literature criticism to find other terms in which to discuss the continuing (re)construction of 'adults' and 'children'.

# 6

# The Reading Child and Other Children: The Psychoanalytic Child and Psychoanalytic Space

*1. A Consideration of some Theoretical Issues in Psychotherapy*

As we have seen, children's literature criticism cannot move away from its many and varied versions of the 'real child'. The children's literature critic's ideas clearly need never be questioned by a confrontation with that figment of his imagination or perception which constitutes his reading 'child'—this is wholly part of his system of beliefs and needs, and need never be substantially challenged. The critic writes about children and books with full control, as the author of his story about himself as critic, the child, and the book. Although many critics, as we have seen, base their claims to authority on their involvement, as teachers, parents, psychologists, or librarians, with 'real children' in the 'real world', they need never test or illustrate their claims in children's literature criticism beyond making them in the first place.

It is a revealing strategy: the notion of the 'knowable real child' is apparently so pervasive and persuasive that each critic assumes to some extent or other that his readers will share his assertions. He assumes that this is what the child is like, and sees little reason to doubt that that is what the child is like for everybody. The assumption of the existence of the 'child' is reflected typically in the 'of course' attitude that I mentioned in Chapter 1: this assumes that 'of course' the child exists and that someone knows what it is and how to deal with it. (We see this position constantly reinforced in society: just try introducing the notion of varying constructed children into a conversation, and see how many people immediately respond by providing you with a list of attributes and characteristics of the child, without addressing your challenge to this very activity.)

To children's literature criticism, and many other areas concerned with children, children are more 'children' than they are 'individuals'. We have also seen that children's literature repeatedly refutes this, claiming that 'individuality' is its priority above all else. I have argued that this is precisely the claim which cannot be sustained, and is undermined within the field itself. To children's literature criticism, the 'child' is an 'individual' *within* the category of 'childhood', but its 'individuality' cannot transcend the category of 'childhood'. In fact, we can reformulate our conclusion with respect to the impossibility of children's literature criticism by saying that this field is torn apart by the paradox of, on the one hand, involuntarily reflecting the disruption of 'childhood' by 'individuality', while on the other hand maintaining an unfailing devotion to the claim that 'childhood' encompasses 'individuality'. Indeed, the paradox within children's literature may be said to reflect a paradox present within our society in a much broader sense, and that is the difficulty of simultaneously placing a high value on the notion of individuality while also being greatly attached to categorization. And, as I have argued, because 'childhood' is so enshrined within the hierarchical structures of our society, there is no solution in simply deciding to allow the 'child' to be an 'individual' amongst 'individuals' rather than a 'child' amongst 'adults', even if there were any possibility of accomplishing this.

We have seen the 'of course' attitude extended by children's literature critics throughout the domain of understanding between human beings. The belief in the ability to 'know' the 'real child' requires a conviction that levels of empathy, sympathy, identification, perception, or communication exist between persons— between 'selves' and 'others'—as the means of attaining communal knowledge and meanings. These are postulations about two-way interactions: assumptions are being made about adults' ability to 'see' children. We have seen Charlotte Huck, for instance, claim that 'Understanding of the child and the accumulated effect of past experiences is gained through observing him in many situations. . . . It is a poor teacher who has to be told what the children's interests are.'[1] Peter Hunt has to save his children's literature criticism by resorting to 'assum[ing] a certain congruence between what you see and what I see and what a child-reader sees; . . . There must be a middle ground of common-sense agreement about what meaning is.'[2] I have suggested throughout that it is the way in which these assumptions concerning self–other observation, understanding, and sharing of meanings are accepted and used that creates another source of the many problems in children's literature criticism. It is a field which has placed itself squarely within the realm of emotional meaning, and which assumes that the emotional meaning of others can be, more or less efficiently, perceived, predicted, and distributed. We have seen how many critics, in the same way as Hunt, seem uneasily (half-)aware of problems in this area and, to varying degrees, introduce assumptions as strategies of defence or camouflage in order to sustain a 'knowledge', and therefore a control, of the 'child' and its supposed emotional attachments and experiences.

We have now left children's literature criticism behind us, however, arguing that it cannot be reformulated from its present position into taking account of the varying constructions of the 'child'. This is bound to raise two important questions: the first will be asked in a practical spirit by those people who now feel lost with respect to (their) children and books, and who will want to know how to deal with giving books to children if children's literature criticism is disposed of; the second question will be how to deal with children other than the reading children we have been examining up until now: if all children besides the reading child are indeed also constructions, then how do we deal further with those constructions?

With respect to the first question, it must be said that I do not believe that there can be any systematic, generalized guidance on choosing books for a person, regardless of age, when it comes to

[1] Charlotte S. Huck, *Children's Literature in the Elementary School* (Holt, Rinehart and Winston, 3rd edn., New York, 1976), 30, 37.

[2] Peter Hunt, *Criticism, Theory, and Children's Literature* (Basil Blackwell, Oxford, 1991), 89.

emotional meaning. Any reader will make use of a book in his own way, and this chapter will serve to demonstrate further why and how I think this to be the case. I have argued that the children's literature criticism we have left behind does not provide the answers or solutions it seeks for itself, but only a false security. Nevertheless, it does reveal the need that makes the provision of this (false) security necessary. The critics reveal throughout their various writings how much they need to feel they know what the 'child' is like, how the 'child's' emotions and thoughts work, and what they represent in terms of, for instance, freedom, innocence, resistence, or primitivism. But I do not intend to supply another mode of false security, and I do not have anything to offer constituting some sort of 'true' security (that could only involve putting forward another candidate version of the 'real' child).

Instead, I suggest that we may be able to think further about both the 'child' and 'individuality' and about attendant questions of emotional meaning and (self–other) communication by turning to particular aspects of psychoanalysis (Sigmund Freud's theories of the structure and function of the human psyche) and psychoanalytic psychotherapy (the application of psychoanalytic principles in the effort to treat or cure emotional difficulties). (To avoid initial confusion I should point out that I will be putting these fields to a different use from that to which we saw Jacqueline Rose put them at the end of the previous chapter.) There are two reasons why psychoanalysis suggests itself as the discipline which may be helpful to us: first (as I have already indicated), children's literature criticism relies on random, loosely formulated ideas about emotional meaning and communication ('identification' being its mainstay), the very processes and characteristics of which are the object of study of psychoanalysis. Secondly, there is a version of psychoanalysis which not only lends support to my claim that *all* 'children' are constructions and inventions, but which also concentrates on ways to work with the idea of the constructed 'individual' ('child' and 'adult')—this despite the fact that to many people the autonomous 'child' will seem to be even more unavoidably present in a therapy session than in children's literature criticism.

This apparent presence of the 'child' in psychotherapy should not mislead us: we have already seen that psychology and adult literary criticism do not help to solve the difficulties of children's literature criticism because they, too, cannot stabilize the 'child' in the ways necessary. It is part of my argument in this chapter that psychotherapy (I will often use this term to cover 'psychoanalysis and psychotherapy' for the sake of ease, and, unless explicitly mentioned, mean *psychoanalytic* psychotherapy by it, not psychotherapies based on other theories) does not offer us the 'real' or 'true' child either—at least not in any simple sense, or in any sense that will resolve the issues of children's literature criticism. We can no more use these disciplines to discover a 'real child' who can be slotted into children's literature criticism to provide it with the stable 'child' it needs, than we could use psychology or adult literary criticism. Psychoanalysis and psychotherapy also construct varying 'children', but exposing this construction does not invalidate their work in the same way that the removal of the 'real child' causes the collapse of children's literature criticism.

I would like to state clearly at this stage that my discussion has no pretensions to contributing to issues within psychotherapy itself. I am using—or, if one prefers, misusing—selected ideas, terminology, and concepts already present in psychoanalysis and psychotherapy to elaborate my thinking with respect to the constructed nature of children as we see it revealed in children's literature criticism. As such, I hope it will be clear that my turning to these fields is not a jump to different problems and issues for their own sake, but a way of showing how the contradictions and instabilities we have analysed within children's literature criticism exist, and are dealt with, in a different context.

One difficulty with plunging into other disciplines to employ their discourse is that this necessitates, along the way, explanations of that discipline itself. When the area under discussion is not necessarily the common currency of conversation, is often misunderstood in many ways, and is subject to many different interpretations (and surrounded by sometimes acrimonious debates), as is the case with psychotherapy, this will mean irritating some readers by over-explaining to avoid (hopefully) confusing others by under-explaining. I would therefore like to ask readers to have patience while I try to clarify what might seem to be extraneous issues. Another difficulty of using many disciplines is, of course, as I have argued throughout this book, that a lack of knowledge, or a very selective or confused knowledge, of the fields concerned may only serve to camouflage the problems which are around. We have seen how child psychology and adult literary criticism are used in this way by children's literary critics. Hopefully, therefore, my explanations of (child) psychotherapy will help to avoid this problem by openly revealing my own ideas and (mis)conceptions about the subject.

The psychoanalyst and developmental psychologist Daniel Stern formulates the constructed 'infant' (the form of 'child' which is most easily accepted as constructed by many people because of the infant's non-verbality) in two ways. First, he comments on construction in terms of the way adults observe infants:

Since we can never crawl inside an infant's mind, it may seem pointless to imagine what an infant might experience. . . . [Yet] what we imagine infant experience to be like shapes our notions of who the infant is. These notions make up our working hypotheses about infancy. As such, they serve as the models guiding our clinical concepts about psychopathology: how, why, and when it begins. They are the wellspring of ideas for experiments about infants: what do they think and feel? These working theories also determine how we, as parents, respond to our own infants, and ultimately they shape our views of human nature. Because we cannot know the subjective world that infants inhabit, we must invent it, so as to have a starting place for hypothesis-making. This book is such an invention. It is a working hypothesis about infants' subjective experience of their own social life.[3]

Secondly, Stern refers to the way an infant is constructed from memory by the adult:

In contrast to the infant as observed by developmental psychology, a different 'infant' has been reconstructed by psychoanalytic theories in the course of clinical practice (primarily with adults). This infant is the joint creation of two people, the adult who grew up to be a psychiatric patient

[3] Daniel Stern, *The Interpersonal World of the Infant: A View From Psychoanalysis and Developmental Psychology* (Basic Books, New York, 1985), 4.

and the therapist, who has a theory about infant experience. This recreated infant is made up of memories, present reenactments in the transference, and theoretically guided interpretations.[4]

(I will be explaining below some of the terminology that Stern uses.)

What some forms of (child) psychotherapy can offer us, then, instead of another 'real child', is suggestions of strategies for negotiating between individuality and generalization and for communicating emotional meaning. By this I mean that psychotherapy works with specific theoretical models of general human emotional structure and development which, however, have to be translated into an application in therapy to the differing cases of distinctive 'individuals'. This is not to say that psychotherapy has pat methods for this procedure: the translation constitutes psychotherapeutic self–other communication, and is a problematic process. The result is various 'styles', within limits, of practising psychotherapy. The thinking in this area questions many of the assumptions about how patients (whether 'child' or 'adult', or 'child' as 'adult' or 'adult' as 'child') can be known, seen, remembered, or understood.

This chapter is therefore divided into two parts: in this first part I will be discussing some of the theoretical ideas in psychotherapy concerning meaning, memory, understanding, and communication. In the second part I will be exploring the writings of several eminent child psychotherapists to show that their 'children' emerge as very different individuals in their work, and that their theories of 'childhood' also differ to various degrees, without this necessarily invalidating any of their approaches for the purposes of psychotherapy. Daniel Stern addresses the presence of these negotiations between theory and practice when he writes that

When I was a resident in psychiatry and in psychoanalytic training, we were always asked to summarize each case with a psychodynamic formulation, that is, an explanatory historical account of how the patient became the person who walked into your office. The account was to begin as early as possible in the patient's life . . . This task . . . was agonizing [to

---

[4] Ibid. 14.

me] because I was caught in a contradiction. On one side, there was the strong conviction that the past influences the present in some coherent fashion. . . . But on the other side, my patients knew so little about their earliest life histories and I knew even less about how to ask about them. So I was forced to pick and choose among those few facts about their infancies that best fit the existing theories and from these selected pickings come up with a coherent historical account. The formulations for all of the cases began to sound alike. Yet the people were very different. . . . This contradiction has continued to disturb and intrigue me.[5]

We also see another aspect of this dilemma echoed in M. Masud R. Khan's caveat with respect to reading various case histories from the work of the famous British child psychoanalyst Donald Winnicott:

In this book [*Therapeutic Consultations in Child Psychiatry*], Dr. Winnicott has concentrated almost exclusively on presenting his clinical material with the minimum of theory. This, however, should not misguide the reader into thinking that this clinical work is the result of mere empathy and inspired hunches. There is a very complex and vast theoretical background to it, which Dr. Winnicott has presented in his various articles and books . . .[6]

The psychoanalyst and therapist Patrick Casement has discussed other important aspects involved in this travelling between theory and practice in his book *On Learning from the Patient.* He reformulates the relationship between the two:

Analytic theories are built up to define more clearly the framework in which analysts and therapists work. These are necessary, if analytic therapy is not to become a matter of inspired guesswork. Theory also helps to moderate the helplessness of not-knowing. But it remains important that this should be servant to the work of therapy and not its master.[7]

This view suggests that psychotherapy can offer ways of accepting specific theories of human development and emotion (a form of

[5] Ibid. p. viii.

[6] Donald Winnicott, *Therapeutic Consultations in Child Psychiatry* (The International Psycho-Analytical Library, no. 87, ed. M. Masud R. Khan) (The Hogarth Press and the Institute of Psycho-Analysis, London, 1971), 397.

[7] Patrick Casement, *On Learning From the Patient* (Tavistock Publications, London, 1985), 4.

'knowing' the 'child'), while on the level of therapeutic practice often allowing oneself not to know the 'child' or 'other' (person). The concept of 'not knowing' is used here in a very specific sense: it does not refer to complacent ignorance, inattention, or carelessness on the part of the therapist, but to the use by the therapist of a form of self-restraint to ensure he does not jump to conclusions about his patient. This self-restraint takes on subtle and complex aspects within the intensive interactions between therapist and patient. In other words, 'not knowing' can be seen as a balancing act that some psychotherapists have developed whereby the individuality of the patient grows out of the use of the theory; the theory supplies the concept that the patient's individuality and sense of him- or herself takes priority in the therapeutic sense. As Casement puts it:

> there is a common myth that the experienced analyst or therapist understands the patient swiftly and unerringly. Some therapists also appear to expect it of themselves; perhaps to gratify an unacknowledged wish to be knowledgeable or powerful. It is not surprising, therefore, how often student therapists imagine that immediate understanding is required of them by patients and supervisors. This creates a pressure to know in order to appear competent. . . . [But] therapists have to tolerate extended periods during which they may feel ignorant or helpless. . . . The experienced therapist or analyst . . . has to make an effort to preserve an adequate state of not-knowing if he is to remain open to fresh understanding.[8]

The ideas involved in Casement's discussion are very complex, and we will explore them further later. But it is important to note here that this type of psychotherapist is taking the concept of individuality very seriously. I would like to propose the general importance for our dealings with the 'child' of this idea that it can be much more important to allow oneself not to know in this way, if this seems to reflect better the actual state of affairs, or if this allows one to achieve or recognize more important goals than 'knowledge'. Casement's suggestions concerning the pressures on therapists to 'know' the patient may, after all, call to mind the ways in which children's literature critics produce their problematic 'knowledge'

---

[8] Ibid. pp. xi, 3–4.

of the 'child'. It may sometimes be better, although often not easier, to be in a state of doubt or non-knowledge than to be in a state of active self-deception with regard to an illusory 'knowledge' of another person. Therefore, in this chapter, ideas about 'not knowing' will be part of the discussion of psychotherapy and of the techniques that are used in psychoanalytic psychotherapy both with children and with adults.

The exploration of construction and knowledge, then, is one reason why I am turning specifically to psychotherapy. The source of the possibility of making this connection between children's literature criticism and psychotherapy can be roughly summarized by saying that they both make claims about being involved with particular forms of *emotional education*: both fields are intensely bound up with the contradictions and complications that this notion entails, and which we analysed and traced in the 'stories of origin'. Children's literature criticism and psychotherapy are both inextricably caught up in the negotiation between individuality and categorization, or generalization, and in the conflict between education and freedom. We can taste something of this overlap in the child analyst Anna Freud's early comment that 'the analyst accordingly combines in his own person two difficult and diametrically opposed functions: he has to analyse and educate, that is to say in the same breath he must allow and forbid, loosen and bind again'.[9] (Later Anna Freud allocated the 'educational function' back to parents and schools.) But, of course, children's literature criticism is not aware of the way its operation is determined by these factors, while psychotherapy addresses them consciously. In other words—just to avoid any possible confusion—I am certainly not agreeing here with children's literature criticism and saying that children's literature is indeed an 'emotional education': I am using this term strictly to indicate that children's literature criticism sees it as such, without being (fully) aware of the difficulties this entails.

These, then, form the two main themes of our discussion: the first theme is that the 'child' is somehow constructed or invented in

[9] Anna Freud, *The Psycho-Analytical Treatment of Children*, trans. Nancy Procter-Gregg (Imago Publishing, London, 1946), 49.

psychotherapy too, and the second theme is that psychotherapy and children's literature criticism both have connections with notions of emotional education, with all the difficulties inherent in that concept. The notion of the construction of the 'child' forms the backdrop to our discussion and re-emerges constantly, so it may be useful to turn first to an examination of the second point.

We have seen that the aim of children's literature criticism is to find the good book for the child, the book which will elicit from the child a response—above all, an emotional response which will allow it to embrace certain values and ideas spontaneously and voluntarily. This is a reformulation of the ideals of the liberal arts education. The valuing of freedom and emotion are the cardinal features: emotional response is supposed to lead to freedom in learning ('I love that book'), and this constitutes the claim of liberation for 'children' through children's literature. A crucial feature of children's literature criticism in this respect is its lack of acknowledgement of its attempt to yoke the cognitive and the emotional aspects of reading: the emotional response or attachment to the book must function both as an end in itself (learning about the emotion) and as the handmaiden to a cognitive appreciation of the ideas and values contained in, or embodied by, the book. In either case, the primary point is for the child to learn what the critic thinks it should learn (even if this is freedom itself). Importantly, this also includes an element of faith in the critics' competence to predict the 'child's' response. We have seen the contradictions between education and liberation expressed in the frustration felt by some children's literature critics: tales abound about children loving Enid Blyton books, while refusing to read someone like Thackeray.

Psychotherapy too aims to affect the emotions of adults and children. It aims to lessen or cure the suffering caused in people by certain types of emotional fears and anxieties. But it takes a much more specific, and very crucial, approach to the relation between cognition and emotion. One of the central points Freud took seriously is that emotions and feelings are often not changed by rational decisions. That is to say, a rational explanation of why you feel the way you do is often not sufficient to make the feelings go away or come back. Rational understanding may sometimes assist in forming one of the paths to further processes affecting the emotions, but it may also block those paths or be irrelevant altogether to the therapeutic process. It is a crucial point, and one which often is still not taken seriously enough: psychoanalytic psychotherapy is in no way merely a rational conversation in which the therapist explains to you what your problems are and where they come from. This will, according to the theories of psychoanalysis, have little effect on the state of the patient on its own, and is not psychoanalysis. It does not take into account any of the theories of psychoanalysis with respect to the dynamics of human emotional life.

In short: for children's literature criticism, emotion opens the gates to emotional, moral, and cognitive learning, with adults prescribing and predicting the type of learning that is desired; for psychotherapy emotion takes clear precedence over cognition (morality should hardly come into the picture at all), and is the area of engagement for its own sake, while the learning to be achieved is defined, to some extent or other, by the patient ('child' or 'adult') *for himself*. This also implies that psychotherapy does not involve the same need as in children's literature criticism for a faith in predictive capacities in the therapist. We have already noted this in Chapter 4, in the quote from Freud in which he argues that one can analyse retrospectively how a person has developed into who they are, but that one would not have been able to predict this in advance. This non-prediction includes the therapist often not knowing how the therapy will develop (and this not knowing is part of the specific therapeutic not knowing we have already started to discuss).

In other words, children's literature criticism is inextricably tied to a *prescriptive* role (even when it does not want to be), whereas psychotherapy is extensively concerned with functioning *non-prescriptively*. This also implies that psychotherapy is even more concerned with ideas about freedom of emotion, thought, and action than children's literature criticism. Psychotherapy, in this sense, participates to an even greater extent in the discourses of freedom which are part of the ideals of liberal humanism. We get some flavour of this in Freud's comment (with respect to the possible involvement of psychoanalysis in educational methods) that '[psychoanalysis] itself contains enough revolutionary factors to ensure that no one educated by it will in later life take the side of reaction and suppression'.[10] Individualism and freedom of feeling, thought, and action are tenets which underpin the aims and methods of psychoanalysis. Daniel Stern formulates the role of culture in this context when he writes that

There is no question that different societies could minimize or maximize this need for intersubjectivity ['potentially shareable subjective experiences']. For instance, if a society were socially structured so that it was assumed that all members had essentially identical, inner subjective experiences, and if homogeneity of this aspect of felt life were stressed, there would be little need, and no societal pressure, to enhance the development of intersubjectivity. If on the other hand a society highly valued the existence and the sharing of individual differences at this level of experience (as ours does), then their development would be facilitated by that society.[11]

We might also refer to the fundamental difference between the prescriptive approach of children's literature criticism and the non-prescriptive stance of psychoanalysis as constituting the difference between the drive (or need) to know and the attempt to learn, or between telling and listening.

The core argument for the psychoanalytic view of the relation between cognition and emotion is Freud's theory that the human psyche operates with a conscious and an unconscious. (These should not be conceived of as static entities, such as parts of the brain; Freud primarily meant them to be considered as descriptions of a dynamic system. He later redivided conscious and unconscious into super-ego, ego, and id, but we need not explore this in detail here.) Rational thought takes place in the conscious, and emotion is involved with both the conscious and the unconscious, but has its most powerful sources in the unconscious. And this is because very powerful types of experiences and feelings are repressed in the unconscious. In other words, although these experiences and

---

[10] Sigmund Freud, *New Introductory Lectures on Psycho-Analysis*, trans. James Strachey (The Penguin Freud Library, 2, ed. James Strachey and Angela Richards) (Penguin, Harmondsworth, 1991), 186.

[11] Stern, *The Interpersonal World of the Infant*, 136–7.

feelings are unconscious, and we consciously know nothing about them, they exercise a strong influence on our emotions and actions in our daily life.

Freud often had to defend and explain the existence of the unconscious—this difficult idea of a hidden and unknown source of many actions and emotions. Here is one such explanation and defence Freud gave, in connection with a patient he treated who suffered from carrying out an obsessional action:

However often the patient repeated her obsessional action, she knew nothing of its being derived from the experience she had had. The connection between the two was hidden from her . . . while she was carrying out the obsessional action [its] sense had been unknown to her . . . both its 'whence' and its 'whither'. . . . Mental processes had therefore been at work in her and the obsessional action was the effect of them; she had been aware of this effect in a normal mental fashion, but none of the mental predeterminants of this effect came to the knowledge of her consciousness. . . . It is a state of affairs of this sort that we have before our eyes when we speak of the existence of *unconscious mental processes*. . . . we will hold fast to [this] hypothesis; and if someone objects that here the unconscious is nothing real in a scientific sense, is a makeshift . . . we can only shrug our shoulders resignedly . . . Something not real, which produces effects of such tangible reality as an obsessional action![12]

The unconscious, then, is never accessible to the conscious. This fundamental characteristic of the Freudian unconscious has been overlooked or misunderstood repeatedly in general portrayals of Freudian theory. But it is only when this idea is taken on board absolutely that we are in a position to understand properly the full implications of Freudian theory for our (or any other) discussion. Freud tells the following anecdote in an attempt to clarify the constant confusion surrounding his thinking in this area. He once met the celebrated Danish scholar Georg Brandes, with whom he had the following exchange (involving, besides the existence of the unconscious, a reference to an important aspect of Freud's theory of childhood sexuality):

[12] Sigmund Freud, *Introductory Lectures on Psycho-Analysis*, trans. James Strachey (The Penguin Freud Library, 1, ed. James Strachey and Angela Richards) (Penguin, Harmondsworth, 1991), 317–18.

'I am only a literary man,' he [Brandes] said, 'but you are a natural scientist and discoverer. However, there is one thing I must say to you: I have never had sexual feelings towards my mother.' 'But there is no need at all for you to have known them,' was my [Freud's] reply; 'to grown-up people those are unconscious feelings.' 'Oh! so *that's* what you think!' he said with relief and pressed my hand.[13]

So, the conscious cannot order the unconscious around, and it cannot 'look' into the unconscious. The unconscious can only be reconstructed in bits from hints provided in a distorted form by dreams, 'parapraxes' (mistakes or accidents, commonly known as 'Freudian slips'), and 'free association' (the procedure in therapy whereby a patient is invited to say whatever comes into his mind without obeying the normal rules of society with respect to conversational coherence, consistency, or subject-matter). The idea of a hidden unconscious expressing itself only in disguised ways immediately introduces the activity of interpretation into therapy. An important part of the therapist's role is to interpret the unconscious meaning of material presented in therapy. Because, according to Freud, precisely the most painful wishes, desires, and fears are repressed in the unconscious, powerful emotions and conflicts are produced by, and much energy is lost to, the effort to keep these feelings 'repressed'. A major aim of psychotherapy is for the analyst or therapist and patient to attempt to lift repression, through interpretation and other means, to allow these bits of the unconscious to become conscious, thereby releasing energy for other activities and resolving some of the conflicts and tensions arising from repression. Freud himself put this as follows:

people usually overlook the one essential point—that the pathogenic conflict in neurotics is not to be confused with a normal struggle between mental impulses both of which are on the same psychological footing. In the former case the dissension is between two powers, one of which has made its way to the stage of what is preconscious or conscious while the other has been held back at the stage of the unconscious. For that reason the conflict cannot be brought to an issue; the disputants can no more come to grips than, in the familiar simile, a polar bear and a whale. A true

---

[13] Freud, *New Introductory Lectures on Psycho-Analysis*, 173.

decision can only be reached when they both meet on the same ground. To make this possible is, I think, the sole task of our therapy.[14]

It should, however, be noted that the unconscious can never entirely become conscious, that it can never be 'empty', and that repression inevitably continues throughout life: it is not this process itself which constitutes emotional disturbances, but the degree to which it needs to take place, and the extent of the problems and symptoms which it produces.

An understanding of the unconscious as a hidden repository of powerful meanings locked away also provides us with the basis of the psychoanalytic theory of memory. Psychoanalysis does not allow for the idea of all past experiences and feelings being accessible for accurate retrieval. When elements of experience are forgotten or remembered, this forgetting or remembering is not seen as an accident or haphazard loss or memorizing, but as a determined result of repression and selective production of memory. Therefore, many memories are stored in the unconscious, and they never disappear: they are forever present in the unconscious, where they are also forever 'present', in the sense that the unconscious is timeless. These are complex concepts, with many implications. We saw Jacqueline Rose employ this notion of the timeless unconscious with its stored memories as a way of tackling a discussion of the 'child' as being forever present, but needing to be repressed, in the 'adult'. We can also note that this theory of memory provides us with the view of the impossibility of 'adults' ever being able simply to remember 'real childhood', even if there were such a 'childhood' to find 'behind' repression. As the psychoanalyst Donald Spence writes:

It was one of Freud's signal achievements to make clear the illusory quality of memory and to show how the mechanisms of displacement and condensation apply to memory as much as they apply to dreams. Although the memory has a feeling of being closer to the real experience, it was Freud's genius to show how this sense is often illusory and how both memory and dream belong to the same group of wish-determined phenomena.[15]

[14] Freud, *Introductory Lectures on Psycho-Analysis*, 484.
[15] Donald Spence, *Narrative Truth and Historical Truth: Meaning and Interpretation in Psychoanalysis* (W. W. Norton, New York, 1982), 59.

The discussion concerning the attempt to understand and interpret the meaning, and affect the emotion, of an 'other', then, is not confused in psychotherapy in the way it is in children's literature criticism. Interpretation and the achievement of effect are in themselves central aims to psychotherapy, and as such have been subject to intense examination, while in children's literature criticism they are largely taken for granted and are bound up with all sorts of extraneous purposes and aims. Whereas in children's literature criticism the processes whereby a book is supposed to affect a child's emotions, and take on personal meaning for him, are essentially taken for granted as being 'that which the good book does', psychotherapy is engaged with examining, in theory and in practice, precisely these processes: how do emotions and personal meaning come about, how can we understand them in others, and how can they be changed?

In other words, children's literature criticism encourages us to assume that communication concerning emotional meaning between 'adult' and 'child' and between 'child' and book—between 'self' and 'other'—is a relatively simple matter. Of course we have seen that children's literature critics often pay due tribute to the idea that these actually may be very complex processes, but the field in fact exists by virtue of its reliance on assumptions that we can, and do, understand and control emotional meaning in others. Psychoanalysis, on the other hand, encourages us to take maximum account of a belief in the great complexity of emotional meaning and communication. These divergences of belief with respect to the degree of difficulty involved in understanding emotion and meaning of course extend well beyond these two specific disciplines. For our specific purposes we turn to the psychoanalytic view because we have noted that children's literature criticism's faith in understanding and in the control of meaning in others leads only to its highly problematic existence as an almost random collection of constructions of 'children'.

The two fields come more closely together again in their consideration of education as 'non-force': one of the features which is most common to the various reading 'children' of children's literature criticism is that this 'child' is seen as being impossible, or difficult, to teach by force. Moreover, this difficulty is seen as being both a part and a result of the 'otherness' of the 'child'. We saw in the 'stories of origin' how this was the legacy of ideas about the need for mass education (Luther and Comenius) and about liberal arts education (the Greeks and Romans, Montaigne, Locke, Rousseau). For an illustration of the connection between freedom and self–other interactions we need only look at many totalitarian political systems, with their partial faith in 'retraining camps' (forced education) and their whole faith in killing the perceived 'other'.

Psychotherapy allies itself wholly with the notion of the difficulty of forced 'education' (treatment). In an overt sense, this has to do with the well-known axiom that it is extremely difficult, if not totally impossible, to treat a patient in psychotherapy who does not want to be treated. (This problem arises, for instance, in the case of prisoners who are obliged to attend therapy sessions—techniques have been developed to attempt to deal with this, but it remains a difficult and limited procedure.) But there are many much more subtle senses in which psychotherapy, in its own terms, can only be an ultimate 'non-force education': first, the unconscious cannot be forced to become conscious, and, secondly, all patients—even those who are enthusiastic about being in therapy—in many senses do not want to change: the illness itself is present because it serves (unconscious) purposes for the patient. Therefore the patient resists interpretation and change. Psychotherapy attempts to apply systems which encourage the patient to stay with the treatment voluntarily through these phases of resistance, and to make it possible for emotional changes to take place in the patient. And, again, the patient plays a role in defining the goals of his treatment, while children's literature criticism defines the aims of reading for the child.

Children's literature criticism has failed us by making claims about the effects of reading on children on which it cannot agree within itself or co-ordinate into a coherent or useful body of theory. Psychotherapy also makes claims about the functioning of its theory and its effectiveness. Many of these claims have been criticized and questioned since the very beginning of the development of psychoanalysis. The most extreme accusation towards psycho-therapy has been that it has no effect at all, but that the therapist (and patient) merely 'see' effects because of their belief in the work. This is another way in which children's literature criticism and psychotherapy are related: as with children's literature criticism, many of psychotherapy's claims are inherently difficult to discuss or 'prove' because they are involved with so many different variables and with the most subjective of perceptions concerning mood and emotional state. There has been research on the effectiveness of psychotherapy with respect to curing diverse emotional problems and disorders which has supported its claims,[16] but there are still problems in describing how psychotherapy works exactly, what causes the effects, and how to teach and apply therapeutic technique.

We are not engaged here in proving or disproving psycho-therapy, but need only note that the very claim of psychotherapy to effectiveness has been implicated, by some critics, in the problems of self–other communication and meaning. It can be stated confidently that the bitterness of the criticism levelled by a critic such as Jan Needle towards a critic such as Michele Landsberg is as nothing compared with the bitterness of the criticism still levelled at psychoanalysis and psychotherapy by those who have no faith in them, or compared with the acrimony of some of the debates within psychotherapy. If acrimony within children's literature criticism derives from its involvement with the 'child', psychotherapy has the problem of addressing not only the 'child' head-on, but also all those subjects which are guaranteed to stir up people's feelings (in more ways than one): aggression, love, hate, sexuality.

What is most relevant about the criticisms levelled at psychotherapy for the purposes of our discussion is that one of the critics' main claims is that psychotherapy produces itself. In other words, psychotherapy is, in the first place, accused of existing only

---

[16] Research on the effectiveness of psychoanalysis and psychotherapy is discussed, for instance, in Robert S. Wallerstein, 'The Psychotherapy Research Project of the Menninger Foundation: An Overview', *Journal of Consulting and Clinical Psychology*, 57/2 (Apr. 1989), 195–205, and Robert S. Wallerstein, 'Followup Psychoanalysis: Clinical and Research Values. Fall of the American Psychoanalytic Association: Evaluation of Outcome of Psychoanalytic Treatment: Should Followup by the Analyst be Part of the Post-termination Phase of Analytic Treatment?', *Journal of the American Psychoanalytic Association*, 37/4 (1989), 921–41.

as a superfluous story the therapist tells about himself, the therapy, and the patient, in the same way that I have analysed children's literature criticism as existing only as a superfluous story the critic tells about himself, the book, and the child. In the second place, if psychotherapy is acknowledged to be effective by its critics at all, it is accused by them of having that effect not because its theories of the human psyche are correct, but because it operates through suggestion or indoctrination. It is central to our interest in these arguments that both these forms of accusation rest on the claim that the therapist is wholly 'inventing' (constructing) the patient, the theory, and the therapy: all these views derive from the broader realm of the problems of self–other interaction we looked at in Chapter 1. Many psychotherapists themselves are not unduly disturbed by the accusations, deriving their faith in their field from the continuing perception of the success of their work in achieving the alleviation or cure of their patients' emotional distress or symptoms. Some analysts also argue, as we will see, that the results of psychoanalysis are not invalidated because of their possible (partial) production through the construction, by therapist and patient together, of a narrative, rather than by the discovery by the therapist of the 'truth' about the patient. (This also relates to our discussion, in Chapter 1, of the relations between 'narrative' and 'science'.) We saw this implied by the fact that Daniel Stern in no way concludes that his comments concerning the construction of the 'infant' result in a refutation of psychoanalysis itself.

Freud himself addressed these types of criticism repeatedly during his life, such as when he wrote that

If [the objections] were justified, psychoanalysis would be nothing more than a particularly well-disguised and particularly effective form of suggestive treatment and we should have to attach little weight to all that it tells us about what influences our lives, the dynamics of the mind or the unconscious. That is what our opponents believe; and in especial they think that we have 'talked' the patients into everything . . . The doctor has no difficulty, of course, in making [the patient] a supporter of some particular theory . . . In this respect the patient is behaving like anyone else—like a pupil—*but this only affects his intelligence, not his illness.*[17]

[17] Freud, *Introductory Lectures on Psycho-Analysis*, 505 (my emphasis).

The idea I am going to work with here is that—as we already saw implied by Daniel Stern's comments—psychotherapy is not prevented from being important or effective through being seen as consisting of the construction of a narrative, part of which may be diverse 'children' or 'adults'. In fact, this constructing activity may constitute (part of) what it means for psychotherapy to be effective, and constitutes an area of negotiation between 'self' and 'other', and between 'individual' and 'childhood' or 'adulthood'. This is the point where I believe children's literature criticism and (child) psychotherapy definitively part ways: children's literature criticism falls apart when the existence of its claimed 'real child' is challenged, whereas (child) psychotherapy does not fall apart when so challenged. And this is because children's literature criticism constructs its various children for no purpose. They are simply created in narrative, published, and have nowhere to go, except to confirm a particular view of the 'child' in the mind of any reader who happens to agree with the critic in question. Psychotherapy, however, it can be argued, creates a narrative by the individual patient and the individual therapist *for that patient*. And that type of narrative is crucial and not arbitrary.

It is the strategies psychotherapy employs to cope with constructed patients (and therapists) and the area between theory and individual which make it a possible model for what our society can do with the notion of all 'children' being constructed. (It will be obvious from my arguments throughout this book that introducing psychotherapy as a possible model has nothing to do with suggesting that people should become a kind of amateur psychotherapist in their dealings with children.) There is a further important aspect of this characteristic of psychotherapy which suggests that it may be a good model for examining ways of working with self–other interactions and 'childhood' and 'individuality': I have discussed the hierarchical structure of the relationship between adults and children within society, and the way this precludes children from defining themselves in the same way that women have been able to start to do in the Western world since the advent of feminism. This structure would appear to be inevitably, inherently, reduplicated within child psychotherapy in the relationship between the therapist and the child patient. In this way the therapist would seem to be in a prime position to impose definitions or narratives on children, even more so than children's literature criticism. But many child psychotherapists have been acutely aware of this hierarchical structure, and have thought about its consequences for their work. Moreover, this situation is not unique to child psychotherapy: adult psychotherapy has to grapple with almost exactly the same hierarchical structures. A therapist is also in a position of power over his adult patient: partially because the patient has put himself into the therapist's hands, and partially because the relationship between therapist and adult patient is often intended to allow for a type of re-creation of a relationship between 'adult' and 'child' (just as the 'child' may be an 'adult' in therapy). But it is still this hierarchical structure which makes it possible for some critics to say that the therapy is 'invented' by the therapist, making the patient 'invisible': the therapist is accused of having full control over the narrative of the therapy and its interpretation, to the exclusion of the patient.

Having introduced some general ideas we can now pose more specific questions about psychotherapy: how does the therapist come to an understanding of his patient? Does the psychotherapist indeed construct his patient in the same way that the children's literature critic constructs his child? If so, does this constructing mean that psychotherapy does not 'exist', involving only a story the therapist tells about himself? Or, at the other extreme, does not the psychotherapist inevitably know what the 'real child' is like through being directly involved with the treatment of many children? These questions will first lead us more deeply into developments and varying opinions in psychotherapeutic theory and practice, after which we will look at the writings of different child psycho-therapists, to illustrate both how they negotiate the application of their theories in practice and how their therapies and 'children' differ.

Psychotherapy, then, is shaped by, and has often had to examine extensively, two crucial issues, which are exactly those points that children's literature criticism elides completely with respect to its 'child': children's literature criticism never discusses how the critic 'knows' the 'child', or how the critic's position relates to 'childhood', while the first crucial issue which psychotherapy raises is that of the precise nature of the relationship between the therapist and the patient. This involves thinking about hierarchy and power. Psychotherapy has had to think about who is 'right', who 'knows' what is true, who produces the narrative of the therapy: that is, it has had to consider the problems of interpretation and dogmatism. In other words, can a therapist 'see' or 'hear' a patient in the patient's terms, do therapists only ever 'see', 'hear', or produce versions of themselves (including their theory), or is the whole process a shared one?

Within psychotherapy the debate has been expressed in terms of a range of therapeutic ideas about the 'presence' of the patient and the therapist, respectively, in the therapy. That is to say, much discussion centres on who has, who can have, and who should have, control over the content and development of the therapy: the therapist or the patient? We can reformulate this dilemma in a different way again, emphasizing its connection with our previous discussions: I have argued that the 'child' has no 'voice' within the hierarchies of our society, because 'adults' either silence or create that voice; therapy thinks about whether the patient ('child' or 'adult') can have a voice, and whether that voice can indeed be heard in its own right by the therapist within the therapeutic setting (even if nowhere else).

One aspect of the therapeutic setting is referred to as the 'psychoanalytic space', by which is meant the psychological arena within which the therapy takes place. The term also implies that psychotherapy believes that it is indeed able to create a 'space' within which the patient can be seen and heard, and that it is a crucial side of its work to create this space with, and for, the patient. Of course, the 'outer limits' of therapeutic space are outlined by the ground rules of the therapeutic setting: psychoanalytic psychotherapists, for instance, do not provide the patient with information about their own lives and opinions (except in special situations); they commit themselves to being present for the patient at the time of their appointment and to being prepared to listen to the patient; and they do not have physical contact with their patients.

With specific reference to child psychotherapy we can say that this is a crucial striving of many child psychotherapists: to create a space within which the 'voice' of children *as 'individuals'* can be heard. We can see a reflection of many nuances of the dilemmas involved in this striving in a statement made by the child psychoanalyst Donald Winnicott:

when I make an interpretation, if the child disagrees or seems to fail to respond, I am immediately willing to withdraw what I have said. Often in these accounts I have made an interpretation and I have been wrong and the child has been able to correct me. Sometimes of course there is a resistance which implies that I have made the right interpretation and that the right interpretation is denied. But an interpretation that does not work always means that I have made the interpretation at the wrong moment or in the wrong way, and I withdraw it unconditionally. Although the interpretation may be correct I have been wrong in verbalising this material in this way at this particular moment. Dogmatic interpretation leaves the child with only two alternatives, an *acceptance* of what I have said as propaganda or a *rejection* of the interpretation and of me and of the whole set-up. . . . Actually I do claim that it is a fact that these interviews are dominated by the child and not by me.[18]

In this sense child psychotherapy, like children's literature criticism—in their joint guise as forms of emotional education—attempts to reconstruct a form of freedom for children within their dependent (non-free) role within society. Children's literature criticism attempts to achieve this by joining in defining the 'child', and seeing forms of freedom in this defined state. Child psychotherapy initially accepts the 'child' as 'child', and then proceeds to attempt to liberate it from its defined status and allow it to be a unique 'individual'—defined by itself. In the non-free situation between adults and children the adults can choose to define the 'child', steered by their own unacknowledged needs, or assume responsibility for self-reflecting on these needs in order to try to create a freedom within non-freedom for children: the freedom to be 'individuals', whether or not as 'child'. Children's 'childness' is thus maximally and minimally defined by their dependence, or ultimate non-freedom, within society. (In many

[18] Winnicott, *Therapeutic Consultations in Child Psychiatry*, 9–10.

respects this discussion can also be applied to the status of adults with respect to the restrictions of society. But, for our purposes, the adult retains a participatory role in the formation of society, despite its reciprocal restrictions, which the 'child' lacks.) During the rest of the discussion, the underlying question will be whether the possibility of hearing the 'voice' of a patient within the structure of psychotherapy—within a psychotherapeutically created space— can suggest anything to us about the possibility of creating a space within which to hear the 'voice' of 'children' as 'individuals' in other settings.

The second of the two crucial issues within psychotherapy, closely related to the first, is that the 'truths' which form the material of the therapy are held to be, at one level or another, *psychological* 'truths', rather than primarily (only) 'provable', 'historical', or 'objective' truths. Or, to put it differently, therapy (to differing extents) places priority on how important an idea or impression is to the patient, rather than simply prioritizing the revelation of a strictly 'provable' or 'objective' 'reality'. These topics instantly raise a huge realm of questions touching both on the wider discussions concerning 'narrative' and 'reality' we have already come across, and on the psychoanalytic ideas about memory that we have also already looked at to some extent. It will be clear that psychotherapy constantly returns us to basic dilemmas about meaning and communication: we have seen these concerns reflected, for instance, in the views of literary theory about whether the author, the text, or the reader—or none of these—is the stable origin of textual meaning. In short, psychotherapy is fully involved and concerned with the general dilemmas of interpretation (in its widest sense).

We must discuss together the question of the relationship between the therapist and the patient and the problem of 'truth' in psychotherapy, as they will prove to be inextricably linked. But first we must return to considering how psychotherapy works in its own terms. An explanation of the way psychotherapy functions automatically engages us in thinking in greater detail about the negotiations between therapist and patient, including the compli- cating factors involved in the patient being able to be heard by the therapist (which is to say, able to be present in the therapy, or contribute to the narrative of the therapy).

In the early days of psychoanalysis, the role of the therapist in achieving results was seen as clearer than it later became: self–other (therapist–patient) relations were described as controlled by the therapist's 'objectivity'. In the development of psychoanalytic theory on the basis of material provided by patients in analysis (analytic theory and practice developed side by side), the emphasis was put on the knowledge of the therapist about the unconscious of the patient. The therapist could interpret the patient's free associations, including his dreams and 'slips', as material from the patient's unconscious, presented in a distorted form. It was also clear from the beginning, however, both that the therapist was not infallible and that interpretation often did not achieve results on its own anyway. With respect to the fallibility of the therapist in interpretation, Freud pragmatically commented that 'whatever in the doctor's conjectures is inaccurate drops out in the course of the analysis; it has to be withdrawn and replaced by something more correct'.[19] But still the therapist always needed first to hang on to interpretations which patients rejected because patients always have degrees of 'resistance' to correct interpretations. After all, these interpretations have to do with the very painful or difficult materials which are in the unconscious for good reasons (from the perspective of the patient). The patient's responses over a period of time convinced the analyst of the ultimate correctness or incorrectness of the interpretation, but, essentially, the analyst held a superior ('objective') position to that of the patient with respect to the knowledge necessary for interpretation.

As psychoanalysis developed (starting with the developments within Freud's own work), this idea of the therapist having some sort of overall objective knowledge of the patient became qualified in detailed and complex ways. To follow this development we first need to understand how psychoanalysis began to describe mechanisms other than the making of interpretations operating within therapy. With respect to interpretation often not producing

---

[19] Freud, *Introductory Lectures*, 505.

results on its own, Freud importantly introduced the process of 'transference' (which we have seen mentioned by Daniel Stern as a factor in the therapist's and patient's creation of the 'infant') as being a central component contributing to the effectiveness of psychoanalysis:

In a whole number of nervous diseases . . . our expectation is fulfilled. By searching for the repression in this way, by uncovering the resistances, by pointing out what is repressed, we really succeed in accomplishing our task—that is, in overcoming the resistances, lifting the repression and transforming the unconscious material into conscious. . . . There are, however, other forms of illness in which, in spite of the conditions being the same, our therapeutic procedure is never successful . . . [and] after a while we cannot help noticing that these patients behave in a quite peculiar manner to us. . . . we find that the cause of the disturbance is that the patient has transferred onto the doctor intense feelings of affection which are justified neither by the doctor's behaviour nor by the situation that has developed during the treatment. . . . This . . . is known by us as *transference* . . . [and] the doctor [also] comes across . . . a hostile or *negative* transference. . . . We overcome the transference by pointing out to the patient that his feelings do not arise from the present situation and do not apply to the person of the doctor, but that they are repeating something that happened to him earlier. In this way we oblige him to transform his repetition into a memory. By that means the transference, which, whether affectionate or hostile, seemed in every case to constitute the greatest threat to the treatment, becomes its best tool, by whose help the most secret compartments of mental life can be opened.[20]

The therapist, then, becomes part of the mental life of the patient, and this often means being put under severe pressure by the patient to meet his demands to repeat a pattern of behaviour which he has previously encountered in his life, even if this involves pain or the ultimate failure of the therapy. As with the misunderstandings concerning the implications of the existence of the unconscious, even people who seem quite familiar with the idea of transference often fail to appreciate its frequent intensity and subtlety: as it is largely an unconscious process, the patient will often be aware only of resulting feelings (which may take many

[20] Ibid. 489, 490, 491, 492, 494, 495, 496.

forms: anger, love, irritation, shame, excessive gratitude) towards the therapist, and not of the fact that these feelings find their basis or origin in past relationships rather than in the actual relationship with the therapist. Likewise, the transference may be very fleeting, ambivalent, or deeply interwoven with other issues, or it may appear as an issue which is actually relevant to the communications between the therapist and the patient. Because of this, it is a very difficult (but essential) matter for therapists to avoid complicity with patients' transferences. And this view of the pressures that transference puts on the therapist begins to alter the image of the therapist as primarily an 'objective' figure. We may also begin to see emerging from the idea of 'transference' influencing the way the patient 'sees' the therapist a useful parallel with one of the ways in which the 'child' is constructed: some analysts, indeed, have noted that 'the concept is widely applied outside psychoanalysis in an attempt to understand human relationships in general'.[21] But 'transference' offers us only one aspect of the interactions between therapist and patient which, used carefully, may suggest parallel (if not identical) processes in the creation of 'adults' and 'children' in the wider context.

The therapist's attempts to avoid complicity with the patient's transferences may be seen to be complicated further by the therapist's own emotional life. This view emerges partially from attempts on the part of therapists to account for therapies which have failed because of their complicity in their patients' transferences. These accounts involve therapists admitting they may have their own feelings about what a patient tells them: they may become shocked, excited, angry, sad, or pleased. Sometimes a therapist may also find himself registering feelings towards the patient: dislike, affection, or impatience. Certain of the therapist's emotional responses to the patient are called 'counter-transferences'. Sandler *et al.*, for instance, refer to Freud's 'letter to his colleague Ferenczi, whom he had analysed, [in which] he apologized for his failure to

---

[21] Joseph Sandler, Christopher Dare, and Alex Holder, *The Patient and the Analyst: The Basis of the Psychoanalytic Process* (George Allen and Unwin, London, 1973), 37.

overcome counter-transference feelings which had interfered with Ferenczi's analysis'.[22]

It is necessary to be careful in a description of 'counter-transference', because there are, in fact, very different views on which part of a therapist's range of responses exactly constitutes a 'counter-transference'. Some of these problems also extend to the description of the patient's 'transference', but 'counter-transference' seems to constitute a particularly thorny issue because it directly concerns the position of therapists themselves. It challenges the possibility of the therapist maintaining an uninvolved, objective stance: it addresses what may be uncomfortable feelings or conflicts in the therapist himself, or types of difficulty or vulnerability with respect to the position of great responsibility he holds in the interaction with his patients. In fact, opinions on 'counter-transference' range from regarding it as a description of undesirable and mistaken (over-)involvement on the part of the therapist, to regarding it as an inevitable and helpful phenomenon which can guide the therapist. According to the latter view, (inner) responses on the part of therapists are inevitable, and important, because the therapists' own feelings are the source of their sensitivity to their patients, and their responses may provide clues to the patients' own feelings or to the responses a patient is trying to provoke in the transference. This may also include the idea that, as the analyst Heimann suggests (quoted by Sandler *et al.*), 'the analyst's unconscious understands that of his patient. This rapport on the deep level comes to the surface in the form of feelings which the analyst notices in response to his patient . . .'.[23]

In any event, when the psychotherapist does register an emotion within himself he is expected to 'catch' himself at this point, and analyse the emotion and its sources carefully, to avoid acting upon it in some unpremeditated way. Effective self-analysis on the part of the therapist, then, becomes seen as an essential prerequisite to the success of the therapy. This in turn requires that the therapist has been in analysis himself as part of his training. Utmost care is required on the part of the therapist because, for the patient, his

[22] Ibid. 62.
[23] Ibid. 65.

behaviour and reactions are of crucial importance. The therapist will act upon his emotions in different ways (within the ground rules of the therapeutic setting mainly by making or not making an interpretation) depending on whether he judges that the emotions he is registering 'belong' to the patient, or are relevant to the patient (at that point in the therapy), or are due to the pressure of a transference, or wholly 'belong' to himself. In this way the therapist is more or less continuously monitoring his own interpretative activity in listening and responding to the patient.

Transference and counter-transference, then, form two principal psychoanalytic descriptions of mechanisms which may operate in self–other interactions. With the advent of counter-transference the status of the therapist as the unfailingly 'objective' factor in the therapy is challenged. Without the therapist as the source of stability for the psychological 'truth' (or 'knowledge') in psychotherapy, the status of the whole exercise is changed: now, either the patient decides what is psychologically 'true' or it becomes a shared process between the therapist and the patient. Daniel Stern notes, for instance, that

Intersubjectivity has currently [1985] become a cardinal issue in psychotherapy, as viewed from the perspective of Self Psychology. The patient–therapist 'system' is seen either implicitly . . . or explicitly as an 'intersection of two subjectivities—that of the patient and that of the analyst . . .—[in which] . . . psychoanalysis is pictured . . . as a science of the intersubjective'.[24]

Stern adds the comment that 'seen in this light, the parent–infant "system" and the therapist–patient "system" appear to have parallels'.[25] Paradoxically, therefore, the role of self-observation on the part of the therapist is increased precisely because more weight is given to the involvement of the therapist in the narrative of the therapy. Self-reflection about this involvement on the part of the therapist becomes seen as necessary for the creation of the

[24] Stern, *The Interpersonal World of the Infant*, 219. Stern is quoting from R. D. Stolerow, B. Brandchaft, and G. E. Atwood, 'Intersubjectivity in Psychoanalytic Treatment: With Special Reference to Archaic States', *Bulletin of the Menninger Clinic*, 47/2 (Mar. 1983), 117–28, 117–18.
[25] Ibid.

maximum space for the patient: it is only when the therapist actively monitors his own 'presence' in the therapy that he can strive towards continuing to create space for the patient's 'presence'.

The degree of 'presence' on the part of therapist and patient, respectively, remains a topic of debate within psychotherapy, and much of the style of each individual therapist depends on his views on the matter. A contingent issue that we have touched on is the extent to which individual therapists believe that the narrative that develops in the therapy is purely a reflection of the objective psychological truth of the patient (which may be believed to encompass various degrees of 'historical truth', as Donald Spence calls it[26]), and the extent to which it is developed to some degree with the incorporation of the language and beliefs of the therapist. Because we have committed ourselves, in accordance with the results of our previous arguments, to the concept of constructed identities and narratives, we will continue to think about psychotherapy, too, as a narrative whose meaning is constructed by therapist and patient together. Now that we have some notion of the issues involved in the negotiation between therapist and analyst, and between theory and practice, in psychoanalysis and psychotherapy, we may turn towards the second part of this chapter: a discussion of the writings of some child psychotherapists, which aims to examine both how they all attempt to ensure they 'hear' their patients' 'voice' and how their children emerge from the texts as 'individuals' in the psychoanalytic space.

*2. On Ways of Hearing and Seeing Patients in some Cases of Child Psychotherapy*

We will be looking principally at texts by Melanie Klein, Donald Winnicott, and Virginia Axline, each of whom was a pioneer in developing aspects of (child) psychotherapeutic theory and practice (as was Anna Freud, but these three therapists form useful contrasts for our discussion). We will find in their work

[26] Spence, *Narrative Truth and Historical Truth*.

considerable overlaps with regard to psychoanalytic theories of child development (the psychoanalytic 'child'), but also a wide range of approaches with respect to therapeutic practice (the 'child' becomes the 'individual').

Before we look at their writings, we must take special note of an important factor in our discussion: when we are looking at case histories we will not be examining child therapies as such, but rather the respective therapists' final text about the therapy. This involves being at several steps' remove from the actual therapy. The reporting of psychoanalytic case histories is a notoriously complex issue (even leaving aside the thorny issue of protecting patients' privacy or anonymity), as Freud himself indicated from the time of his earliest case histories onward:

> The difficulties are very considerable when the physician has to conduct six or eight psychotherapeutic treatments of the sort in a day, and cannot make notes during the actual session with the patient for fear of shaking the patients' confidence and of disturbing his own view of the material under observation. Indeed, I have not yet succeeded in solving the problem of how to record for publication the history of a treatment of long duration.[27]

Donald Spence has studied these difficulties and their consequences in great detail,[28] and we may summarize some of the points he makes by saying, first, that the problems develop because the psychoanalytic 'conversation' disrupts any scheme of conversational rules that might operate in the world at large: free association, silences, non-verbal expressions of emotions such as crying, movement, etc. can all constitute forms of communication in therapy. Secondly, and even more importantly, it is very difficult to incorporate in a text indications of whether, and why, the analyst or patient attributes importance to particular words, silences, or interpretations. Spence suggests that

> It may be necessary to make . . . adjustments in our clinical material in order to give the outside reader the experience of the treating analyst. . . .

[27] Sigmund Freud, *Case Histories I*, trans. Alix Strachey and James Strachey (The Penguin Freud Library, 8, ed. James Strachey and Angela Richards) (Penguin, Harmondsworth, 1990), 38.
[28] Spence, *Narrative Truth and Historical Truth*.

The final arrangement must be presented to the outside reader with the critical material in just the right sequence; only the appropriate [style] will provide the proper context for each utterance. Only then will the outside reader 'hear' each utterance as did the treating analyst and only then will the reader be in a position to understand the analyst's unfolding sense of the hour. It can be argued that Freud appreciated this problem and tried to present his clinical material in a somewhat novelistic manner. But while he was often dramatic and convincing, he was also incomplete and unsystematic, and the omission of certain details cannot help but change the background context in a significant way.[29]

As Spence also points out, taking notes during the session (as Donald Winnicott did), or even having the sessions tape-recorded (as Virginia Axline did), does not solve the difficulties. Both techniques overlook the problem that (psychoanalytic) communication is not purely verbal, and they may fail to reflect the weight of meaning attributed to each communication (the explanation of why it *is* important or meaningful). Spence continues:

The importance of having the proper context as we listen to each utterance cannot be stressed too much. . . . Not only does the written transcript deprive us of tone, pacing, and stress, but it also strips away the fringe of [unverbalized] associations that surrounded each utterance at the time it was spoken and that turned it from a spoken sentence into an evocative communication. . . . What allows the treating analyst to perceive the motivational dimensions of the utterance depends on the context through which he 'hears' the utterance being expressed.[30]

In other words, patient and therapist develop a specific and private narrative between themselves during the course of the therapy.

However, Spence is concerned, in these comments, with attempts to unravel therapeutic reporting for the scientific purposes of the psychoanalytic community, and is therefore primarily concerned with finding an optimal way for these reports to convey the maximum sense of actual therapeutic mechanisms and operations. We are not concerned in the same way with the theories of psychoanalysis in their own right, and we may therefore approach this issue slightly differently. As we have allied ourselves

---

[29] Ibid. 250–1.
[30] Ibid. 252.

with the idea that the meanings of the 'child' are constructed, we have considered that the meanings of 'actual' therapies are also constructed, as are the reports of those therapies. What we do not know is what the precise connections are between the construction of the 'actual' therapy and the construction of the reports: what conclusions does the therapist's style of reporting allow us to draw about his style of therapy?

Spence, we have seen, suggests that the patterns of meaning in the therapy are regulated by a striving to allow a 'private' language increasingly to develop between therapist and patient. (This, in fact, might constitute how the patient 'becomes' most 'individual' in therapy.) The construction of reports, on the other hand, prompts adaptations to the idea of 'public' meanings. After all, reports are written with some purpose of illustration or explanation in mind. I suggest that, for our purposes, we can usefully take into account the way the therapist reflects on his own production of the narrative of the therapy, both in the actual sessions and, subsequently, in the texts. All the therapists we will be looking at provide forms of these 'annotations', and this provides us with additional insight into their own reflections on their interpretative and constructive activities: it is in the 'annotations' that we find further levels of the therapists' 'self-analysis'. I am arguing, then, that the way the therapists make their reports may indeed further reflect aspects of their therapeutic style of practice. I would also suggest that the 'space' the therapist makes for the reader in the text may reflect, or reveal, the extent to which he makes 'space' for the patient in the therapy. Whether or not we are ultimately convinced that an individual person's 'voice' can indeed be 'heard' through these multiple layers of interpretation and construction—first the therapist's listening in the actual session, then his translation of what he heard into a textual report—depends on the extent to which we are convinced that the therapist's strategies for providing space for 'voices' (both in the session and the text) succeed. Ultimately, I am arguing, it is the therapist's 'self-analysis' with regard to the creation of this space that prevents the interpretative levels from silencing the 'voice' of the patient in the same way as happens in the interpretations and observations of the 'child' presented by children's literature critics. It is the continual emphasis on, and the taking into account of, the interpretative and constructive process itself which distinguishes psychotherapy, and its texts, from children's literature criticism.

Each of the therapists we are looking at uses a theoretical version of the psychoanalytic 'child', which provides the frame through which each 'child' patient can emerge—in different ways and, perhaps, to differing extents—as an 'individual' in psychotherapeutic practice. Although I have said that there are overlaps between the various (developmental) theories used by the therapists, they, too, are part of the continuous construction of diverse candidate versions of the 'real child'. For our purposes, we are not so much concentrating on a comparison of the content of these various theoretical versions of psychoanalytic 'children', as on their 'framing' function, which helps to create a space within the therapy in which the patient can become visible to the therapist and from which his voice can be heard. In other words, I am arguing that even if we disagreed with the specific content of psychoanalytic interpretations (which are based on theories about the type of material present in the unconscious), we could still accept that this 'language' can become the bearer of meaningful and effective negotiation and communication between therapist and patient. In this sense, therapy could be accepted as being effective even if its communications and negotiations were regarded as being allegorical or metaphorical, as long as they fulfilled the patient's and the therapist's requirements for communication and interpretation.

Therefore, I am not going to explain the contents of psychoanalytic theories of development in any depth (they will to a limited extent be hinted at by the case history material), beyond drawing out two points that might be argued to be most relevant to the communicative negotiations between patient and therapist, and which may otherwise most mislead readers who do not have a close acquaintance with psychotherapy: first, each of the therapists we are looking at uses toys and drawing as additional media for relaying communications between therapist and patient. We should not take this use of toys (and drawing) as constituting an absolute distinction between 'child' and 'adult' psychotherapy: as I have already pointed out, 'adults' may use many forms of communication within the therapeutic setting (movement, silence, crying, laughing), and 'children' need not use the toys either. It may be noted, for instance, that Freud's 'Little Hans' analysis (the first example of a child analysis; Hans was 5 years of age at the time) took place solely through verbal communication (between Little Hans's father and Little Hans with Freud providing advice and support to the father) before the introduction of 'play therapy'. The toys are there for the use of the patient primarily because Melanie Klein suggested that there are often difficulties attached to asking (young) children to free associate verbally (this requires the ability to follow directions concerning the consequences of self-conscious reflection on the rules of verbal expression, and any of these factors may be a cause of difficulty). Klein further suggested that a 'child's' play displays the same connections with unconscious themes and concerns as free association in 'adults'. With respect to the use of toys it is therefore crucial that the patient should choose his toys himself, and use them as he likes, just as a verbal communication involves the patient's own choice and use of words (which may also be seen as forms of 'toy'). The 'child's' play is seen, then, as being as determined as free association: it is never useless or random or meaningless. We may, then, argue that the use of toys introduces another possible form of control of expression and communication for the patient, and in this way forms part of the patient's 'voice'.

Secondly, the language used by the therapist in making interpretations, in the cases of Melanie Klein and Donald Winnicott, is marked by psychoanalytic theories about childhood sexuality, which are central to many psychoanalytic theories of human development. Again, this should not suggest conclusions about the 'child' or 'adult': these ideas are expressed in some way both to 'children' and 'adults' in psychotherapy. And this is because for psychoanalysis, as we discussed with reference to psychoanalytic theories of memory and Jacqueline Rose's argument, past experience and emotion are forever present in the unconscious of the patient, and form the origin of (or background to) emotional difficulties or illness. Therefore, the interpretations made by therapists about unconscious material may be made in similar terms with patients of any age: explicit references to sexuality and bodily functions may occur in most therapies. Both Klein and Winnicott follow the usual practice of adopting, where possible, the patient's—'adult' or 'child'—own terms for body parts and their functions. This is not always obvious in their writings because, as we have seen, the 'private' language of therapy is vulnerable to retranslation into 'public' language for the purposes of reporting. This adoption of the patient's terms may be seen as another aspect of giving space to the patient's 'voice'. Virginia Axline's work seems an exception as regards the use of references to sexuality and bodily functions, but this is because she follows different ideas concerning the use of the interpretation of unconscious material in therapy.

The two points I have made, then, may serve to alert readers to the fact that the fundamental notion of the timeless unconscious largely breaks down the conventional division between 'child' and 'adult' in psychotherapeutic theory and practice. Any adjustments inspired by the conventional definition of the 'child' take place primarily in terms of the media of communication: they constitute extensions of the potential use in therapy of metaphor, allegory, analogy, symbol, example, and illustration. In other words, all materials and dimensions within the analytic space may be used to contribute to the therapeutic narrative.

The therapists whose work we are looking at present us with a range of therapeutic styles, and these styles, I am arguing, reflect different levels and expressions of concern for the patient's individuality and for the creation of 'space' for the patient (within the overall psychoanalytic 'space'). We will be concentrating on the work of Melanie Klein, Donald Winnicott, and Virginia Axline, with specific reference to the issue of the 'presence' of each therapist in the therapeutic text, and exploring how this may be related to their 'presence' in the actual therapeutic sessions. We will be looking at how the therapists express their views on the relation between therapeutic theory and practice in the 'annotations' they make to specific case histories: that is, their style of presentation of those case histories. With regard to this latter issue it is especially worth noting how the therapists discuss mistakes that they themselves feel they have made: this reveals much of the importance they attach to certain factors concerning their own presence.

Melanie Klein is the therapist who, of the three we are considering, appears most 'present' in her case histories. We will see how her strong 'presence' is constructed by her style of presentation of case work. Klein's focus is strongly centred on interpretation, and the themes which appear from interpretation, and this focus is reflected in her notes: she explains in her introduction to the case history *Narrative of a Child Analysis* that her report is based on 'fairly extensive notes, but I could of course not always be sure of the sequence, nor quote literally the patient's associations and my interpretations'.[31] Klein, like Sigmund Freud, believes it is detrimental to the therapy to take notes within the actual session. Nevertheless, Klein's narrative of the four-month analysis of Richard (an unusually brief analysis, due to disruption from external circumstances to do with the Second World War, which was going on at the time) reads very much as a verbatim report. She usually indicates when her notes were incomplete, explaining at one point, for instance, that 'This is an instance of the difficulty arising from the incompleteness of my notes. The record of this interpretation is misleading, for I would never have given such an interpretation without some material to base it on.'[32]

This attitude marks Klein's narrative throughout: she reports Richard's activities or remarks as the material for her to interpret. This produces a narrative which is a densely knit sequence of 'material' with its accompanying interpretations. Klein—of our three therapists the one working most closely within the model of classical psychoanalysis, with interpretation as the main technique—portrays the interpretative activity in the therapy as being of an awesome intensity. She notes this herself, for she warns that 'There were also hours in which the boy's anxiety made him silent for long periods and he produced less material. It was impossible to describe the nuances of behaviour, gesture, facial expression, and

---

[31] Melanie Klein, *Narrative of a Child Analysis* (The International Psycho-Analytical Library, 55, ed. John D. Sutherland) (The Hogarth Press and the Institute of Psycho-Analysis, London, 1961), 11.

[32] Ibid. 24.

the length of pauses between associations, all of which, as we know, are of particular significance during the analytic work.'[33] At other moments she reminds us that she has condensed several interpretations or events into one passage. Whatever the pragmatic difficulties of such reporting, however, Klein's style emphasizes her preoccupation with interpretation as the technique of effective therapy.

We should again keep in the forefront of our minds here that the aim of interpretation is not primarily to inform the patient rationally of the material in his unconscious: this on its own achieves little or nothing; interpretation achieves its effects by taking place within the dynamic operation of emotions within the therapy—such as transferences—which activate interpretations to allow for what Freud calls 'working through'. Klein describes 'working through':

The necessity to work through is again and again proved in our day-to-day experience: for instance, we see that patients, who at some stage have gained insight, repudiate this very insight in the following sessions and sometimes even seem to have forgotten that they had ever accepted it. It is only by drawing our conclusions from the material as it reappears in different contexts, and is interpreted accordingly, that we gradually help the patient to acquire insight in a more lasting way.[34]

Klein does take account of the fact that silences too may have a function or communicative value of their own. As she writes in a note to a session:

both with adults and with children the analyst has to decide, according to his grasp of the situation, which meaning to attribute to a silence. Many patients have difficulties in starting to speak, and it is, I think, advisable to give them time to overcome their difficulty. But if a silence extends . . . I think it is wrong not to try to interpret the reasons for it, which may be found in the material of the previous session. There are other silences which provide contentment, the pleasure of being with the analyst . . . which I think one should accept without interrupting them by an interpretation. . . . Richard's silence at this juncture in the session was

33 Ibid. 17.
34 Ibid. 12.

obviously a reflective one—his attempt to find out something in himself—
and I did not make any attempt to interrupt that.[35]

It is suggestive, I would argue, however, that this discussion of
silence is a note, or gloss, on a session. A passage from an early
session (the third) in the narrative of the therapy itself is an example
of how 'absent' silences otherwise are from the main narrative (and
may also serve more generally as an instance of Klein's style):

Richard was on time. He soon turned to the map and expressed his fears
about the British battleships being blockaded in the Mediterranean if
Gibraltar were taken by the Germans. They could not get through Suez.
He also spoke of injured soldiers and showed some anxiety about their fate.
He wondered how the British troops could be rescued from Greece. What
would Hitler do to the Greeks; would he enslave them? Looking at the
map, he said with concern that Portugal was a very small country
compared with big Germany, and would be overcome by Hitler. He
mentioned Norway, about whose attitude he was doubtful, though it
might not prove to be a bad ally after all. *Mrs K[lein]* interpreted that he
also worried unconsciously about what might happen to Daddy when he
put his genital into mummy. Daddy might not be able to get out of
Mummy's inside and would be caught there, like the ships in the
Mediterranean. This also applied to the troops which had to be retrieved
from Greece. She [Mrs Klein] referred to what he had said in the first
session about a person standing on his head and dying because his blood
flowed down. This is what he thought might happen to Daddy when at
night he put his genital into Mummy. He was also afraid that Mummy
would be hurt by the tramp-Daddy. Thus he felt anxious about *both*
parents and guilty because of his aggressive wishes against them. His dog
Bobby stood for himself wanting to take his father's place with Mummy
(the armchair standing for the bed), and whenever he felt jealous and
angry, he hated and attacked Daddy in his thoughts . . . This made him
also feel sorry and guilty [Klein's annotation: 'Oedipus situation'].
Richard smiled agreement at Mrs. K's saying that the dog stood for
himself, but disagreed emphatically with the other part of the interpretation, because he would never *do* such a thing. *Mrs K.* explained that the
feeling that he would not really carry out such an attack was a great relief to
him, but pointed out that he might have felt that hostile wishes could be so
powerful that if he wished Daddy to die, he would actually die [Klein's

[35] Ibid. 234–5.

annotation: 'Omnipotence of thought']. (At this point Richard appeared to agree.)[36]

This passage shows how Klein interprets the unconscious content of Richard's comments, tells him about this, and then continues by interpreting his response to the interpretation, and so on. Klein does not 'let up' interpreting because it is her belief that it is this very process of constantly translating conscious material into its unconscious content that underpins the effectiveness of psychoanalysis, by leading to working through and insight. Therefore, everything is material for interpretation, including the agreement or disagreement ('resistance') with interpretations. In connection with this, the passage reveals another important characteristic of Klein's reporting style: Richard's agreement or disagreement with her interpretations are mainly reported not in terms of direct descriptions of his ensuing behaviour or comments, but in terms of her conclusions about whether or not he agreed or disagreed. In this way the reader of the case history is seldom told *how* Richard responded. This is an example, I would like to suggest, of Klein's presence creating a problem for the reader: the reader is forced to accept her perceptions of Richard's responses as correct in order to follow the narrative, and is therefore also encouraged to 'believe' in the correctness of her interpretations and allow a seamless continuation of the narrative.

In other words, it may be that Klein's dense, seamless narrative limits the reader's attempts to make their own decisions about her representation of Richard. The narrative is, in this sense, closed to the reader (or leaves little space for the reader) because of the strength of Klein's presence. Klein herself says of her reporting of Richard's responses to her interpretations—again in a note to a session—that

In the course of this report I indicate at various places Richard's reply to my interpretations: sometimes these replies were negative, even expressing strong objection; sometimes they expressed a definite agreement; and sometimes his attention wandered and he did not appear to hear me. Even when his attention wandered, however, it would be wrong to assume that

[36] Ibid. 27–8.

he did not respond at all. But often I did not or could not record the fleeting effect the interpretation made on him. He might get up, pick up a toy or a pencil or pad. He might interject something which was a further association or a doubt. Therefore my interpretations may frequently appear more lengthy and consecutive than they in fact were.[37]

The question now arises of whether Richard's 'voice' in the therapy is given too little space by Klein in the same way that the reader is given little space in the text. This is not to say that we can draw an easy conclusion that Klein simply 'convinced' Richard of the correctness of interpretations which were in fact incorrect or irrelevant. Freud's argument concerning the difference between convincing a patient of an intellectual dogma and affecting his emotional state may be considered here. And indeed every patient has the ultimate right to veto a therapy by walking out (whether literally or figuratively) and not returning. But there are legitimate questions about whether the therapy's efficacy or fruitfulness may be affected by Klein's approach. We may, for instance, note in the following example that Richard is sometimes reported as expressing discomfort at the apparent intensity of interpretation:

Mrs K. suggested, therefore, that the 'wicked brute' was meant to be Daddy, but it was also meant to be Mummy and Mrs K. Richard strongly objected. He would not call Mrs K. or Mummy such names, for he loved them both. *Mrs K.* interpreted the strength of his conflict when he felt he hated Mummy who was the person he loved most. . . . Richard said, with evident pain, 'Don't say this, it makes me unhappy!' *Mrs K.* interpreted that because her interpretations were often painful, he felt that she was a 'brute'.[38]

Analytically speaking, Richard's pain is a sign of resistance, and therefore an indication that an important area of conflict has been touched on. The issue here is what the best response is to this situation: something important is around, which must be dealt with at some point, in some way, but how and when? Klein's way of helping Richard to come to terms with his resistance and distress is further interpretation. As she writes:

During this session I had given interpretations of a number of anxiety

---

[37] Ibid. 23.        [38] Ibid. 109.

contents. Doubts have often been expressed whether a child—and for that matter an adult—can understand such apparently complicated interpretations. My experience has shown me that there are occasions, not at all infrequent, in which it is essential to bring together in the interpretation several anxiety contents in order to deal with the accumulated anxiety operative at the time. . . . By the end of [this] session [Richard's] anxiety was clearly relieved.[39]

In the session after Richard expresses unhappiness with the interpretations, he asks Klein: 'Do I really think this of all of you? I don't know if I do. How can you really know what I think?'[40] Klein replies 'that from his play, drawings, and what he was saying and doing she gathered some of his unconscious thoughts; but he had just expressed his doubts whether she was right and could be trusted.'[41] In this exchange it is confirmed to Richard that Klein has a privileged knowledge of him, and that her work with him relies on his trusting her 'rightness': where Klein leads, Richard can follow. Klein portrays herself as therapist as a figure of strong presence who 'feeds' her patients what is ultimately the 'good food' of interpretation. Even if the patients initially experience her interpretations as invasive, or as 'bad things' being forced into them, Klein believes further interpretation overcomes these resistances. In a note to a session Klein writes that

I have found with children and adults that gratification about experiencing and recognizing one part of the mind, which until then had been unknown, seems to be both of an intellectual and an emotional nature. . . . Fundamentally, the fact that the analysis has conveyed something to the patient which he feels is helpful and an enrichment revives the earliest experience of being loved and fed.[42]

We can see again in another case history how much Klein believes in the role of interpretation as her primary means of achieving therapeutic effect, when she discusses what she felt to be a mistake in working with her patient Egon. Egon is described as a severely inhibited person, with problems with speaking and a highly apathetic and unspontaneous attitude towards the therapy.

---

[39] Ibid. 171.     [41] Ibid.
[40] Ibid. 111.     [42] Ibid. 243.

Klein discusses her struggle in achieving some progress with Egon:

For several weeks I got Egon to lie on the couch (which he did not refuse to do and apparently preferred to playing games) and tried in various other ways to set the treatment going, till I was forced to recognize that my attempts along these lines were hopeless. . . . the child's difficulty in speaking was so deeply rooted that my first task must be to overcome it analytically. . . . In order to get away from the role of the prying father, against whom his defiance was directed, I played with him for weeks in silence and made no interpretations, simply trying to establish rapport by playing with him. During [several weeks] the details of the game remained absolutely the same . . .[43]

But in a footnote, she criticizes herself for choosing this approach:

Further analysis showed that it had been quite pointless to withhold interpretation of the material for so long. Only after fifteen months, shortly before the termination of the analysis was the inhibition in speech overcome. I have never yet in any analysis seen any advantage follow from such a policy of non-interpretation. In most cases in which I have tried the plan I have very soon had to abandon it because acute anxiety has developed and there has been a risk of the analysis being broken off. In Egon's case, where the anxiety was under such powerful restraint, it was possible to continue the experiment longer.[44]

If Klein has shown us that interpretation is her way of establishing and maintaining a working relationship with her patients, her therapeutic style as we have traced it in her textual representation is not one that all therapists are comfortable with. Although Richard is shown as able to cope with her intensity of interpretation, there are patients who do not respond well to this approach: they may, for instance, leave the therapy, experience feelings of persecution, or even break down. Also, some patients may be preoccupied with being 'good', and they may become compliant with the interpretations for this reason. It is then for the

[43] Melanie Klein, *The Psycho-Analysis of Children*, trans. Alix Strachey, rev. Alix Strachey and H. A. Thorner (vol. ii of *The Writings of Melanie Klein*, The International Psycho-Analytical Library, 22, ed. M. Masud R. Khan) (The Hogarth Press and the Institute of Psycho-Analysis, 1975, rev. edn; original edn. pub. 1932), 68–9.

[44] Ibid. 69.

therapist to perceive the difference between compliance and acceptance of an interpretation as actually meaningful. If this is overlooked, compliance creates a 'false' patient, who is not—or is only partly—able to communicate with the therapist and be affected by the therapy.

If Klein's approach is characterized by a preoccupation with interpretation itself, Donald Winnicott may be described as being more concerned with the timing of interpretation. Winnicott's interest in timing is the consequence of his concern to provide space for, and the possibility of growth in, the patient. He argues that, in order for the interpretation to be helpful to the patient, it needs not to be imposed, but to correspond as much as possible to a state of readiness in the patient to receive the interpretation. According to this view, a therapist who constantly feeds his patient interpretations may be 'force-feeding' the patient. We have seen this articulated in the first section of this chapter, in the quote in which Winnicott argues that, if the patient is not ready for the interpretation, then he has no choice but to accept it 'as propaganda' or reject the therapist and the therapy. Elsewhere he remarks that 'interpretation outside the ripeness of the material is indoctrination and produces compliance',[45] and he addresses the danger of therapists being, in this sense, 'too clever': 'The patient's creativity can be only too easily stolen by a therapist who knows too much.'[46] He also argues, as we saw Patrick Casement do in section 1 of this chapter, that these therapists may be more motivated by their own needs than by the patients' needs. This is, indeed, analogous to my description of children's literature critics, and people working in a highly emotive field such as child abuse and neglect, whose feelings of excitement, anger, or fear may interfere with their ability to register most helpfully, and therefore to attend first and foremost to, the needs of the victims. Both these fields suffer from a lack of consideration of the great difficulties and subtleties involved in negotiating with another individual's emotions and experiences. Yet these difficulties emerge from the

[45] Donald W. Winnicott, *Playing and Reality* (Tavistock Publications, London, 1971), 51.
[46] Ibid. 57.

problematic results of much therapists' work, and also from some interventions in cases of child abuse and neglect.

If Klein, then, as the source of interpretation, is strongly present in her text, while her patient is reported obliquely 'through' her perceptions, Winnicott is present in a less outspoken way, and his patients' responses and activities are presented as direct portrayals. His reports are presented in a more 'open', less dense style than those of Klein; his case histories are often more difficult to follow, because of a diffuse, associative style which often does not provide us with the explanations necessary for creating a seamless, closely knit narrative. The reader needs to 'fill in' the gaps in explanation, and sometimes to supply his own ideas about why Winnicott made certain decisions or interpretations. In this way, the drive to knowledge emerges much more strongly from the work of Klein than from that of Winnicott.

The differences between Klein's and Winnicott's approaches and styles are evident in Winnicott's presentation of the case history *The Piggle* (the pet-name of a girl, Gabrielle):

I have added comments [to the letters of Piggle's parents and to the clinical notes], but not enough—it is hoped—to prevent the reader from developing a personal view of the material and its evolution. . . . In this particular analysis, because of the fact that the child lived a considerable distance from London, the treatment was done 'on demand' . . . On each occasion the analyst had a sense of being informed by the child of a specific problem, although there were many areas of indeterminate play or behaviour or conversation in which there seemed to be no orientation. These phases of indeterminate play were evidently an important feature in that out of the chaos a sense of direction developed and the child became able to communicate out of a sense of real need, a need that had prompted her to ask for another session. I have purposely left the vague material vague, *as it was for me at the time when I was taking notes.*[47]

A passage from the fourth session in *The Piggle* is a further example of the difference between Winnicott's style and Klein's:

Piggle took boats of various colors, and she said the white one was pink.

[47] Donald W. Winnicott, *The Piggle*, ed. Ishak Ramzy (The International Psycho-Analytical Library, 107, ed. M. Masud R. Khan) (The Hogarth Press and the Institute of Psycho-Analysis, London, 1978), 1, 3–4 (my emphasis).

She tried to make the boats stand up upside down, which was impossible (indeterminate play). I said somewhere here: 'Why do you like me?' And she said 'Because you tell me about the babacar [a figure from Piggle's fantasy that frightened her very much].' I had a conversation with her about this because I had said the word wrong, and it was clear that I had not understood properly. I wanted her to help to sort out things in my own mind. *Piggle:* [']There is the black mummy.['] We tried to work out something about whether the black mummy was cross or not. She was making a car go to-and-fro. There was something here that I reintroduced, something to do with mummy being angry with Gabrielle because Gabrielle was angry with mummy for having a new baby. And then mummy seemed to be black. All this was rather vague. She was playing on her own with the toys, *allotting various cars to me or to herself* [Winnicott's gloss on this: '*first sign of the me–not-me theme*']. *Piggle:* [']My shoes are too small; I'll take them off.['] I helped a little. There was something about feet growing. *Piggle:* [']I am growing into a big big girl (and she went on:) pi pi pi (etc., talking to herself). There's a pretty lady waiting for the car, a nice lady to come for the children. The black mummy is naughty.['] [Winnicott's gloss on this: '*Manifestation of anxiety probably due to oedipal fears*'.][48]

We see in this passage, as in all of Winnicott's writing, mentions of vagueness, doubt, and waiting, as companions to the sense of growth, development, and readiness. Note, for example, his reference to his waiting for Piggle to 'help [him] to sort out things in [his] own mind'. The case history is 'opened up' to the reader by Winnicott's refusal to represent as clear and fixed in the text what, at the time, appeared to him to be unclear or unfixed. This applies not just to his perceptions of some of Piggle's play as 'indeterminate', but also to his use of words such as 'somewhere' and 'something', which indicate the unclearness and unfixedness of his perceptions at that point of the session. Winnicott in this way reveals his own states of 'not knowing' during the therapy (the same 'not knowing' that we touched on in section 1 of this chapter).

There are more explicit ways in which Winnicott addresses this issue of 'not knowing' in the therapeutic context: in a note to the third session in *The Piggle*, he writes of the 'Importance of my not

[48] Ibid. 57–8.

*understanding* what she [Piggle] had not yet been able to give me clues for. Only she knew the answers, and when she could encompass the meaning of the fears she would make it possible for me to understand too.'[49] Another example occurs when, in the fifth session, Winnicott notes that 'all this was vague and not clearly articulated. *I let this be so.*'[50]

The contrast with Klein's style is reflected too in Winnicott's comments in *Therapeutic Consultations in Child Psychiatry*, although it should be noted that this work discusses short-term consultations, and not psychotherapies. Nevertheless, the same themes are clearly present:

> *It should be noted that in this work I do not usually make interpretations, but I wait until the essential feature of the child's communication has been revealed. Then I talk about the essential feature, but the important thing is not my talking so much as the fact that the child has reached something.*[51]

Winnicott also argues, crucially, that 'interpretation is not in itself therapeutic, but it facilitates that which is therapeutic, namely, the child's reliving of frightening experiences. With the therapist's ego support the child becomes able for the first time to assimilate these key experiences into the whole personality.'[52] This latter comment perfectly articulates the differences in emphasis between Klein and Winnicott.

Winnicott repeatedly attempts to 'follow' rather than to 'lead' the patient: 'I must be adapted to the child's needs and not requiring the child to adapt to my own';[53] and 'My hope is that by now the reader will have got the feeling that, in spite of my freedom in the use of myself, the structuring of the interview truly comes from the patient.'[54] The regular inclusion of self-critical comments in the reports is another way in which he reveals his striving to follow the patient: with reference to factors influencing his own attitude, for instance, he notes at one point that 'An analyst in supervision with

---

[49] Ibid. 48.
[50] Ibid. 70.
[51] Winnicott, *Therapeutic Consultations in Child Psychiatry*, 69 (author's italics).
[52] Ibid. 214.
[53] Ibid. 224.
[54] Ibid. 334.

me had asked for a . . . child [to treat] at just this time, and I thought of referring Gabrielle to him. This warped me, made me feel guilty, and so I became muddled when I raised the issue with her father.'[55] In the fifth session, Winnicott writes also that 'my notes are relatively obscure because of the heat and my sleepiness'.[56] Similarly, in the ninth session, he writes that 'here I made a definite note that I had been sleepy, but I have no doubt whatever I would have come awake if something had been going on'.[57]

Winnicott, unlike Klein, clearly argues that interpretative activity on the part of the therapist does not consist in interpreting at every moment one correct meaning:

[Gabrielle] was still joining up bits of trains and I said: 'You could be joining up all the different times that you have seen me.' Her reply: 'Yes.' Obviously, there are many interpretations to do with the joining of parts of trains, and one can use this according to the way one feels is most appropriate at the moment, or to convey one's own feelings.[58]

The importance for Winnicott of timing (making an interpretation at the right moment) can again be felt when he remarks that he is making a 'risky' interpretation,[59] or when he remarks in a footnote to an interpretation that 'I think this was wrong; I should have waited for developments.'[60] He sums up this view, finally, when he argues that 'It is not possible for a child of this age to get the meaning out of a game unless first of all the game is *played and enjoyed*. As a matter of principle, the analyst always allows the enjoyment to become established before the content of the play is used for interpretation.'[61]

If Klein writes the therapy as a closed, coherent, seamless narrative—well-knit sequences of reported communication and interpretation—and Winnicott writes the therapy as an open, diffuse, associative account, Virginia Axline, finally, writes the therapy as a closed narrative strongly structured and controlled by her belief that she can allow her patient Dibs to be autonomous and free. We should not be surprised by the apparently paradoxical

[55] Winnicott, *The Piggle*, 73.
[56] Ibid. 67.
[57] Ibid. 115.
[58] Ibid. 77–8.
[59] Ibid. 24, 60.
[60] Ibid. 167.
[61] Ibid. 175.

nature of this statement, for, as we will see, Axline is in a similarly problematic position to the one we are familiar with from children's literature criticism: we have seen children's literature criticism stumble on the conflicts caused by the claim that the 'child' can be known as an autonomous 'reality', and by the accompanying contradictions within the liberal humanist ideal of teaching freedom, and we will see that Axline is caught—again without being aware of it—in exactly the same realm of conflict. Axline believes she can 'hear' and 'see' her patient Dibs correctly without construction or interpretation (in its specific psychoanalytic sense as well as in its wider sense): she believes she can perceive and therefore 'reflect' an autonomous self-constituted 'other', thereby allocating much less complexity to self–other negotiations than do Klein, Winnicott, and the therapists we looked at in section 1. Axline reports herself as echoing her patient Dibs's *conscious* language: she presents herself as being able almost purely to reflect what he says, rather than interpreting (translating) it. Axline hopes in this way to avoid any imposition on Dibs of her 'language' or meanings, and so to minimize her 'presence' in the therapeutic space. She argues that her reflective strategy will give Dibs a sense of safety and of being understood, while wholly prioritizing his language and meanings in their own terms. Yet a passage from Axline's case history of Dibs, as we will see, shows how she does not—and cannot—merely echo Dibs's play and language: to begin with, it is obvious that she by no means simply echoes anything and everything Dibs says. More importantly, the evident selection is only one aspect of what we have argued throughout this book, namely that there is no such thing as pure perception/reflection which avoids the creative and constructive activities involved in the communication of emotional meaning. Axline's case history inadvertently endorses our argument by being as 'closed' in its way as that of Klein: the narrative is strongly structured by Axline's views on Dibs, by the motives she provides for her interventions, and by her explanations of her intentions for Dibs.

Axline's theoretical attitude, however, differs more from the ideas of Klein and Winnicott than theirs do from each other. Klein and Winnicott both base themselves on Freud's theory and practice of psychoanalysis, while Axline was a follower of the therapist Carl Rogers, who developed a form of therapy which he named 'non-directive' therapy. (Axline's is not, therefore, a form of *psychoanalytic* psychotherapy.) Rogerian therapy is not necessarily incompatible with the Freudian explanation of the dynamics of the human psyche, but it concentrates on an extensive creed of individuality, liberty, and, particularly, self-determination, which it translates into a specific therapeutic approach. This approach focuses on the dynamics of *conscious* meaning and communication, although it allows for the idea that unconscious mechanisms may lie beneath these conscious operations. Axline describes this stance as follows: 'Non-directive counseling is really more than a technique. It is a basic philosophy of human capacities which stresses the ability within the individual to be self-directive. . . . It is a real belief in the integrity of the individual.'[62] It will be noted that this comment implies a critique of Freudian psychoanalysis as limiting the self-directiveness of the patient, and his integrity as an individual.

The resulting difference of therapeutic strategy centres on the acknowledgement or denial of the role of interpretation in therapy. While Klein and Winnicott are forced to introduce and consider interpretation because they wish to address the unconscious meanings that they believe to be present in disguised form in the therapeutic space, Axline, because she does not use unconscious meaning, can maintain that she does not make interpretations:

The type of therapy which we are describing is based upon a positive theory of the individual's ability. It is not limiting to any individual's growth. It is outgoing. It starts where the individual *is* and lets that individual go as far as he is able to go. . . . That is why interpretation is ruled out as far as it is possible to do so. What has happened in the past is past history. Since the dynamics of life are constantly changing the relativity of things, past experience is colored by the interactions of life and is constantly changing. Anything that attempts to shackle the individual's growth is a blocking experience. Taking the therapy back into the individual's past history rules out the possibility that he has grown in the meantime and consequently the past no longer has the same significance

[62] Virginia Axline, *Play Therapy* (Churchill Livingston, Edinburgh, 1989 (originally pub. 1947)), 24–5.

that it formerly had. Probing questions are also ruled out for this same reason.[63]

It is clear that Axline is here presenting her own particular view of the psychotherapeutic approaches that she criticizes. However, we have already seen in the first section of this chapter that many psychoanalytic psychotherapists would not agree that, for instance, the use of past history aims to retrieve unchanged historical material for its own sake. Many would question whether this is even an achievable aim. The very changeability of memory, in their view, may illuminate shifts of significance in the therapy: the past is constituted (or (re)constructed) in the present of the therapy (again, this a consequence of the idea of a timeless unconscious). The key point is that Axline's description of her therapeutic stance reveals her essentialist, 'objective' attitude that it is possible to minimize the general processes of interpretation, creation, and construction within the therapeutic space.

What therapeutic technique (or style) results from Axline's theoretical views? Here is a passage from her case history *Dibs: In Search of Self. Personality Development in Play Therapy*, which we can compare with the passages from Klein and Winnicott quoted earlier:

He [Dibs] walked over to the sandbox and stared into the flattened sand and the mixed figures lying around in it. 'Where's my little duck?' he asked. 'You are wondering what happened to the little duck that you left on the top of the mound of sand?' I asked. He turned quickly and looked directly at me. 'That's right,' he said, angrily. 'Where is my little duck?' 'You said you wanted it left there and someone has moved it,' I replied, trying to recapitulate the situation, slowing down his reactions by my responses so that he could more accurately identify his thoughts and feelings. He walked up close to me and looked me straight in the eye. 'That's right,' he said, emphatically. 'Why?' 'You wonder why I didn't see to it that they remained in the same places where you had left them,' I commented. 'Yes,' he said '*Why?*' 'Why do you think I let that happen?' I asked him. 'I don't know,' he said. 'It makes me angry. You should have done it!' Now it was my turn to ask the questions. 'Why should I have done it?' I asked. 'Did I promise you that I would?' He looked down at the floor. 'No,' he replied, his voice dropping almost to a whisper. 'But you wanted me to do it?' 'Yes,' he whispered. 'I wanted you to do it just for me.' 'Other children come in here and play with these things,' I said. 'Some one of them probably moved your duck.' 'And my mountain,' he said. 'My little duck was standing on the top of my mountain.' 'I know,' I said. 'And now your sand mountain is not in there, either, is it?' 'It is gone,' he said. 'And you feel angry and disappointed because of it, don't you?' I asked. Dibs nodded in agreement. He looked at me. I looked at him. What would ultimately help Dibs the most was not the sand mountain, not the powerful, little plastic duck, but the feeling of security and adequacy that they symbolized in the creation he had built last week. Now, faced with the disappearance of the concrete symbols, I hoped he could experience within himself confidence and adequacy as he coped now with his disappointment and with the realization that things outside ourselves change—and many times we have little control over those elements, but if we learn to utilize our inner resources, we carry our security around with us.[64]

This passage illustrates how Axline—unlike Klein and Winnicott—attempts not to engage in a psychoanalytic 'translation' of conscious material into unconscious meaning, and yet it is clear she cannot avoid doing so, despite her own intentions: we may note, for instance, that her comment to Dibs that he 'feel[s] angry and disappointed' because of the removal of the sand mountain constitutes an interpretation. We can also see in this passage how Axline particularly attempts to avoid overtly interpreting (or translating) Dibs's feelings towards her in terms of transference. Crucially (for our purposes), Axline's most explicit statement on the difference between her (and Rogers's) approach and that of Freud centres on her particular understanding of Freudian transference:

Any attitude on the part of the therapist which creates dependence has the same result of creating a fresh maladjustment which in time must also be solved. Probably the most essential differences between therapy with Freudian leanings and non-directive therapy rest on this point. The Freudian view is that considerable dependence and much emotional

[64] Virginia Axline, *Dibs: In Search of Self. Personality Development in Play Therapy* (Penguin, Harmondsworth, 1964), 59–61.

involvement (transference) is a necessary condition of therapy, though this problem of transference must be solved before therapy is complete. Non-directive therapy maintains that such emotional dependence, whether brought on by supportive activities on the part of the therapists or by the taking of responsibility for the client, is a hindrance to them, and that improvement takes place much more rapidly, if, throughout the process, the client's need for dependence is handled in the same fashion as are all his other needs and attitudes, namely, through assisting him to be conscious of these emotionalized attitudes.[65]

This statement (which we need not assume to be an accurate presentation of Freud's views ) conflates various assumptions about the communication of emotional meaning: it presupposes that the patient can, and should, be kept separate from the therapist, and that the therapist can in fact consciously avoid any participation in the creation or interpretation of the therapeutic narrative. This view therefore implicitly takes for granted an extensive control, on the part of the therapist, of the patients' emotions and responses: the non-directive therapist believes she can maintain the patient as an isolated, autonomous individual who is responsible for himself within the therapeutic space.

In other words, Axline reveals here that she believes that the therapist and patient are separate, self-constituted individuals working within a conscious, and therefore consciously controllable, relationship. She assumes, as children's literature critics do, that communication between therapist and patient (or, indeed, adult and child) is self-evident to the extent that the therapists (or critics) need to control this communication. Axline's self-critical anno-tation ('self-analysis') is therefore minimal: she never explores unconscious counter-transference in herself, as Winnicott and Klein do, and only comments on her own adherence to her conscious 'therapeutic rules'. Unlike Winnicott particularly, she does not use the idea that therapists can have unconscious responses—which may influence or, indeed, constitute their perceptions or reactions—to account for the problematic nature of the communication of emotional meaning. We see this concentra-tion on, and faith in, the autonomy and self-constitutedness of both

[65] Axline, *Play Therapy*, 343.

therapist and patient expressed in Axline's description of the ideal therapist:

The therapist's role, though non-directive, is not a passive one, but one which requires alertness, sensitivity, and an ever-present appreciation of what the child is doing and saying. It calls for understanding and a genuine interest in the child. . . . [the therapist] treats [the child] with sincerity and honesty. There is nothing brittle or sugary-sweet about her manner when dealing with him. She is straightforward and feels at ease in his presence. . . . The therapist cannot assume these attitudes. They must be an integral part of her personality. . . . While the non-directive therapist's role seems to be one of passivity, that is far from the actuality. There is no severer discipline than to maintain the completely accepting attitude and to refrain at all times from injecting any directive suggestions or insinuations into the play of the child. . . . The atmosphere must be neutral. . . . An emotional involvement is usually forestalled if she [the therapist] has assimilated the basic principles and attitudes, and is sure in her own mind . . . what she will do if the child should behave in some unpredictable manner (which happens often). . . . The therapist should try to see things through the child's eyes, should try to develop a feeling of empathy with the child.[66]

Axline's statement implies considerable faith in therapists' rational (conscious) control over their own attitudes and responses within the therapy. She reflects the faith of children's literature critics in the ability of 'good' professionals who deal with children to find and implement a 'good' or 'correct' attitude or response towards the 'child'. We may also note how much Axline's language echoes that of children's literature critics: she describes for us what the therapist (and critic) should 'look like', but we are back with all the old, central questions, such as: what does it mean to 'try to see things through the child's eyes'? And how does one actually do it? This faith in the possibility and relative simplicity of the maintenance of separation between therapist and patient is illustrated also by Axline's discussion of a 'mistake' she makes with her patient in her case history. When Dibs unexpectedly puts scouring powder into his mouth, Axline writes:

'Oh no, Dibs!' I exclaimed. 'That's scouring powder. Not good to taste!'

[66] Ibid. 58, 59, 60, 61, 90, 121.

He turned and looked at me coldly. This sudden reaction of mine was inconsistent. . . . 'Why don't you rinse your mouth out with some water?' I suggested. He did. But my reaction had disturbed him. He . . . gave me a cold look. 'I'm sorry, Dibs,' I said. 'I guess I just didn't think. But I didn't like to see you take such a big mouthful of scouring powder.' He bit his lip . . . His sensitive armour was ready to be put on quickly when his feelings were hurt. . . . [Dibs then drops bottles with water] 'They might break and cut!' he cried. 'Are you afraid for me?' 'I think you know how to take care of it,' I said, having learned my lesson.[67]

Axline's faith in the autonomous existence of both therapist and patient, and therefore in conscious-based communication, forms for her the basis of therapeutic interaction. It is reflected too in her writing about her therapies. Axline worked as part of a team who were studying child development, and for this purpose the therapies she carried out were observed by the team through a one-way mirror, and tape-recorded. She therefore claims of her writing of Dibs's case history that

This book was written around those recorded sessions. The records have been edited to disguise all identifying information, to remove false starts, and some repetitious remarks, to facilitate a smoother report. The dialogue between Dibs and his therapist is essentially verbatim in sessions held in the Child Guidance Centre. . . . However, no words were used that were not originally those of Dibs . . .[68]

Axline, then, uses the idea of tape-recording as a reassurance that the 'real' words—and therefore, by implication, the 'real' meanings—of Dibs and herself as therapist are preserved for the reader: she is claiming that both she and Dibs are 'real', or 'exist' in the therapy as autonomous individuals with separable autonomous narratives. We may recall here, in contrast, Donald Spence's argument concerning the limitations of tape-recordings, and we may also notice that Axline reports on and describes Dibs's physical attitudes and activities throughout, as well as including extensive further annotations. It may be important, therefore, to regard her comments about the tape-recordings not as 'proof' of accuracy, but

[67] Axline, *Dibs: In Search of Self*, 127–8.
[68] Ibid. 197–8.

as an additional expression of her concern to confirm her view that she is indeed able to maintain the patient's autonomous existence.

A clash between the claim to grant the patient complete freedom and the simultaneous restriction of the patient's freedom in his attitudes towards, and uses of, the therapist becomes clearly visible at points of explanation and intention in Axline's case history of Dibs. This clash is the result—as in children's literature criticism—of a lack of acknowledgement of the construction of the 'patient' ('child'), and an attendant lack of attention to the complexity of the problem of creating freedom for the patient. It may be confusing that Axline and Winnicott ostensibly share a strong concern with giving the patient space, and with 'following the patient'. Axline, for instance, writes—in the very same words as Winnicott—that 'it is important that the therapist does not get ahead of the child . . . the child leads the way. The therapist follows.'[69] But their respective understandings of what actually constitutes 'following the patient' are quite different, and so, therefore, are the strategies they describe themselves as employing to achieve their aim. Axline is convinced that patients need to aim for her conscious versions of freedom and individuality, while Winnicott tries to allow patients to discover (usually from the unconscious) what they are coming to him for in the first place; Winnicott strives not to determine his patients' therapeutic aims at all (he strives to learn what they in fact may be), while Axline predetermines her patients' needs as being the achievement of what she sees as self-determination and freedom of thought, feeling, and action. In other words, Winnicott works with the idea of the therapy as the shared construction of therapist and patient, within which the therapist makes it possible for therapist and patient to create each other for the needs of the patient; Axline, on the other hand, denies constructive activity of this sort and assumes that her therapist and patient maintain an 'objective', separate existence, with the therapist isolating and prioritizing the autonomous existence of the patient. This complex—and, in the abstract, apparently subtle—difference of emphasis is expressed in a very

[69] Axline, *Play Therapy*, 91, 114.

pronounced way in the respective case histories, as we have seen. Axline is in theory preoccupied with her patients' independence and self-determination, yet she includes in her narrative extensive explanations of her intentions for Dibs and of the way in which her interventions are motivated by conscious aims and goals of her own. The passage quoted above from Dibs's case history is a case in point: 'I hoped that he could experience within himself confidence and adequacy as he coped now with his disappointment and with the realization that things outside ourselves change—and many times we have little control over those elements.'

The incompatibility between Axline's theoretical statements and her closed, controlled narrative force us to consider—as Axline significantly does not—that reflection cannot ever simply be the 'reflection' of pure perception: it is, in fact, a form of interpretation or construction. Axline believes that 'reflection' consists in preserving Dibs's language because she is then ostensibly not changing it or offering him terms other than his own. She believes that as a therapist she can in this way maintain a minimal 'presence' in the patients' therapeutic narrative (or even keep herself wholly separate from it), by preserving herself 'behind' and through 'reflection' as a stable, consistently sympathetic and understanding, figure. Axline does address the problems of reflection indirectly in some of her discussions of sessions. In these comments, she implicitly reveals her (unconscious) awareness of the processes of construction which are involved in her 'reflection': she writes, for instance, of her work with her patient Tom that

in this instance, [I] did not interrupt to reflect back to Tom any feelings that he expressed [in a puppet play]. It seemed he had chosen the medium that would give him the most protection. He was giving a play. He was out of sight. The feelings were flowing freely. It was a legitimate outlet for his remarks. For [me] to interrupt at such a time would have been an invasion of his isolation. Out of respect for his ability to run this by himself, [my] remarks were not intruded.[70]

But she never addresses further the difficulty of the reflecting therapist's involvement in the construction of meanings within the

[70] Ibid. 46.

therapeutic space. The result is that she is forced to claim that she is purely creating space for her patients to be themselves in their own terms, while simultaneously explaining her interventions in terms of her intentions for the patients. In this way—despite her overt preoccupation with freedom, self-determination, and individuality—she presents us with narratives which derive coherence and direction from *Axline's* intentions. Her faith in a level of self-evident self–other existence, separation, perception, and communication in fact leads—as in children's literature criticism—to an *increase* in her control of the narrative of the therapy. Where Winnicott portrays himself as making it possible for Gabrielle to bring to him the communication she needed to bring (whatever it was) and therefore writes an unpredictable and undirected narrative (the reader is made to wait with Winnicott to see what Gabrielle will bring to the therapy from session to session and within each session), Dibs's 'voice' is encompassed by Axline's concern to teach him how to operate best in her terms.

Again—as with Klein's treatment of Richard—despite the contradictions concerning Axline's 'presence', it is not easy to draw conclusions about the effectiveness of the therapy. Axline describes the following coincidental meeting with Dibs two and a half years after the therapy ended:

'. . . I [Dibs] remember how you played with me.' 'What did we play, Dibs?' Dibs leaned toward me. His eyes were shining. 'Everything I did, you did,' he whispered. 'Everything I said, you said.'[71]

Perhaps Dibs was able to make maximal use of the technique used by Axline (as Richard seemed able to cope with Klein's interpretations), and perhaps this in itself made his a suitable case history to use as an illustration of the success of the technique.

Axline, then, is, in theory, as powerfully preoccupied with freedom and self-determination for the patient as most children's literature critics are; she develops explicit therapeutic 'rules' which are designed to develop and uphold the patient's individuality and autonomy ('otherness') within the therapeutic space, just as the critics attempt to do for children's literature criticism. This in itself,

[71] Axline, *Dibs: In Search of Self*, 190.

paradoxically, closes Axline's therapeutic narrative to the reader, just as it limits the therapeutic space for the patient—it is the paradox of the literary pluralist critic who cannot escape a prescriptive stance which 'knows' the 'child'. Where Winnicott writes of patients making use of him in different ways, Axline predetermines her role as therapist as much as Klein does. She implicitly expresses the paradox of her position (and that of children's literature critics) when she writes:

Since the element of complete acceptance of the child seems to be of such vital importance, it is worth a more penetrating study. Acceptance of what? The answer seems to be that it is acceptance of the child and a firm belief that the child is capable of self-determination. It seems to be a respect for the child's ability to be a thinking, independent, constructive human being.[72]

Axline wants her patient to 'exist' unconstructed, but the status of that existence is prescribed by her—as it always is in children's literature criticism: it is an existence as an autonomous, self-constituted individual.

I hope I have been able to convey some inkling of three dedicated therapists' struggles with emotional meanings and communications. To differing extents each discerns problems with dealing with these meanings and communications, and formulates solutions to these difficulties. I would like, finally, to suggest a conclusion from our examination of the writings of these three therapists which will be of relevance to children's literature criticism. On the one hand, Melanie Klein and Virginia Axline—as I have presented them—may be said to share views and strategies, and therefore problems, with all the children's literature critics. In their writing, whatever their best intentions, they create a text in which they, as therapists, present the narratives of their patients. They themselves are stable figures: Klein portrays herself as interpreting; Axline portrays herself as reflecting; and both regard this as their fixed and proper role.

Donald Winnicott, on the other hand, is, in my view, the only one of the three therapists who offers us a parting of the ways with

[72] Axline, *Play Therapy*, 19.

respect to the attitudes and problems of children's literature criticism and other fields which 'know'—that is, constantly produce definitions or descriptions of—the 'child'. And this is because Winnicott the therapist, in his case histories, invites his patients and readers to create him. He does not portray himself as a stable figure, external to the patient's narrative or to the reader's narrative. We are forced, while reading *The Piggle*, for instance, to construct or 'invent' (partially at least) Winnicott as a therapist: to supply our own ideas about why or what he did. Winnicott offers us perhaps the best example of how a therapist can allow the patient to be himself in the therapy—as in the narrative—by inviting the patient to 'write' the therapist who writes the narrative of the therapy.

Winnicott's acute awareness of—and painstaking striving to make space for—this complex process of mutual construction contrasts powerfully with the self-defeating operations of a children's literature criticism struggling to preserve the 'real child' for its own needs. Winnicott's effort to make it possible for the patient to use the therapist in any way necessary to that patient translates into the idea that a book gains whatever importance it may have for any reader at any time precisely by allowing the reader the space to inscribe the text in his own way into his narrative of emotional meaning—by making it possible for the reader to create his own use for the book, whatever that may be.

# Bibliography

This bibliography includes all the references in the book, as well as additional titles which have influenced my thinking.

APPLEBEE, ARTHUR N., *The Child's Concept of Story: Ages Two to Seventeen* (University of Chicago Press, Chicago, 1978).

ARIÈS, PHILIPPE, *Centuries of Childhood* (Penguin, Harmondsworth, 1973).

ARISTOTLE, *Politics*, trans. H. Rackham (The Loeb Classical Library) (William Heinemann, London, 1959).

—— *Nichomachean Ethics*, trans. H. Rackham (The Loeb Classical Library) (William Heinemann, London, 1975).

—— *The Poetics of Aristotle*, trans. and commentary Stephen Halliwell (University of North Carolina Press, Chapel Hill, NC, 1987).

AXLINE, VIRGINIA M., *Play Therapy* (Churchill Livingston, Edinburgh, 1989 (originally pub. 1947)).

—— *Dibs: In Search of Self. Personality Development in Play Therapy* (Penguin, Harmondsworth, 1964).

BARTHES, ROLAND, *Image, Music, Text*, essays selected and trans. Stephen Heath (Fontana, London, 1977).

—— *Roland Barthes by Roland Barthes*, trans. Richard Howard (Macmillan, London, 1977).

—— *On Racine*, trans. Richard Howard (Performing Arts Journal Publications, New York, 1983).

BEATTIE, JOHN, *Other Cultures: Aims, Methods and Achievements in Social Anthropology* (Cohen and West, London, 1964).

BECK, FREDERICK A. G., *Greek Education 450–350 BC* (Methuen, London, 1964).

BEEHLER, RODGER, and DRENGSON, ALAN R. (eds.), *The Philosophy of Society* (Methuen, London, 1978).

BEEKMAN, DANIEL, *The Mechanical Baby: A Popular History of the Theory and Practice of Child Raising* (Dennis Dobson, London, 1977).

BETTELHEIM, BRUNO, *The Children of the Dream* (Macmillan, London, 1969).

—— *The Uses of Enchantment* (Knopf, New York, 1976).

BLISHEN, EDWARD (ed.), *The Thorny Paradise: Writers on Writing for Children* (Kestrel Books, London, 1975).

BOAS, GEORGE, *The Cult of Childhood* (Studies of the Warburg Institute, 29; ed. E. H. Gombrich) (Warburg Institute, University of London, 1966).

BONNER, STANLEY F., *Education in Ancient Rome: From the Elder Cato to the Younger Pliny* (Methuen, London, 1977).

BOOTH, WAYNE CLAYTON, *The Rhetoric of Fiction* (University of Chicago Press, Chicago, fifth impression, 1965).

BOWEN, JAMES, *A History of Western Education*, i: *The Ancient World: Orient and Mediterranean, 2000 BC–AD 1054* (Methuen, London, 1972).

BOWER, GORDON H., and HILGARD, ERNEST R., *Theories of Learning* (Prentice-Hall, Englewood Cliffs, NJ, 5th edn., 1981).

BRIGGS, JULIA, 'Awkward Questions', *Times Literary Supplement* (1–7 Apr. 1988), 372.

BRODERICK, DOROTHY M., *Image of the Black in Children's Fiction* (R. R. Bowker, New York, 1973).

BRUNER, JEROME, *Actual Minds, Possible Worlds* (Harvard University Press, Cambridge, Mass., 1986).

BURKE, KENNETH, *A Grammar of Motives* (Prentice-Hall, New York, 1945).

BUTTS, DENNIS, 'Introduction', in Butts (ed.), *Stories and Society: Children's Literature in its Social Context* (series: Insights, gen. ed. Clive Bloom) (Macmillan, London, 1992), pp. x–xvi.

CARPENTER, HUMPHREY, and PRICHARD, MARI (eds.), *The Oxford Companion to Children's Literature* (Oxford University Press, corrected repr., Oxford, 1984).

CASEMENT, PATRICK, *On Learning From the Patient* (Tavistock Publications, London, 1985).

CASSIRER, ERNST, *An Essay On Man: An Introduction to a Philosophy of Human Culture* (Yale University Press, New Haven, Conn., 1944).

CHAMBERS, NANCY (ed.), *The Signal Approach to Children's Books* (Kestrel Books, London, 1980).

CHILDREN'S RIGHTS WORKSHOP (eds.), *Sexism in Children's Books: Facts, Figures and Guidelines* (Papers on Children's Literature, 2, ed. the Children's Rights Workshop) (Writers and Readers Publishing Co-operative, London, 1976).

CHUKOVSKY, KORNEI, *From Two to Five*, trans. and ed. Miriam Morton (University of California Press, Berkeley, Calif., 1963).

CICERO, *On Oratory and Orators*, trans. J. S. Watson (Henry G. Bohn, London, 1855).

CLIFFORD, JAMES, *The Predicament of Culture: Twentieth-Century Ethnography, Literature, and Art* (Harvard University Press, Cambridge, Mass., 1988).

COLLINGWOOD, R. G., *The Idea of History* (Oxford University Press, Oxford, 1961).

COLLINSON, ROGER, 'The Children's Author and His Readers', *Children's Literature in Education*, 10 (Mar. 1973), 37–49.

COMENIUS, JOHN AMOS, *The Great Didactic*, introd. and trans. M. W. Keatinge (Adam and Charles Black, London, 1896).

COTT, JONATHAN, *Pipers at the Gates of Dawn: The Wisdom of Children's Literature* (Viking, London, 1984).

COVENEY, PETER, *Poor Monkey: The Child in Literature* (Rockliff, London, 1957).

CULLER, JONATHAN, *On Deconstruction: Theory and Criticism After Structuralism* (Cornell University Press, Ithaca, NY, 1982).

—— *Barthes* (Modern Masters Series, ed. Frank Kermode) (Fontana, London, 1983).

DARTON, F. J. HARVEY, *Children's Books in England: Five Centuries of Social Life* (first pub. Cambridge University Press 1932; 3rd edn. rev. Brian Alderson, Cambridge University Press, Cambridge, 1982).

DAVIDSON, THOMAS, *Aristotle and Ancient Educational Ideals* (William Heinemann, London, 1904).

DE BEAUVOIR, SIMONE, *The Second Sex*, trans. and ed. H. M. Parshley (Penguin, Harmondsworth, 1972).

DE CASTELL, SUZANNE, LUKE, ALLAN, and EGAN, KIERAN, *Literacy, Society, and Schooling: A Reader* (Cambridge University Press, Cambridge, 1986).

DE MAUSE, LLOYD (ed.), *The History of Childhood* (Psychohistory Press, New York, 1974).

DERRIDA, JACQUES, *Of Grammatology*, trans. Gayatri Chakravorty Spivak (Johns Hopkins University Press, Baltimore, 1976).

—— *La Carte postale de Socrate à Freud et au-delà* (series La Philosophie en Effet) (Aubier-Flammarion, Paris, 1980).

DE STERCK, M., LANNOY, L., BACCARNE, R., *et al.* (eds.), *Jeugdboekengids. Schrijver Gezocht. Encyclopedie van de Jeugdliteratuur (Guide to Children's Books. Writer Wanted. Encyclopedia of Children's Literature)* (Lannoo/Van Holkema en Warendorf, Tielt, 1988).

DE VRIES, ANNE, *Wat Heten Goede Kinderboeken? De Theoretische Opvattingen over Kinderliteratuur en de Praktijk van de Boekbeoordeling in Nederland 1880–1980: Academisch Proefschrift voor de V.U. (What Are Said to be Good Children's Books? Theoretical Ideas about Children's Literature and the Practice of Judging Books in The Netherlands 1880–1980)* (Em. Querido's Uitgeverij b.v., Amsterdam, 1989).

DE WAAL, FRANS, *Chimpanzee Politics: Power and Sex Among Apes* (Counterpoint, Unwin Paperbacks, London, 1982).

DILTHEY, WILHELM, *Introduction to the Human Sciences*, trans. and introd. essay by Ramon J. Betanzos (Wayne State University Press, Detroit, 1988).

DIXON, BOB, *Catching Them Young*, i: *Sex, Race and Class in Children's Fiction* (Pluto Press, London, 1977); ii: *Political Ideas in Children's Fiction* (Pluto Press, London, 1977).

DREVER, JAMES, *Greek Education: Its Practice and Principles* (Cambridge University Press, Cambridge, 1912).

DUSINBERRE, JULIET, *Alice to the Lighthouse: Children's Books and Radical Experiments in Art* (Macmillan, London, 1987).

EGOFF, SHEILA, STUBBS, G. T., and ASHLEY, L. F. (eds.), *Only Connect: Readings on Children's Literature* (Oxford University Press, Toronto, 1969).

ELLIS, JOHN M., *Against Deconstruction* (Princeton University Press, Princeton, NJ, 1989).

FISHER, MARGERY, . . . *Intent Upon Reading: A Critical Appraisal of Modern Fiction for Children* (Brockhampton Press, Leicester, 1961).

FLEW, ANTHONY, *An Introduction to Western Philosophy: Ideas and Argument from Plato to Sartre* (Thames and Hudson, London, 1971).

FOUCAULT, MICHEL, *Madness and Civilization: A History of Insanity in the Age of Reason*, trans. Richard Howard (Tavistock Publications, London, 1967).

FOX, GEOFF, *et al.* (eds.), *Writers, Critics, and Children: Articles from 'Children's Literature in Education'* (Heinemann Educational Books, London, 1976).

FREEMAN, DEREK, *Margaret Mead and Samoa: The Making and Unmaking of an Anthropological Myth* (Harvard University Press, Cambridge, Mass., 1983).

FREEMAN, KENNETH J., *Schools of Hellas: An Essay on the Practice and Theory of Ancient Greek Education* (Macmillan, London, 1907).

FREUD, ANNA, *The Psycho-Analytical Treatment of Children*, trans. Nancy Procter-Gregg (Imago Publishing, London, 1946).

FREUD, SIGMUND, *Case Histories I*, trans. Alix Strachey and James

Strachey (The Penguin Freud Library, 8, ed. James Strachey and Angela Richards) (Penguin, Harmondsworth, 1990).

—— *Case Histories II*, trans. James Strachey, comp. and ed. Angela Richards (The Penguin Freud Library, 9) (Penguin, Harmondsworth, 1990).

—— *Introductory Lectures on Psycho-Analysis*, trans. James Strachey (The Penguin Freud Library, 1, ed. James Strachey and Angela Richards) (Penguin, Harmondsworth, 1991).

—— *New Introductory Lectures On Psycho-Analysis*, trans. James Strachey (The Penguin Freud Library, 2, ed. James Strachey and Angela Richards) (Penguin, Harmondsworth, 1991).

—— *The Interpretation of Dreams*, trans. James Strachey (The Penguin Freud Library, 4, ed. James Strachey and Angela Richards) (Penguin, Harmondsworth, 1991).

—— *On Sexuality*, trans. James Strachey, comp. and ed. Angela Richards (The Penguin Freud Library, 7) (Penguin, Harmondsworth, 1991).

FRYE, NORTHROP, *Anatomy of Criticism: Four Essays* (Princeton University Press, Princeton, NJ, 1957).

GAY, PETER, *The Enlightenment: An Interpretation*, ii: *The Science of Freedom* (Wildwood House, London, 1970, repr. 1979).

GEERTZ, CLIFFORD, *Local Knowledge: Further Essays in Interpretive Anthropology* (Basic Books, New York, 1983).

—— *Works and Lives: The Anthropologist as Author* (Stanford University Press, Stanford, Calif., 1988).

GENETTE, GERARD, *Narrative Discourse*, trans. Jane E. Lewin (Basil Blackwell, Oxford, 1980).

GLAZER, JOAN I., and WILLIAMS III, GURNEY, *Introduction to Children's Literature* (McGraw-Hill, New York, 1979).

GOODMAN, NELSON, *Ways of Worldmaking* (Hackett, Indianapolis, 1978).

—— *Of Mind and Other Matters* (Harvard University Press, Cambridge, Mass., 1984).

GRAFF, HARVEY J., *The Labyrinths of Literacy: Reflections on Literacy Past and Present* (Falmer Press, London, 1987).

GWYNN, AUBREY, *Roman Education from Cicero to Quintilian* (Russell and Russell, New York, 1964).

HAND, NIGEL, 'Criticism and the Children's Fiction Industry', *Children's Literature in Education*, 12 (Sept. 1973), 3–9.

HARDING, D. W., 'Considered Experience: The Invitation of the Novel', *English in Education*, 2/1 (1967), 3–14.

HAVILAND, VIRGINIA (ed.), *Children's Literature: A Guide to Reference Sources* (Library of Congress, Washington, DC, 1966).

—— (ed.), *Children and Literature: Views and Reviews* (The Bodley Head, London, 1973).

HAZARD, PAUL, *Books, Children and Men*, trans. Marguerite Mitchell (The Horn Book Inc., Boston, 1947; this edn. repr. 1958).

HEIMERIKS, NETTIE, and VAN TOORN, WILLEM (eds.), *De Hele Bibelebontse Berg: De Geschiedenis van het Kinderboek in Nederland en Vlaanderen van de Middeleeuwen tot Heden (The Whole 'Bibelebonts' Mountain: The History of the Children's Book in The Netherlands and Flanders from the Middle Ages to the Present Day)* (Em. Querido's Uitgeverij b.v., Amsterdam, 1989).

HIRSCH, E. D. (Jr.), *Validity in Interpretation* (Yale University Press, New Haven, Conn., 1967).

HOGGART, RICHARD, *The Uses of Literacy: Aspects of Working-Class Life. With Special References to Publications and Entertainments* (Chatto and Windus, London, repr. 1971).

HOMER, *The Iliad*, trans. and introd. Martin Hammond (Penguin, Harmondsworth, 1987).

HUCK, CHARLOTTE S., *Children's Literature in the Elementary School* (Holt, Rinehart and Winston, 3rd edn., New York, 1976).

HUNT, PETER, *Criticism and Children's Literature: Theory and Practice* (Department of English, University of Wales Institute of Science and Technology, Cardiff, 1985).

—— (ed.), *Children's Literature: The Development of Criticism* (Routledge, London, 1990).

—— *Criticism, Theory, and Children's Literature* (Basil Blackwell, Oxford, 1991).

INGLIS, FRED, *The Promise of Happiness: Value and Meaning in Children's Literature* (Cambridge University Press, Cambridge, 1981).

—— *Popular Culture and Political Power* (Harvester Wheatsheaf, Brighton, 1988).

ISER, WOLFGANG, *The Act of Reading: A Theory of Aesthetic Response* (Johns Hopkins University Press, Baltimore, 1978).

ISOCRATES, *Isocrates*, vol. i, trans. George Norlin (The Loeb Classical Library) (William Heinemann, London, 1961); vol. ii, trans. George Norlin (The Loeb Classical Library, William Heinemann, London, 1929).

JAUSS, HANS ROBERT, *Toward an Aesthetic of Reception*, introd. Paul de

Man, trans. Timothy Bahti (series: Theory and History of Literature, ed. Wlad Godzich and Jochen Schulte-Sasse, 2) (Harvester, Brighton, 1982).

JENKINSON, A. J., *What do Boys and Girls Read?* (Methuen, 2nd edn., London, 1946).

JENKS, CHRIS (ed.), *The Sociology of Childhood: Essential Readings* (Batsford Academic and Educational Ltd., London, 1982).

KANT, IMMANUEL, *Prolegomena to Metaphysic: Kant's Critical Philosophy for English Readers*, ed. John P. Mahaffy and John H. Bernard (Macmillan, London, 1889).

KERTZER, ADRIENNE E., 'Inventing the Child Reader: How We Read Children's Books', *Children's Literature in Education*, 15/1 (Spring 1984), 12–21.

KIMMEL, ERIC A., 'Children's Literature Without Children', *Children's Literature in Education*, 13/1 (Spring 1982), 38–43.

KIRKPATRICK, D. L. (ed.), *Twentieth-Century Children's Writers* (Macmillan, London, 1978).

KLEIN, MELANIE, *The Psycho-Analysis of Children*, trans. Alix Strachey, rev. Alix Strachey and H. A. Thorner (vol. ii of *The Writings of Melanie Klein*, The International Psycho-Analytical Library, 22, ed. M. Masud R. Khan) (The Hogarth Press and the Institute of Psycho-Analysis, London, 1975 (original edn. pub. 1932)).

—— *Narrative of a Child Analysis* (The International Psycho-Analytical Library, 55, ed. John D. Sutherland) (The Hogarth Press and the Institute of Psycho-Analysis, London, 1961).

KNUTTEL-FABIUS, ELIZE, *Oude Kinderboeken (Old Children's Books)* (originally pub. Martinus Nijhoff, The Hague, 1906; this facsimile edn. Interbook International, Schiedam, 1977).

KRUPNICK, MARK, 'Introduction', in Krupnick (ed.), *Displacement: Derrida and After* (Indiana University Press, Bloomington, Ind., 1983), 1–17.

KUHN, REINHARD, *Corruption in Paradise: The Child in Western Literature* (published for Brown University Press by University Press of New England, Hanover, NH, 1982).

KUJOTH, JEAN SPEALMAN (comp.), *Reading Interests of Children and Young Adults* (Scarecrow Press, Metuchen, NJ, 1970).

LANDSBERG, MICHELE, *Reading for the Love of It: Best Books for Young Readers* (Prentice Hall, New York, 1987).

LEAVIS, F. R., *The Great Tradition: George Eliot, Henry James, Joseph Conrad* (Chatto and Windus, London, 1948).

—— *Anna Karenina and Other Essays* (Chatto and Windus, London, 1967).

LEAVIS, Q. D., *Fiction and the Reading Public* (Chatto and Windus, London, repr. 1968).

LEE, CAROL, *Friday's Child: The Threat to Moral Education* (Thorson's Publishing Group, Wellingborough, 1988).

LEESON, ROBERT, *Children's Books and Class Society: Past and Present*, ed. The Children's Rights Workshop (Papers on Children's Literature, 3) (Writers and Readers Publishing Co-operative, London, 1977).

LENG, I. J., *Children in the Library* (University of Wales Press, Cardiff, 1968).

LENTRICCHIA, FRANK, *After the New Criticism* (Athlone Press, London, 1980).

LIENHARDT, GODFREY, 'The Observers Observed', *Times Literary Supplement* (26 Aug.–1 Sept. 1988), 925.

LOCKE, JOHN, *The Educational Writings of John Locke: A Critical Edition*, introd. and ed. James L. Axtell (Cambridge University Press, Cambridge, 1968).

—— *An Essay Concerning Human Understanding* (*The Clarendon Edition of the Works of John Locke*, gen. ed. P. H. Nidditch *et al.*) (Clarendon Press, Oxford, 1975, repr. with corrections, 1979).

—— *Some Thoughts Concerning Education* (*The Clarendon Edition of the Works of John Locke*, gen. ed. John W. Yolton, ed. and introd. John W. Yolton and Jean S. Yolton) (Clarendon Press, Oxford, 1989).

LONSDALE, BERNARD J., and MACKINTOSH, HELEN K., *Children Experience Literature* (Random House, New York, 1973).

LURIE, ALISON, *Don't Tell the Grown-Ups: Subversive Children's Literature* (Bloomsbury, London, 1990).

LUTHER, MARTIN, and ERASMUS, DESIDERIUS, *Luther and Erasmus: Free Will and Salvation* (Erasmus, *De Libero Arbitrio*, trans. and ed. E. Gordon Rupp and A. N. Marlow; Luther, *De Servo Arbitrio*, trans. and ed. Philip S. Watson and B. Drewery) (The Library of Christian Classics, 17, ed. John Baillie *et al.*) (SCM Press, London, 1969).

—— *First Principles of the Reformation or the Ninety-Five Theses and the Three Primary Works*, trans. and introd. Henry Wace and C. A. Buchheim (John Murray, London, 1883).

MACCANN, DONNARAE, and WOODARD, GLORIA (eds.), *The Black American in Books for Children: Readings in Racism* (Scarecrow Press, Metuchen, NJ, 1972).

—— *Cultural Conformity in Books for Children: Further Readings in Racism* (Scarecrow Press, Metuchen, NJ, 1977).

MARROU, HENRI-IRÉNÉE, *Histoire de l'éducation dans l'antiquité* (Éditions du Seuil, 2nd edn., Paris, 1950).

MATTERA, GLORIA, 'Bibliotherapy in a Sixth Grade' (Ed.D., The Pennsylvania State University, 1961, microfilm-xerography by University Microfilms International, Ann Arbor, Mich., 1978).

MEEK, MARGARET, WARLOW, AIDAN, and BARTON, GRISELDA (eds.), *The Cool Web: The Pattern of Children's Reading* (The Bodley Head, London, 1977).

MEHL, DIETER, 'The Audience of Chaucer's Troilus and Creseyde', in Beryl Rowland (ed.), *Chaucer and Middle English Studies in Honour of Rossel Hope Robbins*, (George Allen and Unwin, London, 1974), 173–87.

MILL, JOHN STUART, *On Liberty, Representative Government, The Subjection of Women: Three Essays*, introd. Millicent Garrett Fawcett (Oxford University Press, London, first pub. 1912, repr. 1969).

MINNIS, A. J., 'Chaucer and Comparative Literary Theory', in Donald M. Rose (ed.), *New Perspectives in Chaucer Criticism* (Pilgrim Books, Norman, Okla., 1981).

MONSON, DIANNE L., and PELTOLA, BETTE J. (comp.), *Research in Children's Literature: An Annotated Bibliography* (International Reading Association, Newark, Del., 1976).

MONTAIGNE, MICHEL EYQUEM DE, *The Teacher's Montaigne*, trans. and introd. Geraldine E. Hodgson (Blackie's Library of Pedagogics, Blackie and Son, London, 1915).

MULHERN, FRANCIS, *The Moment of 'Scrutiny'* (New Left Books, London, 1979).

NAGEL, THOMAS, *The View From Nowhere* (Oxford University Press, Oxford, 1986).

NEEDLE, JAN, 'Personal View', *Sunday Times* (31 July 1988), G4.

NEHAMAS, ALEXANDER, *Nietzsche: Life as Literature* (Harvard University Press, Cambridge, Mass., 1985).

NIETZSCHE, FRIEDRICH, *Beyond Good and Evil: Prelude to a Philosophy of the Future*, trans. Helen Zimmern (*The Complete Works of Friedrich Nietzsche*, vol. xii, ed. Oscar Levy) (George Allen and Unwin, London, 1923).

—— *The Will to Power*, ed. Walter Kaufmann, new trans. Walter Kaufmann and R. J. Hollingdale (Vintage Books, New York, 1968).

NORTON, DONNA E., *Through the Eyes of a Child: An Introduction to Children's Literature* (Charles E. Merrill, Columbus, Oh., 1983).

NORVELL, GEORGE W., *The Reading Interests of Young People* (Michigan State University Press, East Lansing, Mich., 1973).

PATON WALSH, JILL, 'The Writer's Responsibility', *Children's Literature in Education*, 10 (Mar. 1973), 30–7.

PHILLIPS, ROBERT (ed.), *Aspects of Alice: Lewis Carroll's Dreamchild as Seen through the Critics' Looking-Glasses 1865–1971* (Penguin, Harmondsworth, 1971).

PIAGET, JEAN, and INHELDER, BÄRBEL, *The Psychology of the Child*, trans. Helen Weaver (Routledge and Kegan Paul, London, 1969).

PLATO, *The Laws*, trans. and introd. Trevor J. Saunders (Penguin, Harmondsworth, 1970).

—— *Protagoras*, trans. with notes by C. C. W. Taylor (Clarendon Press, Oxford, 1976).

—— *Republic*, vol. i, books I–V, trans. Paul Shorey (The Loeb Classical Library, ed. G. P. Goold) (William Heinemann, London, 1978); vol. ii, books VI–X, trans. Paul Shorey (The Loeb Classical Library, ed. G. P. Goold) (William Heinemann, London, 1942).

POSTMAN, NEIL, *The Disappearance of Childhood* (Delacorte Press, New York, 1982).

QUINTILIAN, *Institutes of Oratory or: Education of an Orator in 12 Books*, vol. i, trans. John Selby Watson (George Bell and Sons, London, 1903); vol. ii, trans. John Selby Watson (George Bell and Sons, London, 1905).

REES, DAVID, 'Enigma Variations: William Mayne', *Children's Literature in Education*, 19/2 (Summer 1988), 94–105.

RICHARDS, I. A., *Principles of Literary Criticism* (Routledge and Kegan Paul, London, 1928).

RIEMENS-REURSLAG, J., *Het Jeugdboek in de Loop der Eeuwen (Children's Books through the Centuries)* (first pub. The Hague, 1949; facsimile edn. pub. Interbook International, Schiedam, 1977).

RIMMON-KENAN, SHLOMITH, *Narrative Fiction: Contemporary Poetics* (series: New Accents, ed. Terence Hawkes) (Methuen, London, 1983).

RORTY, RICHARD, *Contingency, Irony, and Solidarity* (Cambridge University Press, Cambridge, 1989).

ROSE, JACQUELINE, *The Case of Peter Pan or: The Impossibility of Children's Fiction* (series: Language, Discourse, Society, ed. Stephen Heath and Colin MacCabe) (Macmillan Press, London, 1984).

ROUSSEAU, JEAN-JACQUES, *Émile*, trans. Barbara Foxley (Everyman's Library no. 518) (J. M. Dent and Sons, London, first pub. in this edn. 1911, repr. 1950).

—— *The Social Contract and Discourses*, trans. and introd. G. D. H. Cole (Everyman's Library) (J. M. Dent and Sons, London, repr. 1968).

RUDMAN, MASHA KABAKOW, *Children's Literature: An Issues Approach* (D. C. Heath, Lexington, Mass., 1976).

RUSK, ROBERT R., *The Doctrines of the Great Educators* (Macmillan, London, 1957).

RUSSEL, D. A., and WINTERBOTTOM, M. (eds.), *Ancient Literary Criticism: The Principal Texts in New Translations* (Clarendon Press, Oxford, 1972).

RUSTIN, MARGARET, and RUSTIN, MICHAEL, *Narratives of Love and Loss: Studies in Modern Children's Fiction* (Verso, London, 1987).

SADKER, MYRA POLLACK, and SADKER, DAVID MILLER, *Now upon a time: A Contemporary View of Children's Literature* (Harper and Row, New York, 1977).

SALWAY, LANCE (ed.), *A Peculiar Gift: Nineteenth Century Writings on Books for Children* (Kestrel Books, Penguin, Harmondsworth, 1976).

SANDLER, JOSEPH, DARE, CHRISTOPHER, and HOLDER, ALEX, *The Patient and the Analyst: The Basis of the Psychoanalytic Process* (George Allen and Unwin, London, 1973).

SHAHAR, SHULAMITH, *Childhood in the Middle Ages* (Routledge, London, 1990).

SHAVIT, ZOHAR, *Poetics of Children's Literature* (University of Georgia Press, Athens, Ga., 1986).

SIDNEY, PHILIP, *An Apology for Poetry or: The Defence of Poesy*, ed. Geoffrey Shepherd (Thomas Nelson and Sons, London, 1965).

SMITH, JAMES A., and PARK, DOROTHY M., *Word Music and Word Magic: Children's Literature Methods* (Allyn and Bacon, Boston, Mass., 1977).

SMITH, LILLIAN H., *The Unreluctant Years: A Critical Approach to Children's Literature* (American Library Association, Chicago, 1953).

SPENCE, DONALD P., *Narrative Truth and Historical Truth: Meaning and Interpretation in Psychoanalysis* (W. W. Norton, New York, 1982).

SPINK, JOHN, *Children as Readers: A Study* (Clive Bingley, London, 1989).

SPIVAK, GAYATRI CHAKRAVORTY, *In Other Worlds: Essays in Cultural Politics* (Routledge, London, 1988).

STAINTON ROGERS, REX, and STAINTON ROGERS, WENDY, *Stories of Childhood: Shifting Agendas of Child Concern* (Harvester Wheatsheaf, London, 1992).

STERN, DANIEL, *The Interpersonal World of the Infant: A View from Psychoanalysis and Developmental Psychology* (Basic Books, New York, 1985).

STINTON, JUDITH (ed.), *Racism and Sexism in Children's Books* (Writers and Readers Co-operative, London, 1979).

STROHM, PAUL, 'Chaucer's Audience(s): Fictional, Implied, Actual', *Chaucer Review*, 18/2 (1983), 137–45.

SULEIMAN, S.R., and CROSMAN, INGE (eds.), *The Reader in the Text: Essays on Audience and Interpretation* (Princeton University Press, Princeton, NJ, 1980).

TOWNSEND, JOHN ROWE, *A Sense of Story: Essays on Contemporary Writers for Children* (Longman, London, 1971).

—— *Written for Children: An Outline of English-Language Children's Literature* (2nd rev. edn., Penguin, Harmondsworth, 1983).

TRILLING, LIONEL, *Beyond Culture: Essays on Literature and Learning* (Martin Secker and Warburg, London, 1966).

TUCKER, NICHOLAS, *What is a Child?* (series: The Developing Child, ed. J. Bruner, M. Cole, B. Lloyd) (Fontana/Open Books, London, 1977).

—— *The Child and the Book: A Psychological and Literary Exploration* (Cambridge University Press, first pub. 1981, Canto edn., Cambridge, 1990).

VIVES, JUAN LUIS, *On Education: A Translation of the De Tradendis Disciplinis of Juan Luis Vives*, introd. and trans. Foster Watson (Cambridge University Press, Cambridge, 1913).

WADSWORTH, BARRY J., *Piaget for the Classroom Teacher* (Longman, London, 1978).

WALL, BARBARA, *The Narrator's Voice: The Dilemma of Children's Fiction* (Macmillan, London, 1991).

WALLERSTEIN, ROBERT S., 'Followup Psychoanalysis: Clinical and Research Values. Fall of the American Psychoanalytic Association: Evaluation of Outcome of Psychoanalytic Treatment: Should Followup by the Analyst be Part of the Post-termination Phase of Analytic Treatment?', *Journal of the American Psychoanalytic Association*, 37/4 (1989), 921–41.

—— 'The Psychotherapy Research Project of the Menninger Foundation: An Overview', *Journal of Consulting and Clinical Psychology*, 57/2 (Apr. 1989), 195–205.

WASHBURNE, CARLETON, and VOGEL, MABEL, *What Children Like to Read: Winnetka Graded Book List. The Results of a Statistical Investigation as to the Books Enjoyed by Children of Various Ages and Measured Degrees of Reading Ability* (Rand McNally, Skokie, Ill., 1926).

WELLEK, RENÉ, *Concepts of Criticism*, ed. and introd. Stephen G. Nichols Jr. (Yale University Press, New Haven, Conn., 1963).

WHITE, DOROTHY NEAL, *About Books for Children* (Oxford University Press, New York, 1949).

WHITEHEAD, FRANK, *et al.*, *Children and their Books* (Schools Council Research Studies, Macmillan Education, London, 1977).

WIEDEMANN, THOMAS, *Adults and Children in the Roman Empire* (Routledge, London, 1989).

WINNICOTT, DONALD W., *Collected Papers: Through Paediatrics to Psycho-Analysis* (Tavistock Publications, London, 1958).

—— *Playing and Reality* (Tavistock Publications, London, 1971).

—— *Therapeutic Consultations in Child Psychiatry* (The International Psycho-Analytical Library, 87, ed. M. Masud R. Khan) (The Hogarth Press and the Institute of Psycho-Analysis, London, 1971).

—— *The Piggle: An Account of the Psychoanalytic Treatment of a Little Girl*, ed. Ishak Ramzy (The International Psycho-Analytical Library, 107, ed. M. Masud R. Khan) (The Hogarth Press and the Institute of Psycho-Analysis, London, 1978).

—— *Holding and Interpretation: Fragment of an Analysis*, introd. M. Masud R. Khan (The International Psycho-Analytical Library, ed. Clifford Yorke, 115) (The Hogarth Press and the Institute of Psycho-Analysis, London, 1986).

—— *Home is Where We Start from: Essays by a Psychoanalyst* (Penguin, Harmondsworth, 1986).

WINTLE, JUSTIN, and FISHER, EMMA (eds.), *The Pied Pipers: Interviews with the Influential Creators of Children's Literature* (Paddington Press, New York, 1974).

ZIMET, SARA GOODMAN, *Print and Prejudice* (with an additional chapter by Mary Hoffman) (Hodder and Stoughton, London, 1976).

# Index